T0186103

Lecture Notes of the Institute for Computer Sciences, Social Informatics and Telecommunications Engineering 510

Editorial Board Members

Ozgur Akan, *Middle East Technical University, Ankara, Türkiye*
Paolo Bellavista, *University of Bologna, Bologna, Italy*
Jiannong Cao, *Hong Kong Polytechnic University, Hong Kong, China*
Geoffrey Coulson, *Lancaster University, Lancaster, UK*
Falko Dressler, *University of Erlangen, Erlangen, Germany*
Domenico Ferrari, *Università Cattolica Piacenza, Piacenza, Italy*
Mario Gerla, *UCLA, Los Angeles, USA*
Hisashi Kobayashi, *Princeton University, Princeton, USA*
Sergio Palazzo, *University of Catania, Catania, Italy*
Sartaj Sahni, *University of Florida, Gainesville, USA*
Xuemin Shen ⓘ, *University of Waterloo, Waterloo, Canada*
Mircea Stan, *University of Virginia, Charlottesville, USA*
Xiaohua Jia, *City University of Hong Kong, Kowloon, Hong Kong*
Albert Y. Zomaya, *University of Sydney, Sydney, Australia*

The LNICST series publishes ICST's conferences, symposia and workshops.
  LNICST reports state-of-the-art results in areas related to the scope of the Institute.
  The type of material published includes

- Proceedings (published in time for the respective event)
- Other edited monographs (such as project reports or invited volumes)

  LNICST topics span the following areas:

- General Computer Science
- E-Economy
- E-Medicine
- Knowledge Management
- Multimedia
- Operations, Management and Policy
- Social Informatics
- Systems

Sérgio Ivan Lopes · Paula Fraga-Lamas ·
Tiago M. Fernándes-Camáres · Babu R. Dawadi ·
Danda B. Rawat · Subarna Shakya
Editors

Smart Technologies for Sustainable and Resilient Ecosystems

3rd EAI International Conference, Edge-IoT 2022
and 4th EAI International Conference, SmartGov 2022
Virtual Events, November 16–18, 2022
Proceedings

Springer

Editors
Sérgio Ivan Lopes ⓘD
Instituto Politécnico de Viana do Castelo
Viana do Castelo, Portugal

Paula Fraga-Lamas ⓘD
Universidade da Coruña
A Coruña, Spain

Tiago M. Fernándes-Camáres ⓘD
Universidade da Coruña
A Coruña, Spain

Babu R. Dawadi ⓘD
Tribhuvan University
Kathmandu, Nepal

Danda B. Rawat ⓘD
Howard University
Washington, WA, USA

Subarna Shakya ⓘD
Tribhuvan University
Kathmandu, Nepal

ISSN 1867-8211   ISSN 1867-822X (electronic)
Lecture Notes of the Institute for Computer Sciences, Social Informatics
and Telecommunications Engineering
ISBN 978-3-031-35981-1   ISBN 978-3-031-35982-8 (eBook)
https://doi.org/10.1007/978-3-031-35982-8

© ICST Institute for Computer Sciences, Social Informatics and Telecommunications Engineering 2023

This work is subject to copyright. All rights are reserved by the Publisher, whether the whole or part of the material is concerned, specifically the rights of translation, reprinting, reuse of illustrations, recitation, broadcasting, reproduction on microfilms or in any other physical way, and transmission or information storage and retrieval, electronic adaptation, computer software, or by similar or dissimilar methodology now known or hereafter developed.
The use of general descriptive names, registered names, trademarks, service marks, etc. in this publication does not imply, even in the absence of a specific statement, that such names are exempt from the relevant protective laws and regulations and therefore free for general use.
The publisher, the authors, and the editors are safe to assume that the advice and information in this book are believed to be true and accurate at the date of publication. Neither the publisher nor the authors or the editors give a warranty, expressed or implied, with respect to the material contained herein or for any errors or omissions that may have been made. The publisher remains neutral with regard to jurisdictional claims in published maps and institutional affiliations.

This Springer imprint is published by the registered company Springer Nature Switzerland AG
The registered company address is: Gewerbestrasse 11, 6330 Cham, Switzerland

Preface

We are delighted to jointly introduce the proceedings of the 4th edition of the European Alliance for Innovation (EAI) International Conference on Smart Governance for Sustainable Smart Cities (SmartGov 2022) and the 3rd edition of the EAI International Conference on Intelligent Edge Processing in the IoT Era (Edge-IoT 2022). These conferences brought together researchers, developers, and practitioners around the world who are leveraging and developing smart technologies for smarter and more resilient systems. The theme of SmartGov 2022 was "to promote the development of secure and sustainable smart cities with smart governance", while the theme of Edge-IoT 2022 was "to address the decentralization of contemporary processing paradigms, notably Edge processing, focusing on the increasing demand for intelligent processing at the edge of the network, which is paving the way to the Intelligent IoT Era".

Both the EAI SmartGov 2022 and EAI Edge-IoT 2022 conferences were co-located with the EAI SmartCity360 international convention; this 8th EAI International Convention on Science and Technologies for Smart Cities brought a holistic approach covering all aspects of science and technologies for Smart Cities. The convention presented an excellent platform to meet, connect, and engage with some of the brightest minds that are shaping the future of the cities we live in.

The technical program of Edge-IoT 2022 consisted of 6 full papers presented in two oral sessions: Session 1 – Edge-IoT Applications; and Session 2 – IoT Architectures, Forecasting and Adversarial Training. The Edge-IoT 2022 conference is covered by chapters 1–6. The technical program of EAI SmartGov 2022 consisted of 6 full papers, including 2 invited papers in oral presentation sessions at the main conference tracks. The SmartGov 2022 conference is covered by chapters 7–12. The conference tracks of SmartGov 2022 were: Track 1 – AI and Machine Learning for Smart Governance; Track 2 – Smart Transportation.

Coordination with the Steering Chair Imrich Chlamtac and the General Chairs, Danda B. Rawat from SmartGov 2022, and Sérgio Ivan Lopes from Edge-IoT 2022, was essential for the success of both conferences. We sincerely appreciate their constant support and guidance. It was also a great pleasure to work with such an excellent organizing committee team for their hard work in organizing and supporting the conferences. In particular, for SmartGov 2022, the Technical Program Committee, led by our TPC Chairs, Babu R. Dawadi and Kayhan Zrar Ghafoor completed the peer-review process of technical papers and created a high-quality technical program. Similarly, for Edge-IoT 2022, the Technical Program Committee, led by our TPC Chairs, Paula Fraga-Lamas and Tiago Fernándes-Camáres, completed the peer-review process in a timely manner. We are also grateful to our conference manager, Kristina Havlickova, for her support and to all authors who submitted their papers to these conferences.

We strongly believe that the SmartGov and Edge-IoT conferences provided a good forum for all researchers, developers, and practitioners to discuss all science and technology aspects that are relevant to smart governance, IoT, and intelligent edge processing.

We also expect that in the future these conferences will be as successful and stimulating as indicated by the contributions presented in this volume.

Babu R. Dawadi
Danda B. Rawat
Subarna Shakya
Sérgio Ivan Lopes
Paula Fraga-Lamas
Tiago M. Fernándes-Camáres

EAI Edge-IoT 2022 Conference Organization

Steering Committee

Imrich Chlamtac   University of Trento, Italy
Sérgio Ivan Lopes   Instituto Politécnico de Viana do Castelo, Portugal

Organizing Committee

General Chair

Sérgio Ivan Lopes   Instituto Politécnico de Viana do Castelo, Portugal

General Co-chairs

Mauro Migliardi   University of Padova, Italy
Pedro Santos   CISTER, Instituto Politécnico do Porto, Portugal

TPC Chairs and Co-chairs

Paula Fraga-Lamas   Universidade da Coruña, Spain
Tiago M. Fernández-Caramés   Universidade da Coruña, Spain

Workshops Chair

António Moreira   Instituto Politécnico do Cávado e do Ave, Portugal

Publicity and Social Media Chair

Pedro Pinto   ESTG - Politécnico do Porto, Portugal

Publications Chairs

Alessio Merlo   University of Genoa, Italy
Luca Verderame   University of Genoa, Italy

Web Chair

Silvestre Malta   Instituto Politécnico de Viana do Castelo, Portugal

Technical Program Committee

Cezary Orłowski	WSB University in Gdańsk, Poland
Catarina Silva	Universidade de Coimbra, Portugal
Paula María Castro Castro	Universidade da Coruña, Spain
Dixys Leonardo Hernández Rojas	Technical University of Machala, Ecuador
Chi-Hua Chen	Fuzhou University, China
Luca Bianconi	Gruppo Sigla s.r.l., Italy
Pedro Miguel Moreira	Instituto Politécnico de Viana do Castelo, Portugal
Teodoro Aguilera Benítez	University of Extremadura, Spain
Paulo Leitão	Instituto Politécnico de Bragança, Portugal
Josu Bilbao	IKERLAN Technology Center, Spain
Felix Freitag	Technical University of Catalonia, Spain
Fernando J. Álvarez Franco	Universidad de Extremadura, Spain
Daniel Albuquerque	Instituto Politécnico de Viseu, Portugal
Luís Ferreira	Instituto Politécnico do Cavado e do Ave, Portugal
António M. R. Cruz	Instituto Politécnico de Viana do Castelo, Portugal
Paulo Pedreiras	Universidade de Aveiro, Portugal
Alberto Sillitti	Innopolis University, Russia
Luigi Benedicenti	University of New Brunswick, Canada
Ilsun You	Soonchunhyang University, South Korea
Fang-Ye Leu	Tunghai University, Taiwan
Kangbin Yim	Soonchunhyang University, South Korea
Carlo Ferrari	Università degli Studi di Padova, Italy
Francesco Palmieri	Università degli Studi di Salerno, Italy
Riccardo Pecori	Università del Sannio, Italy
Valentina Casola	Università "Federico II" di Napoli, Italy
Alessandra De Benedictis	Università "Federico II" di Napoli, Italy
Massimiliano Rak	Università della Campania Luigi Vanvitelli, Italy
Alexandre Meslin	Pontifical Catholic University of Rio de Janeiro, Brazil
Luís Barreto	Instituto Politécnico de Viana do Castelo, Portugal
Ahmad Keshavarz	Persian Gulf University, Iran
Habib Rostami	Persian Gulf University, Iran
Anjus George	Oak Ridge National Laboratory, USA

EAI SMARTGOV 2022 - Conference Organization

Steering Committee

Imrich Chlamtac   University of Trento, Italy
Danda B. Rawat   Howard University, USA

Organizing Committee

General Chair

Danda B. Rawat   Howard University, USA

General Co-chairs

Subarna Shakya   Tribhuvan University, Nepal

TPC Chairs

Babu R. Dawadi   Tribhuvan University, Nepal
Kayhan Zrar Ghafoor   Salahaddin University-Erbil, Iraq

Sponsorship and Exhibit Chair

Danda B. Rawat   Howard University, USA

Workshops Chair

Vijay K. Shah   George Mason University, USA

Publicity and Social Media Chair

Eric Mohati   George Mason University, USA

Publications Chairs

Danda B. Rawat   Howard University, USA
Babu R. Dawadi   Tribhuvan University, Nepal

Web Chair

Babu R. Dawadi   Tribhuvan University, Nepal

Panels Chair

Jamie Galán Jimenéz ·   University of Extremadura, Spain

Administration/Management (EAI Conference Manger)

Kristina Havlickova

Technical Program Committee

Marco Polverini	University of Rome, Italy
Pradip Paudyal	Nepal Telecommunications Authority, Nepal
Gajendra Sharma	Kathmandu University, Nepal
Rajeeb Kr. Kantha	Savonia University, Finland
Sanjeeb Pd. Panday	Tribhuvan University, Nepal
Pietro Manzoni	Technical University of Valencia, Spain
Bimal Acharya	Nepal Telecom, Nepal
Dibakar Raj Panta	Tribhuvan University, Nepal
Aakash Gautam	San Francisco State University, USA

Contents

Edge-IoT Applications

A Cost-Effective Thermal Imaging Safety Sensor for Industry 5.0
and Collaborative Robotics 3
  Daniel Barros, Paula Fraga-Lamas, Tiago M. Fernández-Caramés,
  and Sérgio Ivan Lopes

Edge Computing with Low-Cost Cameras for Object Detection in Smart
Farming 16
  Bruno Cardoso, Catarina Silva, Joana Costa, and Bernardete Ribeiro

Evaluating Maximum Operating Distance in COTS RFID TAGS for Smart
Manufacturing 29
  André Pinto, Rolando Azevedo, and Sérgio Ivan Lopes

IoT Architectures, Forecasting and Adversarial Training

Philippine Stock Direction Forecasting Utilizing Technical, Fundamental,
and News Sentiment Data 43
  Sean Arthur E. Sombrito, Kenneth John G. Gonzales,
  Jan Kyle Lewis T. Nolasco, and Nestor Michael C. Tiglao

IoT Architectures for Indoor Radon Management: A Prospective Analysis 59
  Oscar Blanco-Novoa, Paulo Barros, Paula Fraga-Lamas,
  Sérgio Ivan Lopes, and Tiago M. Fernández-Caramés

Adversarial Training for Better Robustness 75
  Houze Cao and Meng Xue

Artificial Intelligence and Machine Learning for Smart Governance

Integrating Computer Vision and Crowd Sourcing to Infer Drug Use
on Streets: A Case Study with 311 Data in San Francisco 87
  Hye Seon Yi, Tanvir Bhuiyan, and Sriram Chellappan

Machine Learning Approach to Crisis Management Exercise Analysis:
A Case Study in SURE Project 102
  Henry Joutsijoki, Sari Mäenpää, Ilari Karppi, and Iina Sankala

Quantitative Evaluation of Saudi E-government Websites Using a Web
Structure Mining Methodology 117
   Tahani M. Alqurashi and Zahyah H. Alharbi

Extracting Digital Biomarkers for Unobtrusive Stress State Screening
from Multimodal Wearable Data 130
   Berrenur Saylam and Özlem Durmaz İncel

Smart Transportation

Continuous Measurement of Air Pollutant Concentrations in a Roadway
Tunnel in Southern Italy 155
   Saverio De Vito, Antonio Del Giudice, Gerardo D'Elia,
   Elena Esposito, Grazia Fattoruso, Sergio Ferlito, Fabrizio Formisano,
   Giuseppe Loffredo, Ettore Massera, Girolamo Di Francia,
   Patrizia Bellucci, and Francesca Ciarallo

Rating Urban Transport Services Quality Using a Sentiment Analysis
Approach 166
   Orlando Belo and Ricardo Milhazes

Author Index 177

Edge-IoT Applications

A Cost-Effective Thermal Imaging Safety Sensor for Industry 5.0 and Collaborative Robotics

Daniel Barros[1]([⊠]), Paula Fraga-Lamas[2,3], Tiago M. Fernández-Caramés[2,3], and Sérgio Ivan Lopes[1,4,5]

[1] ADiT-Lab, Instituto Politécnico de Viana do Castelo, Viana do Castelo, Portugal
`danielbarros@ipvc.pt, sil@estg.ipvc.pt`
[2] Department of Computer Engineering, Faculty of Computer Science,
Universidade da Coruña, 15071 A Coruña, Spain
`{paula.fraga,tiago.fernandez}@udc.es`
[3] Centro de Investigación CITIC, Universidade da Coruña, 15071 A Coruña, Spain
[4] CiTin - Centro de Interface Tecnológico Industrial, Arcos de Valdevez, Portugal
[5] IT - Instituto de Telecomunicações, Campus de Santiago, 3810-193 Aveiro, Portugal

Abstract. The Industry 5.0 paradigm focuses on industrial operator well-being and sustainable manufacturing practices, where humans play a central role, not only during the repetitive and collaborative tasks of the manufacturing process, but also in the management of the factory floor assets. Human factors, such as ergonomics, safety, and well-being, push the human-centric smart factory to efficiently adopt novel technologies while minimizing environmental and social impact. As operations at the factory floor increasingly rely on collaborative robots (CoBots) and flexible manufacturing systems, there is a growing demand for redundant safety mechanisms (i.e., automatic human detection in the proximity of machinery that is under operation). Fostering enhanced process safety for human proximity detection allows for the protection against possible incidents or accidents with the deployed industrial devices and machinery. This paper introduces the design and implementation of a cost-effective thermal imaging Safety Sensor that can be used in the scope of Industry 5.0 to trigger distinct safe mode states in manufacturing processes that rely on collaborative robotics. The proposed Safety Sensor uses a hybrid detection approach and has been evaluated under controlled environmental conditions. The obtained results show a 97% accuracy at low computational cost when using the developed hybrid method to detect the presence of humans in thermal images.

Keywords: Industry 5.0 · Safety · Human-centric · Thermal Imaging · Cobots

1 Introduction

With the introduction of new paradigms such as Industry 4.0 [1–4] and Industry 5.0 [5–8] a new focus to improve safety conditions for operators in an industry

© ICST Institute for Computer Sciences, Social Informatics and Telecommunications Engineering 2023
Published by Springer Nature Switzerland AG 2023. All Rights Reserved
S. I. Lopes et al. (Eds.): Edge-IoT 2022/SmartGov 2022, LNICST 510, pp. 3–15, 2023.
https://doi.org/10.1007/978-3-031-35982-8_1

setting has been made. With Industry 4.0, the focus was on the technological revolution, with the implementation of Cyber-Physical Systems (CPS), Industrial Internet of Things (IIoT) devices, Cloud Computing solutions, or Artificial Intelligence (AI) enabled systems, with the main goal of making industrial production lines more efficient, flexible and with higher quality standards. Currently, Industry 5.0 emerges as an evolution, unlike the revolutionary Industry 4.0, in the sense that it is focused on human-centricity, sustainability, and resilience [9]. In manufacturing, Industry 5.0 is aimed at combining computation skills with human intelligence and resources in a collaborative setting to further increase a company's value and customer satisfaction [10]. In an environment where humans and collaborative robots must interact and work together, one aspect that cannot be forgotten is safety, both in terms of the safety of the human operators and the safety and integrity of products and production lines.

This paper proposes a cost-effective safety sensor that uses low-cost thermal imaging, to be deployed on factory floors for detecting and counting, in real-time, humans in distinct zones of an image. Thus, enabling safety in Industry 5.0 environments that may include Collaborative Robots (CoBots) and humans in the loop. The adoption of Thermal imaging for this purpose, increases the probability of detection of humans in low visibility conditions, when compared with conventional RGB cameras [11]. Moreover, it increases the system's sensitivity to nonmedical grade human-related activities [12,13], since it focuses on heat sources detection. However, other redundant safety measures should also be considered. The sensor uses a hybrid method to determine if a human is present in a thermal image and if that human has crossed a virtual fence or is in a specific area. The obtained results show that the developed methods for detecting the human presence in a frame are able to yield a reasonably high accuracy at low computational complexity.

The rest of this paper is structured as follows. Section 2 describes the most relevant works regarding safety sensors for Industry 5.0 and human detection using low-cost thermal imaging. Section 3 presents the proposed system architecture and the devised hybrid detection approach. Section 4 analyzes the obtained results. Finally, Sect. 5 is dedicated to conclusions and future work.

2   Related Works

Multiple works have previously addressed the problem of monitoring and detecting the presence of humans in different environments. For instance, in [14] the authors propose and develop a system capable of detecting humans. For such a purpose they study different identification algorithms (such as HoG, Viola James, and YOLOv3) and analyze the impact of the use of different resolutions on latency time. Specifically, the paper describes a system that consists of four sensors (two eight-megapixel cameras and two ultrasound sensors), which are aimed at being mounted onto the base of a robot. The sensing module of the system uses background subtraction to extract contours and then applies identification algorithms.

Another relevant contribution is presented in [15], where the authors describe a wide-band radar sensor that is continuously monitoring human distance to a collaborative robot. The use of an RF transmitter with large bandwidth results in a high range resolution, allowing the authors to estimate better the distance of a human to the sensor. The presented device, according to the authors, suffers from high complexity, due to the use of high-level signal processing algorithms, reduced spatial resolution and a narrow field of view. Similarly, in [16], the authors present a new method, based on Shape Context Descriptor with Adaboost cascade classifiers, for detecting pedestrians in thermal images. The developed method is proved to have a high human detection rate but suffers from high computational costs.

In [17] it is presented a multi-modal sensor array for safe human-robot interactions. The sensor array consists of ST Micro-electronic VL6180X time-of-flight (ToF) sensors that measure the time the light needs to travel to an object and back to the sensor. For force sensing, eight Melexis MLX90393 sensors are used.

In relation to the used sensors, the authors of [18] present a survey regarding the multiple types of available thermal sensors, including FLIR Lepton 2.0, MLX90640 and others, as well as other sensors commonly used in different industries. Then, the paper discusses the employment of thermal sensors in Heating, Ventilation, and Air Conditioning (HVAC) systems, and for the automotive and manufacturing industries. Also, the authors, during the discussion, present a comparison of different detection algorithms such as AdaBoost, KNN, GNB and SVM, showing that the surveyed sensors are able to estimate occupancy with a 100% accuracy when mounted on the ceiling and a 98.6% accuracy when mounted on a wall. In [12], Braga et al. present the assessment procedure and the results obtained when comparing the performance of two low-cost thermal imaging cameras with a more expensive flagship device for medical screening purposes. Results have shown that, although not being medical grade devices, such cameras can be used for elevated temperature detection events.

Finally, another example of thermal imaging sensors for occupancy estimation is detailed in [21]. The authors compare three thermal sensors (MLX90393, GridEye, and FLIR Lepton 2.0) in terms of their resolution, cost or Field of View (FOV), among other specifications. The presented solution makes use of a combination of active frame analysis, component analysis, feature extraction and classification that can be implemented in various smart building applications.

3   Design and Implementation of the Proposed System

The solution presented in this paper is aimed at implementing a cost-effective solution, capable of being installed on factory floors, offices or even outdoors. In addition, the devised system is also intended for being as a one-size-fits-all type of solution, with minimal intervention and adjustment needs, thus being able to operate in different environmental conditions.

The component selection can be divided into three subsystems: processing, sensor interface and thermal image sensor.

– Processing subsystem. For image processing, we opted for Espressif ESP32 [22], due to its low cost, high availability, low power consumption, good efficiency, Bluetooth and Wi-Fi communication capabilities, and also an I2C port for direct interfacing with the sensor interface (i.e., with PureThermal2 module), the power consumption of the ESP32 is about 215 mW in active mode and 19 mW in deep sleep mode [23].
– Sensor interface. For the experiments performed for this paper, the PureThermal2 module was selected due to its low cost and native integration of a Micro-USB port, which enables easy connectivity and is capable of allowing communications via I2C, UART and JTAG [24]. The PureThermal2 module includes a STM32F412 [25], whose firmware may be modified for performing certain processing tasks (e.g., image processing), but, actually, for the work presented in this paper, image processing is performed on the ESP32.
– Thermal image sensor. For the implemented system, the FLIR Lepton 3.5 sensor was selected [26]. Such a sensor is capable of outputting 160×120 pixels images, with thermal sensitivity of less than 50 mK (0.050°C) and a horizontal FOV of 57°. In terms of power consumption, the FLIR Lepton 3.5 consumes nominally 150 mW while operating, 650 mW during the shutter event and 5 mW on standby.

Figure 1 illustrates the conceptual framework, in which it is possible to observe the sensor module used to implement the safety sensor. Additionally, Fig. 2 depicts the operational flowchart of the proposed safety sensor.

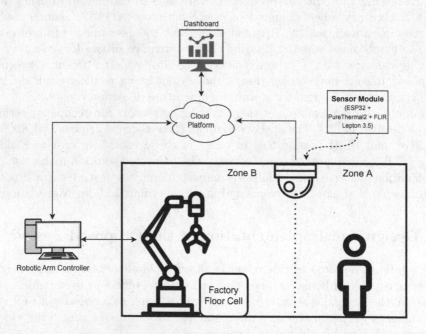

Fig. 1. Conceptual framework of the proposed Industry 5.0 use case.

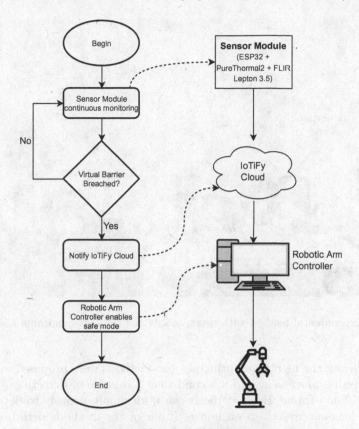

Fig. 2. Operational flowchart.

3.1   Experimental Testbed

An experimental testbed, cf. Fig. 3, was built to prove whether the use of a thermal imaging sensor would be a capable solution to detect, accurately, persons in a real environment. For such a purpose, a Raspberry Pi 3B was connected via Micro-USB to the PureThermal2 Module with the FLIR Lepton 3.5 camera. Then, the testbed was placed on a vantage point that monitored a research lab, which is frequently used by people. The acquisition of frames was carried out during afternoons, having a large window on the left side of the frame, irradiating heat, which appeared to be negligible due to the high dynamic range of the Flir Lepton 3.5.

3.2   Hybrid Detection Approach

The used detection approach was devised on one simple principle: every human is considered to be a body of heat, and as a such, any body of heat with a shape similar to a human may be considered as one. This principle is only valid with the use of a thermal imaging camera, as a normal RGB camera is not capable of detecting sources of heat.

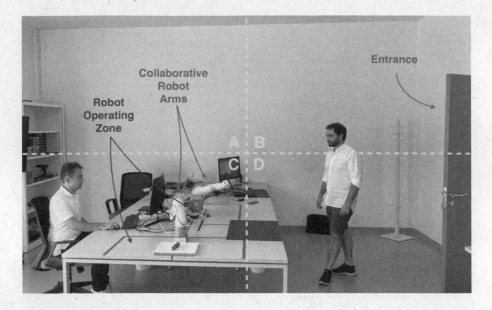

Fig. 3. Experimental testbed with users, cobots and the four quadrants identified.

Considering the mentioned principle, two methods were proposed: one capable of detecting movement and a second that is capable of detecting regions of interest within a frame. Both methods can work simultaneously to determine if there are humans present in an image. If one of the methods determines that there is a human presence, the result is predicted as a positive detection. Only if both methods determine that there is no human present, then the result is negative (i.e., no humans have been detected).

Figure 4 depicts the proposed detection approach consisting of Method A and B. Method A focuses on Movement Detection and consists in the use of two sequential frames: one that will serve as a basis for the comparison and another one that is compared to the previous one.

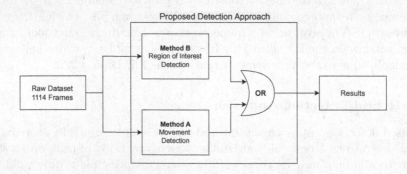

Fig. 4. Proposed Detection Approach.

This method uses the direct subtraction of the image matrices to generate a new frame (i.e., the first frame is used as a background, so it is considered as the reference frame). Subsequent frames are then subtracted to the background. This operation has two possible outcomes:

1. The output of the absolute difference results in a new frame with pixel values averaging zero or near zero. This implies that there are no new relevant updates in the new frame, so it can be concluded that there is no movement. In this case, the new image frame will serve as the new background for the comparison with the next frame. This assures that the next comparison is always performed with the most recent reference to compensate for temperature increases during the day and other external factors.
2. If the absolute difference results in a group of pixels (also called active pixels) that have values near a reference value, then a major update is detected, so the likelihood of existing movement is very high. To achieve higher confidence when detecting movement, a comparison needs to be made and it is made using a threshold. Such a threshold is defined as a percentage of active pixels. For the test presented in this paper, the number of pixels in a frame was considered. For example, for a frame of 19,200 pixels (that is the image size for a resolution of 160×120 pixels), if at least 5% of those pixels (i.e., 960 pixels) are considered as active, then it can be determined with certainty that there was movement. If that value is lower than the threshold, then there is no significant movement and no detection is signalized by the algorithm. The percentage of pixels needed for the frame to be considered as a positive is a value that can be adjusted for different conditions or to improve the algorithm sensitivity.

Figure 5 shows the flowchart of the proposed method. Inanimate objects that have heat are discarded with this approach because, although they may have a certain amount of heat that may be identified as a body of heat, when subtracting the sequence of images, only the bodies of heat that moved are shown.

Method B uses a Region of Interest Approach, which consists in using a single 160×120 pixels frame that is then divided into four 80×60 pixels quadrants. Such quadrants do not hold much data on their own, but when compared to the entire frame, they can help to determine if that quadrant has any significance. This comparison is made using the mean value of all the pixels in the total frame with each quadrant, so if the original frame (i.e., entire) has a mean value of X, a quadrant will be considered of interest if its mean is at least 20% larger (this value can be adjusted). As it will be later shown in Sect. 4, this method yields good results for detecting regions of interest in the frame and, when compared with method A, it shows increased accuracy in detecting stationary persons in different parts of the frame. However, one problem that was identified occurs when the body of heat is in the center of the frame, resulting in it being divided into four different quadrants and averaging the values by the frames. Nonetheless, this method can be easily implemented, allowing, if needed, to only monitor a single quadrant (or more) of the image frame. Figure 6 details the flowchart of the proposed method B.

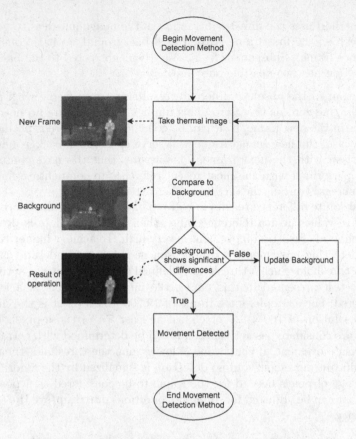

Fig. 5. Method A - Movement Detection Approach.

4   Results

A script was created for the experimental testbed to first gather the data to be used in the testing of the proposed human-detection methods. Such a script took four consecutive frames every second and was executed continuously for four consecutive days. During that period, 1114 frames were taken and then used to create the reference dataset. Such frames consisted of 1057 frames that contain one or more persons, while the remaining 57 frames had no body of heat present in the frame, except for different types of electrical and electronics equipment, which emitted small portions of heat. Both A and B methods were evaluated individually and combined, as previously described in Fig. 4. The results are presented below in confusion matrixes where the output of each run of the methods is flagged as True Positive (TP), True Negative (TN), False Positive (FP) or False Negative (FN). Then, the accuracy can be obtained using Eq. 1:

$$((TP + TN)/(TP + TN + FP + FN)) * 100 \tag{1}$$

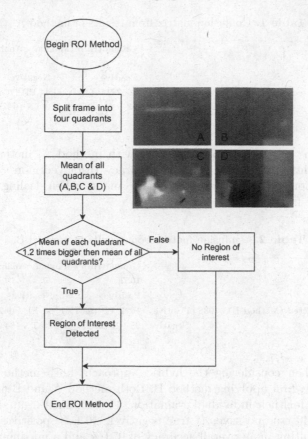

Fig. 6. Method B - Region of Interest Approach.

Regarding the sole application of method A, its results are shown in the confusion matrix presented in Table 1. The results yielded 1101 positives and 12 negatives, of which 1057 were true positives, 44 were false positives and 12 were false negatives (there were no false negatives). These results show what seems at first a high number of false positives, but this is because of the dataset in which the method is being applied: some frames changed substantially from one day to another, so some new frames were flagged as positives despite being actually negatives. Nonetheless, considering a final Industry 5.0 implementation, having a higher number of false positives can be considered safer than having more false negatives. Overall, method A achieved a 94.5% accuracy with a maximum detection latency of 7 ms per frame.

The results of the application of method B are shown in the confusion matrix presented in Table 2. As it can be observed, 1027 were true positives, 11 were false positives, 48 were true negatives and 28 were false negatives. These results show that method B presents an accuracy using Eq. 1 of 96.5% and a maximum

Table 1. Confusion matrix from results of method A.

			Groundtruth (Manually Analized)	
			1057	57
			Positive	Negative
Predicted (Method A)	1101	Positive	1057 TP (100 %)	44 FP (77.2 %)
	12	Negative	12 FN (1.1 %)	0 TN (0 %)

latency of 6 ms per frame. In comparison with method A, method B besides showing a slightly higher percentage of accuracy, displayed more capabilities in detecting stationary people and better performance when dealing with sudden changes in the frame layout.

Table 2. Confusion matrix from results of method B.

			Groundtruth (Manually Analized)	
			1057	57
			Positive	Negative
Predicted (Method B)	1038	Positive	1027 TP (97.1%)	11 FP (19.2%)
	76	Negative	28 FN (2.6%)	48 TN (84.2%)

Finally, when considering the hybrid approach, both methods were used simultaneously, first applying method B. Both method A and B used the same parameters as for their individual evaluation. The obtained results indicate that there were 1040 true positive, 41 true negatives, 16 false positives and 17 false negatives, resulting in an overall accuracy of 97.0% and a maximum of 10 ms of detection latency.

It is worth noting that the proposed hybrid approach allows for a good trade-off between performance and computing power, because it does not rely on compute-intense algorithms to identify humans or shapes of humans in a frame, like most Machine Learning (ML) or AI algorithms available. Moreover, both methods A and B only use basic matrix operations to perform the analysis and comparison, and no previous training is required. So 97% accuracy means that this solution can be easily implemented in an edge-like device (e.g., an ESP32) that has low energy consumption, low footprint, low complexity and low cost. Nonetheless, in case of trying to achieve a 99.9% accuracy, some trade-offs would have to be made, mainly in the computational capabilities of the proposed solution (Table 3).

Table 3. Confusion matrix from results of both methods combined.

			Groundtruth (Manually Analized)	
			1057	57
			Positive	Negative
Predicted (Both Methods)	1056	Positive	1040 TP (98.4%)	16 FP (28%)
	58	Negative	17 FN (1.6%)	41 TN (71.9%)

5 Conclusion and Future Work

This paper described the design and implementation of a real-time cost-effective thermal imaging safety sensor that can be used within the scope of the Industry 5.0 paradigm to trigger different safety states in manufacturing processes that rely on collaborative robotics. Therefore, it enables the protection against possible incidents or accidents or the optimization of the energy efficiency of the deployed industrial devices and machinery. The overall cost of the prototype is approximately €200, which is roughly the same cost of other solutions that use cloud computing instead of edge computing [19], but more costly when compared to solutions that only use the sensor for gathering data [14,20], although the latter demand for powerful servers for processing. However, if industrialized, the cost of the proposed solution should reduce considerably, depending on the quantity produced. The proposed method, in contrast to recent literature, avoids relying on complex ML or AI algorithms that require prior training and provides a low energy consumption, low footprint, low complexity and low-cost solution that can be easily deployed instead on a cloud platform on Edge computing devices. The proposed solution can also be deployed with minimal intervention and tuning requirements, thus being able to operate in different environmental conditions. Two approaches were evaluated. First, a movement detection approach achieved a 94.5% of accuracy, and 7 ms maximum detection latency. Second, a region of interest approach achieved a 96.5% of accuracy, and 6 ms of latency. In addition, a hybrid approach that combined both methods simultaneously to determine whether a human is present in a thermal image and whether he/she has crossed a virtual fence or is in a specific area was tested. The results of the hybrid approach showed a promising accuracy of 97%, and 10 ms of maximum latency.

The obtained results were performed with pre-recorded frames. Thus, the next step will consist in using the hardware presented in Sect. 3 so that the execution of the algorithms can be carried out in real time. From there, with the implemented solution, more analyses and evaluations can be performed, such as the evaluation of the sensor under various failure modes of the components, stress tests, the evaluation of the computational complexity of the pipeline, the assessment of the system latency, to determine the average life time of the sensor, the comparison with other detection algorithms in the same conditions, as well as other solutions using different technologies (e.g., 24 GHz mmWave Sensors [27,28]). Moreover, determining the long-term maintenance cost of the proposed solution is also interesting as future work.

Acknowledgment. This work is a result of the project TECH-Technology, Environment, Creativity and Health, Norte-01-0145-FEDER-000043, supported by Norte Portugal Regional Operational Program (NORTE 2020), under the PORTUGAL 2020 Partnership Agreement, through the European Regional Development Fund (ERDF). P.F.L and T.M.F.C. have been supported by Centro de Investigación de Galicia "CITIC" for a three-month research stay in Instituto Politécnico de Viana do Castelo between 15 June and 15 September 2022. CITIC, as Research Center accredited by

Galician University System, is funded by "Consellería de Cultura, Educación e Universidades from Xunta de Galicia", supported in an 80% through ERDF Funds, ERDF Operational Programme Galicia 2014–2020, and the remaining 20% by "Secretaría Xeral de Universidades" (Grant ED431G 2019/01). In addition, this work has been funded by the Xunta de Galicia (by grant ED431C 2020/15), the Agencia Estatal de Investigación of Spain, MCIN/AEI/10.13039/501100011033 (by grant PID2020-118857RA-I00 (ORBALLO)) and ERDF funds of the EU (FEDER Galicia 2014–2020 & AEI/FEDER Programs, UE).

References

1. Patnaik, Srikanta (ed.): New Paradigm of Industry 4.0. SBD, vol. 64. Springer, Cham (2020). https://doi.org/10.1007/978-3-030-25778-1
2. di Nardo, M.D., Forino, D., Murino, T.: The evolution of man-machine interaction: the role of human in Industry 4.0 paradigm **8**(1), 20–34 (2020)
3. Vidal-Balea, A., Blanco-Novoa, O., Fraga-Lamas, P., Vilar-Montesinos, M., Fernández-Caramés, T.M.: Creating collaborative augmented reality experiences for industry 4.0 training and assistance applications: performance evaluation in the shipyard of the future. Appl. Sci. **10**(24), 9073 (2020)
4. Fraga-Lamas, P., et al.: Design and empirical validation of a Bluetooth 5 fog computing based industrial CPS architecture for intelligent industry 4.0 shipyard workshops. IEEE Access **8**, 45496–45511 (2020)
5. Zizic, M.C., Mladineo, M., Gjeldum, N., Celent, L.: From Industry 4.0 towards Industry 5.0: a review and analysis of paradigm shift for the people, organization and technology. Energies **15**, 5221 (2022)
6. Huang, S., Wang, B., Li, X., Zheng, P., Mourtzis, D., Wang, L.: Industry 5.0 and society 5.0-comparison, complementation and co-evolution. J. Manuf. Syst. **64**, 424–428 (2022)
7. Fraga-Lamas, P., Varela-Barbeito, J., Fernández-Caramés, T.M.: Next generation auto-identification and traceability technologies for Industry 5.0: a methodology and practical use case for the shipbuilding industry. IEEE Access **9**, 140700–140730 (2021)
8. Fraga-Lamas, P., Lopes, S.I., Fernández-Caramés, T.M.: Green IoT and edge AI as key technological enablers for a sustainable digital transition towards a smart circular economy: an industry 5.0 use case. Sensors **21**(17), 5745 (2022)
9. Xu, X., Lu, Y., Vogel-Heuser, B., Wang, L.: Industry 4.0 and Industry 5.0-inception, conception and perception. J. Manuf. Syst. **61**, 530–535 (2021)
10. Maddikunta, P.K.R.: Industry 5.0: a survey on enabling technologies and potential applications. J. Ind. Inf. Integr. **26**, 100257 (2022)
11. Rocha, D., Rocha, P., Ribeiro, J., Lopes, S.I.: Identification and classification of human body parts for contactless screening systems: an edge-AI approach. In: Paiva, S. et al. (eds.) Science and Technologies for Smart Cities. SmartCity 360 2021. Lecture Notes of the Institute for Computer Sciences, Social Informatics and Telecommunications Engineering, vol. 442. Springer, Cham (2021). https://doi.org/10.1007/978-3-031-06371-8_7
12. Braga, B., Queirós, G., Abreu, C., Lopes, S.I.: Assessment of low-cost infrared thermography systems for medical screening in nursing homes. In: 2021 17th International Conference on Wireless and Mobile Computing, Networking and Communications (WiMob), pp. 157–162 (2021)

13. Lopes, S.I., Pinho, P., Marques, P., Abreu, C., Carvalho, N.B., Ferreira, J.: Contact-less smart screening in nursing homes: an IoT-enabled solution for the COVID-19 era. In: 2021 17th International Conference on Wireless and Mobile Computing, Networking and Communications (WiMob), pp. 145–150 (2021)
14. Gradolewski, D., et al.: A distributed computing real-time safety system of collaborative robot. Elektronika Ir Elektrotechnika **26**(2), 4–14 (2020). https://doi.org/10.5755/j01.eie.26.2.25757
15. Zlatanski, M., Sommer, P., Zurfluh, F., Madonna, G.L.: Radar sensor for fenceless machine guarding and collaborative robotics. In: 2018 IEEE International Conference on Intelligence and Safety for Robotics (ISR), pp. 19–25 (2018)
16. Wang, W., Zhang, J., Shen, C.: Improved human detection and classification in thermal images. In: 2010 IEEE International Conference on Image Processing, pp. 2313–2316 (2010)
17. Abah, C., Orekhov, A.L., Johnston, G.L.H., Yin, P., Choset, H., Simaan, N.: A multi-modal sensor array for safe human-robot interaction and mapping. In: 2019 International Conference on Robotics and Automation (ICRA), pp. 3768–3774 (2019)
18. Altaf, M.A., Ahn, J., Khan, D., Kim, M.Y.: Usage of IR sensors in the HVAC systems, vehicle and manufacturing industries: a review. IEEE Sens. J. **22**(10), 9164–9176 (2022)
19. Saponara, S., Elhanashi, A., Gagliardi, A.: Implementing a real-time, AI-based, people detection and social distancing measuring system for Covid-19. J. Real-Time Image Proc. **18**, 1937–1947 (2021). https://doi.org/10.1007/s11554-021-01070-6
20. Real-time Human Detection with OpenCV. (n.d.). Accessed 18 Aug 2022. thedatafrog.com/en/articles/human-detection-video
21. Chidurala, V., Li, X.: Occupancy estimation using thermal imaging sensors and machine learning algorithms. IEEE Sens. J. **21**(6), 8627–8638 (2021)
22. ESP32 Wi-Fi & Bluetooth MCU I Espressif Systems. www.espressif.com/en/products/socs/esp32. Accessed 11 Nov 2022
23. ESP32-DevKitC V4 real current consumption in deep sleep mode. lucidar.me/en/esp32/power-consumption-of-esp32-devkitc-v4/. Accessed 11 Nov 2022
24. PureThermal 2 - FLIR Lepton Smart I/O Module by GetLab — GroupGets. group gets.com/manufacturers/getlab/products/purethermal-2-flir-lepton-smart-i-o-module. Accessed 11 Nov 2022
25. STM32F412 - STMicroelectronics. www.st.com/en/microcontrollers-microproces sors/stm32f412.html. Accessed 11 Nov 2022
26. Lepton LWIR Micro Thermal Camera Module — Teledyne FLIR. www.flir.com/products/lepton/?model=500-0771-01&;vertical=microcam&;segment=oem. Accessed 11 Nov 2022
27. Rohling, H., Heuel, S., Ritter, H.: Pedestrian detection procedure integrated into an 24 GHz automotive radar. In: IEEE Radar Conference 2010, pp. 1229–1232 (2010). https://doi.org/10.1109/RADAR.2010.5494432
28. Jacobi, R., Manager, M.: Choosing 60-GHz mm Wave sensors over 24-GHz to enable smarter industrial applications Artem Aginskiy

Edge Computing with Low-Cost Cameras for Object Detection in Smart Farming

Bruno Cardoso[1] , Catarina Silva[1](✉) , Joana Costa[1,2] ,
and Bernardete Ribeiro[1]

[1] Center for Informatics and Systems (CISUC), University of Coimbra, Coimbra, Portugal
{catarina,joanamc,bribeiro}@dei.uc.pt
[2] School of Technology and Management, Polytechnic Institute of Leiria, Leiria, Portugal

Abstract. Cameras are becoming a key device for edge computing in several Internet of Things (IoT) applications, including Smart Farming (SF). With low-cost cameras it becomes possible to create less expensive IoT networks using such devices on the edge to do most of the work, such as capturing, processing, and sending images. This allows the use less fog and cloud resources, saving them for the most complex calculations, such as the use of deep learning. However, with low-cost devices, memory and computational power restrictions arise, especially in the detection of objects, such as agricultural pests, where it is especially relevant to take into account features such as image quality and size. These two features influence the choice of cameras to be used on the edge and can make the application of IoT networks not appropriate or too expensive, due to memory consumption by the computation in the several stages, namely to send high resolution images. In this work, we evaluate the impact of using low-cost cameras on the edge for pest detection in Smart Farming, contributing to the general use of Smart Farming and allowing farmers to make more informed decisions. To make the evaluation, we studied the impact of image quality and size on the performance of object detection models. For that, we trained a model using high-resolution images and then we used this model in different test datasets, composed of the same images but with different resolutions and sizes. The results show that it is possible to use lower-resolution images without decreasing significantly the models performance, confirming that is possible to use low-cost/low-resolution cameras at the edge.

Keywords: Edge Computing · Deep Learning · Internet of Things · Low-Cost Cameras · Smart Farming

1 Introduction

IoT can be defined as a network composed of (any)thing(s). The goal of this type of network is to connect those things, that can be almost any device with a processor, to obtain, transmit, and store data. The users of the network can use the obtained data to get insights about any subject of their interest. Smart Farming (SF) has emerged with the use of IoT to increase the capacity and the quality of agricultural production. In Smart

© ICST Institute for Computer Sciences, Social Informatics and Telecommunications Engineering 2023
Published by Springer Nature Switzerland AG 2023. All Rights Reserved

S. I. Lopes et al. (Eds.): Edge-IoT 2022/SmartGov 2022, LNICST 510, pp. 16–28, 2023.
https://doi.org/10.1007/978-3-031-35982-8_2

Farming, data can be used, among others, to maximize the use of space, minimize water consumption, and integrated pest control. Recent advances in IoT, such as reducing hardware dimension and increasing computing power on the edge, have facilitated SF. As a result, devices on the edge are becoming more and more relevant for obtaining economical and reliable data without compromising quality. Also, the chosen devices for the edge influence the entire IoT network, considering that the appropriate choice of devices can make it possible to use less computing power on the fog or on the cloud without loss of performance.

Currently, in pest detection, technicians must collect data from the fields in various forms, e.g., traps with insects, specimens in crops, etc. Then, they need to get back to the lab, analyze the materials to extract information that can be used to support farmers' decisions, notably on how and when to use pesticides. SF approaches make it possible to enhance part of the technicians' work with automatic monitoring systems. Such systems are usually composed of sensors/microcontrollers (on the edge), with attached sensors and cameras, programmed to send images/information that can be used as input to possibly intelligent models (which run on fog or cloud), prepared/trained to perform the desired task.

In this work, we study the impact of using low-cost cameras on the edge in model performance for pest detection. Intelligent detection models are usually trained using high-resolution images. However, after training, the object detection models may have to be used with lower-resolution images. The edge can have memory restrictions that do not allow obtaining and sending high-resolution images to the fog or the cloud. The quality of the images obtained on the edge can influence the performance of object detection models, especially with small objects like pests usually are. In this sense, we propose to address the effect of using low-cost cameras in model performance in SF, contribution to the development of efficient low-cost monitoring systems and to the generalization of SF. The proposed approach consisted in the selection of a public dataset with high-resolution images for pest detection and a State-Of-The-Art model for object detection. Then, the dataset was divided into a training dataset and a test dataset that was compressed to several lower-resolutions. Next, we trained the model with the high resolution images of the train dataset and we tested the model on the lower-resolution images of the several test datasets. Finally, to find if it is possible to use low-resolution cameras, we evaluated the performance of the object detection model on each test dataset.

The rest of the paper is structured as follows. Section 2 introduces the Smart Farming scenario, detailing the main challenges. Section 3 describes the data processing used in SF, including a compression technique to obtain lower-resolution images. Section 4 presents the object detection problem including possible approaches, and Sect. 5 presents the proposed approach detailing the experimental setup. Section 6 presents and analyzes the results. Finally, Sect. 7 concludes and delineates future research lines.

2   Smart Farming: Pest Detection

Agriculture has been evolving in a remarkable way with the use of intelligent methodologies and applications in different areas, e.g., prediction of diseases and pests or the forecast of the best time for harvesting. However, agricultural technology has immense challenges due to diseases and pests spread by globalization and aggravated by climate change. To tackle these challenges, technological tools that allow early detection of pests in the field are becoming instrumental.

In this work we focus on pest detection, more specifically the whitefly (WF) that can be captured using sticky traps as the yellow sticky trap represented in Fig. 1. Yellow sticky traps are a commonly used method for catching whiteflies. This trap usually consists of a rectangular piece of yellow plastic with an adhesive sticker on the surface to catch small insects.

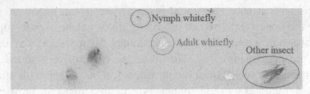

Fig. 1. Example of an image of a yellow sticky trap with different pests annotated.

The impact of whiteflies is one of the biggest challenges for producers who have to adopt pest control to minimize the losses [1]. Pest control starts by preventing pests, for example, by keeping the crop clean, monitoring them (using yellow sticky traps), counting the number of plagues trapped, and setting a threshold for this counting. Lastly, if the count exceeds the threshold, chemical control can be used through pesticides, or biological control, through predatory insects. Thus, appropriate monitoring can reduce pesticides use while improving harvest quality and maximizing crop yields.

3 Data Architectures and Lower-Resolution Images

With the advent of IoT, large amounts of data from source devices such as cameras, humidity, temperature, or soil moisture sensors are available for processing. This section provides some background on the data processing for SF and on image compression to obtain lower-resolution images.

3.1 Data Processing

Depending on the goal, environmental conditions, and network access, SF applications normally use two (edge-cloud or edge-fog) or three (cloud-fog-edge) types of processing to extract information from that data [2], as depicted in Fig. 2.

- **Cloud computing** allows the generation and management of services in a virtualized, shared, and dynamic way (depending on the user's needs) quickly and easily. Its main feature is to provide a service tailored to the user, accessible anywhere (with an Internet connection), allocating only the necessary resources and allowing for an easy and quick readjustment, accounting, and monitoring of consumed resources. Cloud computing provides cost savings, efficiency, scalability, and reliability of services. But it also offers disadvantages such as low latency (making real-time data analysis

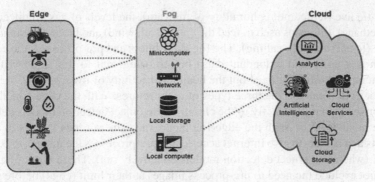

Fig. 2. Data processing for SF (adapted from [3]).

difficult), high bandwidth consumption, and high-power consumption. This type of computing has been used mainly in a centralized way (all kinds of data processing and analysis on the cloud). This centralized way can make the use of SF challenging, for example, in remote areas (without Internet access) or when there are limited resources on the cloud.

- **Fog computing** brings data storage and processing closer to the location where that data is obtained and is very useful when real-time data processing is required or when there is no Internet. The fog layer allows performing operations (such as data processing) outside the cloud that would not be possible due to the low computing power of edge devices. The fog layer can contain several nodes (distributed in multiple locations), with different computational and storage resources, connected to the data collection devices (edge) or the cloud through communication protocols. Usually is used as a bridge between edge computing and cloud computing (reducing the resources used by the cloud).
- **Edge computing** is performed on the devices used to collect the data. Edge computing features are similar to fog computing: low latency, mobility of your nodes, and low bandwidth consumption. However, compared to fog computing, edge computing has less computational power and storage capacity, which makes it infeasible to store large amounts of data or, in some cases, to pre-process that data. Due to these features, combining edge computing with fog computing or cloud computing can be useful.

Smart Farming uses the edge-fog architecture when real-time information is needed. Among others, aquaculture uses this type of architecture to minimize freshwater needs, using sensors to collect data on the edge (such as dissolved oxygen, water level, and water temperature) and monitoring that data in real-time on the fog [4].

The edge-cloud architecture is used when it is necessary to process large amounts of data. Crop managers use this architecture to monitor irrigation systems. On the edge, the sensors are placed in different nodes of the irrigation system to measure water pressure and flow and in the crop to obtain information about the soil (moisture, pH). The collected data is stored and processed on the cloud to define priorities in water consumption [5].

The edge-fog-cloud architecture (Fig. 2) is used when it is necessary to pre-process data before sending it to the cloud. Livestock producers use this architecture to monitor the amount of feed used. On the edge, the sensors collect information about the conditions where cattle live (temperature, humidity of the yarn), the levels of gas produced by the cattle (methane), the crops used to feed the cattle (soil, wind) and biometric signals from the cattle (temperature, breathing). The fog layer filters and pre-processes the collected data (removes noise and redundant data) before being sent to the cloud. The cloud displays temporal information about the health and activity of livestock [6].

Pest detection can use the three types of architectures. With the edge-fog, the camera/sensor sends images directly to the cloud, where object detection models detect and count the number pests. With the edge-fog cloud, the camera sends images to the fog, which acts as a router (to give Internet access) and pre-processes the images to be sent to the cloud (where the object detection models effectively run). These types of architectures do not exclude the need to pre-process images at their limit (edge) before sending them to the fog or the cloud. Because of that, the edge device must have computational power to connect to the camera, take an image of the trap, encode the image, connect to WiFi and finally send the encoded image to the fog or edge, as shown in Fig. 3. Due to the low memory capacity of the sensors/microcontrollers on the edge, it may not be possible to complete all those steps for high-resolution images and can be useful to use lower-resolution (or compressed) images instead.

3.2 Lower-Resolution Images (Image Compression)

Joint Photographic Experts Group (JPG) is the most common format for digital images. This format stores images in a rasterized format where images are a pixel matrix of different colors that form a picture. Each pixel is composed of a 3-dimensional vector (in color images), with the elements of that vector specifying the pixel's color within a color space, i.e., RGB (Red, Green, Blue). This type of image (due to the use of pixels) loses quality when compressed. Lossy compression involves the elimination of some pixels. Each pixel compares to the neighboring pixels during the compression process, and if the information is the same, they are considered redundant and removed. The compression process happens in three steps (see Fig. 4):

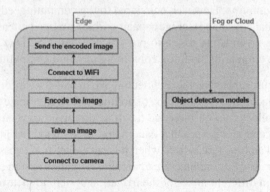

Fig. 3. Steps performed on the edge to send images to fog or cloud.

1. **Forward Transform:** Split the pixel matrix into non-overlapping 8 × 8 blocks (subsampling) and create a new matrix where the original pixel matrix scale is converted

from 0 to 255 to -128 to 127 (converts the pixel scale from a positive scale to a centered scale at zero).

2. **Quantization:** Apply the discrete cosine transformation (DCT) to convert the pixels from the spatial domain to the frequency domain. Then each element of the new matrix is divided by the corresponding element of the pre-defined JPEG Standard quantization matrix. The result is rounded to an integer value, causing a loss of information. This step transforms most pixels with the highest frequency into zero value pixels.

3. **Entropy Encoding:** For each 8 × 8 block, pixels are selected in zigzag to join adjacent pixels. Then, the pixels are encoded using the Huffman algorithm to assign a unique binary code to each pixel. At this stage, the pixel values are converted to binary, allowing to reduce the size of the image [7].

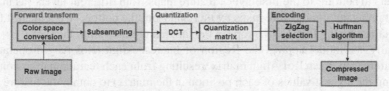

Fig. 4. Compression steps (adapted from [7]).

4 Object Detection Models

Computer vision (CV) can replace Human-visual tasks such as pest detection and counting. Pest detection can use image classification or object detection models to detect pests in images. Image classification is most used when only one class is associated with an image. For example, when we want to classify an image containing pests or not. In pest detection, it's not the goal to classify the trap as containing pests or not, but rather to detect the multiple pests in the same trap. In that case, it is necessary to adapt classification models. It is required to obtain the top image of the trap, do the pre-processing to remove the bottom, segment the image to extract the insects and choose their most relevant features to classify each pest. This process can be complex and replaced by object detection models to automatically process the trapped images (considering the pests as objects).

There are two types of object detection models, those that look twice at the image, i.e., the region-based convolutional neural networks (R-CNN), and those that look only once at the image, i.e., the YOLO [8]. The most recent models, with better results in some cases, are the YOLO. One of the most recent versions is the YOLOv5 model that we are focusing on in this work.

4.1 You Only Look Once (YOLOv5)

This model consists of three stages. The first stage extracts the most critical features of each image. Then the second stage generates the same object with different scales. Finally, the last refines the anchor boxes to obtain the final detections (see Fig. 5).

1. **Backbone:** In the backbone, YOLO uses the CSPDarknet-53 (Cross Stage Partial Darknet-53) neuronal network as a feature extractor, dividing the feature map obtained in the Darknet-53 base layer into two parts with only one of these parts subjected to the following convolution layers of the Darknet-53 network. In contrast, the other part combines through a transition layer with the feature map resulting from the convolution process.

To allow images of different sizes YOLOv5 uses a spatial pyramid pooling (SPP) layer instead of the original Darknet-53 pooling layer. SPP applies a series of pooling layers to the feature map to result in a fixed-size vector that feeds the first layer of the artificial neural network.

2. **Neck:** The PANet (Path Aggregation Network) is used to combine information from the feature maps obtained from the convolution layers of the CSPDarknet-53.

The PANet starts by obtaining new feature maps by joining, from the top (from the last layer) to bottom (to the first layer), feature maps from different layers (as in FPN), then obtaining the final feature maps by merging from the bottom (from the last feature map obtained by the FPN) to the top (to the first feature map from the FPN).

Finally, the model applies the Region of Interest Align (RoI Align) operation in each feature map. Each RoI Align matrix, resulting from each feature map, is combined (choosing the highest values of each position in the matrix) to obtain the feature maps.

3. **Head:** Two parts divide the final stage: predict the dimensions of the bounding boxes and classify the object. First, for each pixel of the feature maps, compare the anchor boxes with the annotations that overlap. Then, remove the anchor boxes that worst fit (with less overlapping) using non-maximum suppression. Finally, the crossed binary entropy function uses the remaining bounding rectangles to get the information loss [9–11].

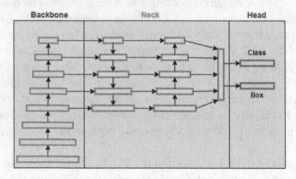

Fig. 5. YOLOv5 general architecture (adapted from [12]).

5 Proposed Approach and Experimental Design

The main goal of this work is to evaluate the use of low-cost cameras for object detection, namely in pest detection. This goal is relevant because it allows assessing the best hardware to use on the edge to assure no loss of performance (in the object detection models), optimization of the computation devices on fog or cloud and choosing the most suitable communication protocol to send images/information. The proposed approach includes the following steps:

1. **Dataset selection** Choose the dataset to use.
2. **Model selection** Choose the object detection model and the evaluation metric for assessment.
3. **Hardware selection** Choose the hardware (camera) to get the images.
4. **Image compression** Compress the test subset images to different dimensions and sizes.
5. **Model comparison** Evaluate the performance of the chosen (final) object detection model in the test datasets (with different resolutions and sizes).

This approach makes it possible to evaluate which hardware (and configuration) is most suitable for obtaining the images, as well as to assess the influence of image compression on model performance and image transmission and to estimate the use of cheaper hardware for pest detection.

5.1 Dataset

The images used belong to a dataset [13] that contains 284 images of yellow sticky traps with two types of whiteflies (both with WF annotation) and the predatory insects Macrolophus (MR) and Nesidiocoris (NC). This dataset contains 5611 annotated instances of whiteflies, 1341 annotated instances of Macrolophus, 511 annotated instances of Nesidiocori, and some unannotated WF instances. We removed from [13] the MR and NC annotations, images with annotations that did not overlap with the whiteflies, and images that did not contain whiteflies. The final dataset comprises 147 images with 4939 WF annotations. We divided the whole dataset into a training dataset with 117 images and a test dataset with 30 images (see Fig. 1 for an example).

The whitefly pest usually affects tomato crops. Some common species of whiteflies are Trialeurodes vaporariorum and Bemisia tabaci. These two types of whitefly are very similar, and only a skilled technician (e.g. biologist) can distinguish them. This pest in the egg has an oval shape. It begins to look like a moth in childhood, and in adulthood, it resembles a white moth. These insects can reach up to 1.5 mm and 3.0 mm in length as adults.

5.2 Model and Evaluation Metrics

We chose the YOLOv5 model, described in Subsect. 4.1. The implementation of this model [14] was made public with four versions obtained by changing the number of layers and neurons from the same architecture. The YOLOv5 (Small) is the less deep version, the YOLOv5 (XLarge) is the deepest version, the YOLOv5 (Medium) and YOLOv5 (Large) depths are between the first two versions. To detect and count the whiteflies we chose the deepest version, the YOLOv5 (XLarge).

We chose the number of WF correctly detected to evaluate the model performance. In pest detection we are interested in detecting the maximum number of pests per image even if the false positive rate increases. That is, it is much more penalizing for farmers not to detect a pest than it is to detect a false positive.

This metric allows comparing the detections from the selected/final model with the technician's detections (technicians who annotated the dataset). Also, due to the low resolution of the test dataset images, it is difficult to annotate them, making it hardly possible to correctly assess the model's accuracy, i.e., the mean average precision.

5.3 Hardware

The selected hardware for the edge was the ESP32-Cam. The ESP32 is a low-cost, low-power microcontroller. This microcontroller is particularly suitable for pest detection, as it might be used for long periods without needing an external power source. The ESP32 has only 520 kb of total memory, with 320 kb of DRAM memory (for storage), 192 kb of IRAM memory (for instructions), and the rest is RTC memory (memory that persists when the device is in standby). The attached camera to the ESP32 was the OV2640, which is a low-cost (one of the most affordable) camera whose main parameters are the frame_size that enables to configure the image size (320 × 240, 352 × 288, 640 × 480, 800 × 600, 1024 × 768, 1280 × 1024 and 1600 × 1200) and jpeg_quality, which allows defining the quality of the images by choosing an integer between 10 (best quality) and 63 (worst quality) [15].

5.4 Image Compression

The test dataset images were compressed and resized (using the image compression technique described in 3.2) to sizes and dimensions compatible with the chosen hardware (Esp32-Cam). They were resized to 6 dimensions (between 1600 × 1200 and 320 × 240) and 7 sizes (between 125 KB and 5 KB). For the maximum dimension allowed by Esp32-Cam (1600 × 1200) the maximum size of the trap image is 125 KB (when using jpeg_quality = 10) and the minimum size (when using jpeg_quality = 63) is 45 KB. For the minimum dimension allowed by Esp32-Cam (320 × 240) the maximum size of the trap image is 5 KB (when using jpeg_quality = 10).

Figure 6 shows the compression of an image of the dataset. The left is part of the original image with dimensions 5184 × 3456 and 1044 KB in size. In the center is the same image compressed to 1600 × 1200 and 124 KB. On the right, the image is compressed to 1600 × 1200 and 51 KB.

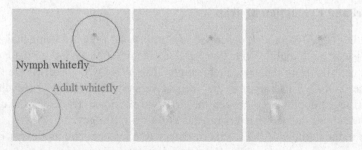

Fig. 6. Compression effect on a dataset image.

6 Experimental Results

Table 1 presents the results on the number of whiteflies detected in the test dataset considering the image dimensions (allowed by ESP32-Cam and the 5184 × 3456 dimension used to train the models) and the maximum, intermediate and minimum size for these dimensions. For example, for 1600 × 1200 resolution, the maximum size of each image is 125 KB (an image in the test set averages 125 KB when using `jpeg_quality = 10`) and the minimum size is 45 KB.

Table 1. YOLOv5 (XLarge) performance (number of whiteflies detections) for different image dimensions and sizes.

	5184x3456	1600x1200	1280x1024	1024x768	800x600	640x480	352x288	320x240
1050 KB	1371							
125 KB		1243						
75 KB		1238	1229					
45 KB		1233	1219	1204				
25 KB			1207	1186	1147			
15 KB				1154	905	497		
10 KB					602	237	4	
5 KB						14	1	0

- 12.2% more detections than dataset technicians
- Between 0.6% and 1.7% more detections than dataset technicians
- Between 0.2% and 6.1% less detections than dataset technicians
- Between 25.9% and 100% less detections than dataset technicians
- Invalid dimension or size

The technicians, that annotated the dataset, detected 1222 whiteflies in the test dataset, while using object detection models to identify whiteflies in images with the dimension 5184 × 3456 it is possible to increase the detection up to 1371, increasing the number of whiteflies detected by 12.2%.

Some of the reasons for technicians not detecting the same pests as the object detection model can be, among others, the method used by technicians to count the pests or the lack of time to count all the pests in all the images. In order to evaluate the detections made by the object detection model we submitted these results to experienced technicians that analyzed in detail the images and confirmed the correctness of the obtained results.

The most used method by technicians (count whiteflies only in a strip of the trap) can identify more than 90% of the total whiteflies in half of the traps [16]. As the object detection models for some camera resolutions do not present significant losses (and in some cases improves the detection) concerning the technicians, it becomes possible to use low-resolution cameras (like ESP32-Cam).

ESP32-Cam only allows images up to 1600×1200. Despite that, using ESP32-Cam, it is possible to increase the number of detected whiteflies (between 0.6% and 1.7%) when compared to dataset technicians. 75 KB or 45 KB images must be used with dimensions of 1600×1200 to achieve this result.

Using images with 1280×1024 dimensions and between the sizes of 45 KB and 25 KB, the number of whiteflies detected, when compared with the technicians, is reduced between 0.24% and 1.22%. Using images with 1024×768 dimension or 800×600 dimension and 25 KB, the number of whiteflies detected is reduced between 1.5% and 6.1%.

For images smaller than 15 KB and between 800×600 and 320×240 dimension, the number of detected whiteflies is reduced between 25.9% and 100%.

The experimental results show that it is preferable to reduce the image size rather than its dimension. For example, 1600×1200 images range from 125 KB to 45 KB depending on image quality, and 1200×1204 from 75 KB to 25 KB. Looking at Table 1 it is possible to see that it is preferable to use 1600×1200 images with lower-quality (45 KB) than 1200×1024 images with higher quality (75 KB). This happens for all image sizes, showing that by reducing the size and keeping the dimensions, it is possible to detect more whiteflies. This is especially relevant because, to send the images to the fog or cloud, we usually encode those images in a base64 string, which increases the string size by 33% [17]. Hence, this size reduction can be helpful not only to allow the use of low-cost edge devices, but also to allow sending encoded images.

7 Conclusions and Future Work

In this work, we studied the impact of using lower-resolution images, compatible with low-cost cameras, in model performance for Smart Farming, more specifically for pest detection. While the training of object detection models requires high-resolution images so that technicians can identify the objects to annotate, after training it is possible to use these models with lower-resolution images without losing significant performance. The obtained results show that it is possible to reduce the image size and dimension from 5184×3456 to 1600×1200 without decreasing significantly the models performance, it decreases from 12.2% to between 0.6% and 1.7% more detections than the technicians. Even for lower-sizes and dimensions (1280×1204 and 1024×768) the results continue to be good, between 0.2% and 6.1% less detections than technicians. Also, the results show that it is preferable to reduce the size of the images than its dimension to not lose the performance. In edge devices where memory constraints arise these results are especially relevant.

The studied images sizes and dimensions are compatible with low-cost cameras definitions (like ESP32-Cam), making it possible to say that it is possible to use low-cost devices for pest detection. The obtained results contribute to the general use of Smart Farming and to the development of more efficient monitoring systems. Also, low-cost devices on the edge usually imply low power consumption, making it possible to improve the life of these devices using these results. This is especially useful in Smart Farming, where most of the time there are external power sources constraints.

Future work will focus on the development of different IoT network architectures for automatic pest control, namely with low-cost cameras on the edge.

References

1. Ortiz, O.: Tropical whitefly project progress report. In: Impact Evaluation, vol. 69, pp. 249–311 (2007)
2. Kalyani, Y., Collier, R.: A systematic survey on the role of cloud fog, and edge computing combination in smart agriculture. Sensors 17, 5922 (2021). https://doi.org/10.3390/s21175922
3. Cao, H., Wachowicz, M., Renso, C., Carlini, E.: Analytics everywhere: generating insights from the Internet of Things. IEEE Access 7, 71749–71769 (2019). https://doi.org/10.1109/ACCESS.2019.2919514
4. Romli, M., Daud, S., Zainol, S., Kan, P., Ahmad, Z.: A automatic RAS data acquisition and processing system using fog computing, In: IEEE 13th Malaysia International Conference on Communications, pp. 229–234 (2017). https://doi.org/10.1109/MICC.2017.8311764
5. Ahumada, L., Faz, J., Romero, M., Luque, R.: Proposal for the design of monitoring and operating irrigation networks based on IoT, cloud computing and free hardware technologies. Sensors 19, 2318 (2019). https://doi.org/10.3390/s19102318
6. Alonso, R., Candanedo, I., Garcıa, O´., Prieto, J., Gonz´alez, S.: An intelligent edge-IoT platform for monitoring livestock and crops in a dairy farming scenario. Ad Hoc Netw. 98, 102047 (2020). https://doi.org/10.1016/j.adhoc.2019.102047
7. Skodras, A., Christopoulos, C., Ebrahimi, T.: The JPEG 2000 still image compression standard. IEEE Signal Process. Mag. 18(5), 36–58 (2021). https://doi.org/10.1109/79.952804
8. Jayavrinda, V., Saravanan, C., Mahanti, G.K.: Wavelet and JPEG based image compression: an experimental analysis. In: Proceedings on International Conference and workshop on Emerging Trends in Technology, pp. 36–42 (2012). Int. J. Comput. Appl.
9. Redmon, J., Divvala, S., Girshick, R., Farhadi, A.: You only look once: unified, real-time object detection. In: 2016 IEEE Conference on Computer Vision and Pattern Recognition (CVPR), pp. 779–788 (2016). https://doi.org/10.1109/CVPR.2016.91
10. Tan, S., Lu, G., Jiang, Z., Huang, L.: Improved YOLOv5 network model and application in safety helmet detection. In: IEEE International Conference on Intelligence and Safety for Robotics, pp. 330–333 (2021). https://doi.org/10.1109/ISR50024.2021.9419561
11. He, K., Gkioxari, G., Dollar, P., Girshick, R.: Mask R-CNN. In: 2017 IEEE International Conference on Computer Vision (ICCV), pp. 2980–2988 (2017). https://doi.org/10.1109/ICCV.2017.322
12. Wang, C.-Y., Bochkovskiy, A., Liao, H.-Y.: ScaledYOLOv4: scaling cross stage partial network. arXiv:2011.08036, pp. 13029–13038 (2020)
13. Guo, P., Xue, Z., Long, L.R., Antani, S.: Cross-dataset evaluation of deep learning networks for uterine cervix segmentation. Diagnostics 10, 44 (2020). https://doi.org/10.3390/diagnostics10010044
14. Nieuwenhuizen, A., Hemming, J., Suh, H.: Detection and classification of insects on stick-traps in a tomato crop using Faster RCNN. In: The Netherlands Conference on Computer Vision (2018)
15. Jocher, G., Chaurasia, A., Stoken, A., Borovec, J.: NanoCode012, ...: ultralytics/yolov5: v6.1 - TensorRT, TensorFlow Edge TPU and OpenVINO Export and Inference (2022)

16. Sarjerao, B., Prakasarao, A.: A low-cost smart pollution measurement system using REST API and ESP32. In: 3rd International Conference for Convergence in Technology, pp. 1–5 (2018). https://doi.org/10.1109/I2CT.2018.8529500
17. Heinz, K., Parrella, M., Newman, J.: Time-efficient use of yellow sticky traps in monitoring insect populations. J. Econ. Entomol. **85**(6), 2263–2269 (1992)
18. Costa, C., Ferreira, C., Basti~ao, L., Ribeiro, L., Silva, A., Oliveira, J.: Dicoogle - an open source peer-to-peer PACS. In: J Digit Imaging **24**, 848–856 (2011). https://doi.org/10.1007/s10278-010-9347-9

Evaluating Maximum Operating Distance in COTS RFID TAGS for Smart Manufacturing

André Pinto[1](✉), Rolando Azevedo[1], and Sérgio Ivan Lopes[1,2,3]

[1] CiTin - Centro de Interface Tecnológico Industrial,
4970-786 Arcos de Valdevez, Portugal
{andre.pinto,rolando.azevedo}@citin.pt
[2] ADiT-Lab, Instituto Politécnico de Viana do Castelo,
4900-348 Viana do Castelo, Portugal
sil@estg.ipvc.pt
[3] IT - Instituto de Telecomunicações, Campus Universitário de Santiago,
3810-193 Aveiro, Portugal

Abstract. Supply chain management, inventory control, operations traceability, and many other applications within the scope of Industry 4.0 and smart manufacturing scenarios, can benefit from Radio Frequency IDentification (RFID), namely in the UHF band due to higher data rate transmission, effective multiple tag readability and lower cost. However, the adoption of such technology depends on specific application domain requirements that may be unique for specific industrial sectors. One important criterion is the maximum operating distance (MOD), which, depending on the application domain, may be critical for effective deployment. This work presents the experimental evaluation of MOD regarding 16 distinct commercial off-the-shelf (COTS) RFID tags in real-world environments. Results have shown that considering the specifications provided by the RFID TAG suppliers, it is not straightforward to design an RFID-based system to be directly scaled and deployed in a complex environment, based only on the RFID TAG specs. The properties of RFID TAGs, such as size and encapsulation type, are relevant for increased range and optimal MOD performance.

Keywords: RFID · UHF · IIoT · Industry 4.0 · Smart Manufacturing

1 Introduction

Industry 4.0 and smart manufacturing can benefit from Radio Frequency IDentification (RFID) technologies, particularly in the UHF band due to its higher data rate transmission, efficient multiple TAGs readability, and lower cost [1]. RFID enables passive wireless data transmission and processing, being mainly adopted for 1) short-range, proximity authentication, and access control [2,3]; and 2) long-range, tracking and tracing applications [4,5]. Industrial application scenarios may include supply chain management, inventory control, and

© ICST Institute for Computer Sciences, Social Informatics and Telecommunications Engineering 2023
Published by Springer Nature Switzerland AG 2023. All Rights Reserved
S. I. Lopes et al. (Eds.): Edge-IoT 2022/SmartGov 2022, LNICST 510, pp. 29–39, 2023.
https://doi.org/10.1007/978-3-031-35982-8_3

operations traceability, among others. Nevertheless, the adoption of a specific commercial off-the-shelf (COTS) RFID tag depends on certain industry-specific application requirements, such as the maximum operating distance (MOD) [6–8], which might be crucial for cost-effective deployment.

Industrial environments are susceptible to uncertain conditions that can change rapidly [9]. Short-range RFID systems are more adaptable to these changing environments, but when considering high-range applications, it is necessary to design optimized RFID systems for better performance [9]. One of the most relevant characteristics is the maximum read or write distance that an RFID TAG can have, concerning an RFID reader [10]. This distance parameter is defined as the maximum operating distance (MOD), cf. [6–8]. MOD is highly dependent on several environmental characteristics which, in a real industrial environment, are impossible to control or keep stabilized. The predictive and systematic formulation of the MOD during the design of an RFID-based system has been the subject of discussion in different studies [10–12]. However, there is no model capable of predicting all parameter configurations of an RFID system involving high-dispersion objects with different interrogation powers, namely in real and complex environments [10]. Since RFID TAGs respond to the power emitted by the reader by varying their input impedance and thus modulating the backscatter signal, it is possible to decompose the performance characteristics of a TAG into two main parameters, the sensitivity (the minimum signal strength power for a defined position), and the range (the maximum distance in free space) at which is possible to read and/or write in the tag [10,12]. Therefore, to select an established set of RFID TAGs that should be used with COTS RFID-based system architectures, a real-world experimental characterization is a straightforward, reliable, and accurate method for characterizing the MOD according to a fixed transmitted power by the RFID reader.

In this study, we experimentally evaluated the MOD for 16 commercial-of-the-shelf RFID TAGS in distinct geometries. Results have shown that considering the specifications provided by the RFID TAG suppliers, it is not straightforward to design an RFID-based system to be directly scaled and deployed in a complex environment, based only on the RFID TAG specs. The properties of RFID TAGs, such as size and encapsulation type, are determinants in longer range and optimal MOD performance.

This document is organized as follows: Sect. 2 presents the materials used and the adopted experimental methodology; Sect. 3 presents the results and their discussion. Lastly, in Sect. 4, conclusions are undertaken, and future work avenues are put forward.

2   Materials and Methods

For the analysis of MOD in RFID TAGs, three parameters can be controlled, 1) the power applied to the transmitting antenna, 2) the distance between the RFID TAG and the RFID reader, and 3) the distance between the TAG and the central axis perpendicular to the antenna plane. A study that includes real-world conditions during evaluation can be based on fixing the transmitted power and varying the distance from the RFID TAG in relation to the RFID reader [12], when it operates as an RF transponder. A method and architecture considering a real-world environment have been used to evaluate the MOD for distinct RFID TAGs. This method, consists of the evaluation of detected EPC (Electronic Product Code), in a specific distance, between the TAG and the RFID Reader, as well as the comparison of each TX Power from the reader at that specific distance. That is, for each TAG in a specific position, 15 EPC identification processes have been performed. The adopted evaluation setup consists of an RFID TAG in a static position and a UHF antenna attached to a commercial-of-the-shelf (COTS) RFID reader, the ThingMagic M6e Nano UHF RFID Reader Technology that is available in a Raspberry Pi 4 shield board provided by SB Components [13]. Thereafter, and considering the TAG in the same position, an increment was made to the value of the power to be emitted by the reader. The selected RFID UHF HAT allows a maximum TX power to the antenna of 27 dBm. Figure 1 depicts the block diagram of the hardware used in the experiment.

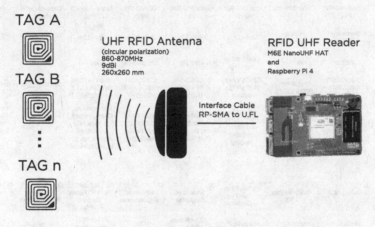

Fig. 1. Block diagram for the UHF RFID experimental setup.

The evaluation setup includes a UHF antenna placed in a horizontal position, face down. The main characteristics of the antenna are as follows: operating frequency 865–868 MHz; circular polarization; gain 9 dBi; normal impedance 50 Ohms; maximum power 10 W; dimensions $260 \times 260 \times 40$ mm; weight 1.1 Kg; operating Temperature: $-40\,^{\circ}$C to $65\,^{\circ}$C; and IP65 protection degree.

2.1   COTS RFID Tags Description

The evaluated RFID tags were selected from a pack of UHF tags commercially available at atlasRFIDstore [14]. All TAGS are recognized by the RAIN association and have been designed by different commercial TAG suppliers for a wide range of applications. The evaluated pack comprises the following main features:

– Worldwide UHF frequency coverage;
– High-quality UHF RFID tags built with Impinj M700 series, Impinj Monza R6 series, or Impinj Monza 4 series built-in integrated circuits;
– 16 distinct UHF RFID tags and inlays that can be attached to a variety of surfaces with different form factors and tag materials such as wet inlays, labels, hard tags, wristbands, laundry tags, and cards;
– Designed for several application domains including retail, supply chain management, inventory, logistics, sports timing, asset tracking, healthcare, and more.

Figure 2 depicts the overall RFID TAGs evaluated and describes its main characteristics, namely, the Chip Type, operating frequency, read range, tag form factor, size, and typical application domains.

	A. Avery Dennison AD-237r6	B. CCRR E68	C. Confidex Carrier Tough Slim	D. Confidex Ironside Micro	E. Confidex Silverline Blade II™	F. HID Global PVC	G. HID Global LinTRAK C15-MRI	H. HID Global SlimFlex™ Seal
Impinj Tag Chip Type	Monza R6	Monza R6-P	Monza 4QT	Monza 4QT	M730	Monza 4QT	Monza R6-P	Monza R6-P
Frequency	Global (860-960 MHz)	Global (860-960 MHz)	Global (865-928 MHz)	Global (865-928 MHz)	FCC (902-928 MHz)	Global (860-960 MHz)	Global (860-960 MHz)	Global (860-960 MHz)
Read Range (m)	Greater than 4.57 m	Testing Recommended	Up to 12 m	Up to 5 m	Up to 10 m	Up to 12 m	Up to 5 m	Up to 8 m
Tag Form Factor	Wet Inlay	Wet Inlay	Label Encased Hard Tag	Hard Tag	Hard Label Tag	Card Tag	Soft Tag	Flexible Hard Tag
Size (mm/inches)	73.18 x 17.678 mm (2.881 x 0.696 in)	94 x 28 mm (3.70 x 1.10 in)	122 x 18 x 2 mm (4.80 x 0.71 x 0.08 in)	27 x 27 x 5.5 mm (1.06 x 1.06 x 0.22 in)	60 x 25 x 1.4 mm (2.36 x 0.98 x 0.055 in)	85.6 x 54 x 0.76 mm (3.4 x 2.1 x 0.03 in)	66 x 15 mm (2.6 x 0.6 in)	85 x 25 x 3 mm (3.3 x 1 x 0.1 in)
Typical Applications	Apparel, Retail, Asset Tracking	Race Timing, Asset Tracking, Supply Chain Management, Inventory and Logistics	Returnable Transit Items and Plastic Container Tracking	Returnable Transit Items and Industrial Asset Tracking	Manufacturing, Automotive, IT Asset Tracking, Healthcare	Parking Access, Closed Payment Systems, NFC Applications, Access Control, Loyalty Schemes	Laundry, Textile	Asset Tracking, Logistics, Returnable Transit Items, Waste Management

	I. HuTag XC2	J. Omni-ID Exo 750	M. SIVA Foam Backed DogBone	N. Smartrac DogBone	O. Smartrac Squarewave	P. Vulcan RFID™ Foam Backed Wristband	Q. Vulcan RFID™ Flame	R. Xerafy Data Trak II
Impinj Tag Chip Type	Monza R6-P	Monza 4QT	Monza R6-P	M750 or Monza R6-P	M730	Monza R6 or Monza R6-P	Monza R6-P	Monza 4E
Frequency	FCC (902-928 MHz)	Global (860-930 MHz)	Global (860-960 MHz)	Global (860-960 MHz)	Global (860-960 MHz)	Global (860-960 MHz)	Global (860-960 MHz)	FCC (902-928 MHz)
Read Range (m)	Up to 8 m (Horizontal), Up to 4 m (Vertical)	Up to 11 m	Up to 6.1 m	Up to 20 m or Up to 16 m	Testing Recommended	Testing Recommended	Testing Recommended	Up to 4.5 m (On Metal), Up to 2.5 m (Off Metal)
Tag Form Factor	Hard Tag	Hard Tag	Foam Backed Tag	Wet Inlay	Wet Inlay	Wristband Tag	Wet Inlay	Hard Tag
Size (mm/inches)	50.5 x 44.5 x 12 mm (1.98 x 1.74 x 0.47 in)	51 x 48 x 12.6 mm (2.01 x 1.8 x 0.50 in)	99 x 31.75 x 3 mm (3.89 x 1.25 x 0.12 in)	97 x 27 mm (3.8 x 1.1 in)	97 x 15 mm (3.8 x 0.6 in)	279.4 x 34.9 mm (11 x 1.375 in)	47.50 x 13.38 mm (1.870 X 0.526 in)	38 x 13 x 4 mm (1.5 x 0.51 x 0.16 in)
Typical Applications	Race Timing	Automotive Supply Chain, Logistics, Tote Tracking	Race Timing	Universal	Universal	Large-scale Access Control	Retail, Supply Chain, Asset Tracking	Logistics, Warehousing, IT Asset Tracking

Fig. 2. UHF RAIN RFID sample pack TAGs comparison. Adapted from [14].

2.2 Experimental Procedure

For each of the RFID TAG identified in Fig. 2, an experimental procedure was implemented to evaluate the MOD for each distinct RFID TAG, over a given fixed power assigned to the RFID reader, according to the diagram in Fig. 3.

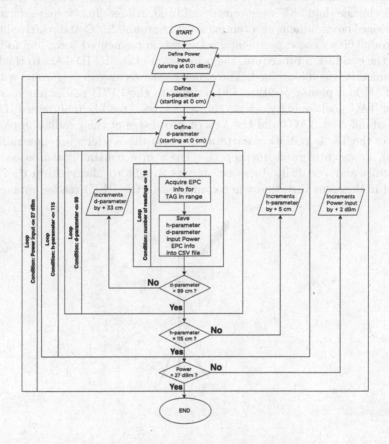

Fig. 3. Experimental procedure diagram.

In this setup, the control unit of the power applied to the RFID reader antenna was the UHF HAT shield that contains the M6e Nano Integrated Circuit (IC) from ThingMagic. Although this configuration allows the simultaneous reading/identification of multiple TAGs, it has the limitation of allowing only one identification process every second. The identification process was configured to repeat 15 times for each position, and automated using a python script. The position of the TAGs regarding the RFID reader antenna has been changed along two axes, height (h) and width (d), measured from the antenna centroid, as illustrated in Fig. 4. For each value of h, 24 positions were measured, starting from 0 to 115 cm, with 5 cm steps. The maximum distance, 115 cm, was defined having in mind the limitations of the experimental setup, namely by the limitation of the support used. For each value of d, 4 positions have been performed, from 0 to 99 cm, with steps of 33 cm. Regarding the transmitted power, for each of the respective positions defined by h and d, power was changed between 0 and 27 dBm, with 2 dBm steps. The experimental procedure consisted in acquiring 15 readings of the EPC of each RFID TAG under evaluation, for each value of the height, width, and power, respectively. Only readings with an EPC code detection higher than 98% were considered valid. All readings were performed in a conditioned environment at a temperature of around 21°C and relative humidity of around 60%. The experimental setup was implemented according to Fig. 4. During the evaluation procedure, the orientation of the RFID TAG to the RFID reader antenna was maintained. The experiment was always performed with the RFID TAG in a planar position and parallel to the RFID reader antenna. The study of TAG positioning vis-à-vis the reader was steadily maintained. Due to the use of different TAGs and the lack of knowledge of their radiation patterns (not only the TAGs radiation pattern, but also the reader's antenna radiation pattern), it was preferable to keep the TAGs in a constant orientation, both horizontally and vertically. Likewise, it was sought to always keep the TAGs oriented in the same direction when compared to the RFID reader antenna.

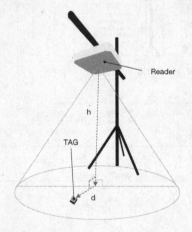

Fig. 4. Experimental setup adopted to evaluate the RFID TAG MOD with both height-h and width-d parameters identified.

All EPC data acquired from the identified RFID TAGs have been stored externally and subsequently processed. Lastly, a statistical and comparative analysis has been performed to understand if the MOD defined for each position has been achieved. Thus, only readings, for each position, that comprised 98% of EPC effective readings for the respective TAG under analysis were considered valid.

3   Results and Discussion

Figure 5 depicts the results obtained for the MOD in the 16 RFID evaluated TAGs, cf. Fig. 2, as a function of height (h) and width (d), according to the experimental setup defined in Fig. 3.

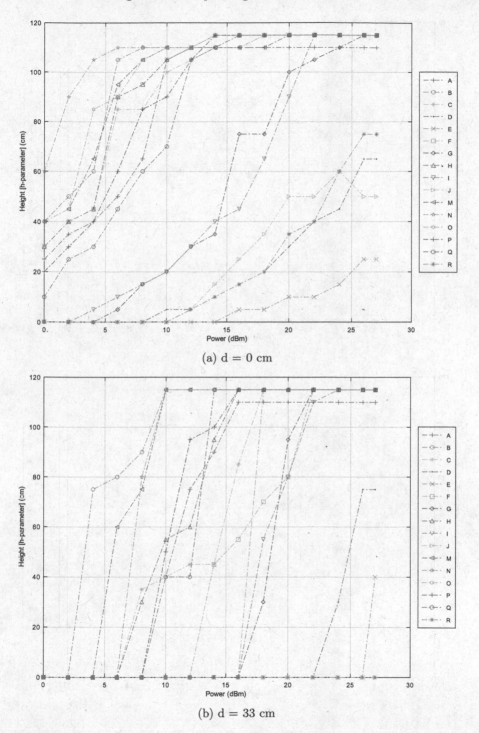

(a) d = 0 cm

(b) d = 33 cm

Fig. 5. Maximum Operating Distance as a function of height (h) and width (d), according to the experimental procedure described in Fig. 3, for the 16 RFID evaluated TAGs, cf. Fig. 2.

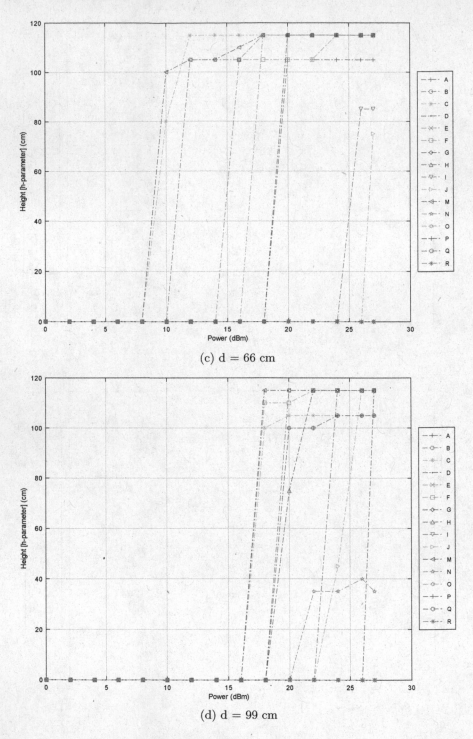

(c) d = 66 cm

(d) d = 99 cm

Fig. 5. (*continued*)

From the results obtained, it was observed that by maintaining the same test conditions, namely for different power and position settings, and for different RFID TAGs, distinct MOD values have been observed, despite the specifications put forward by the manufacturer. Another observation, is that the RFID TAGs with smaller dimensions (*e.g.* TAGs D, G, I, J and R) and with hard (*e.g.* TAGs D, E, I, J and R) and/or thick (*e.g.* TAGs I, J and R) encapsulation types, demonstrated lower MOD for higher h and d values (Fig. 5).

The experimental procedure was performed for the 16 TAGs identified in Fig. 2, according to the method depicted in Fig. 3. In the cases where variations were made due to TAG positioning error or even due to carelessness when performing the test, there was a higher variability in the number of readings for the smaller RFID TAGs (*e.g.* D, E and R), especially for lower power values and longer distances between the TAG and the antenna. This becomes even more observable when the TAG was centered towards the antenna, i.e., $d = 0$ cm, and for lower power values.

Despite the specifications provided by the RFID TAG manufacturers, who indicate a maximum readable range with the respective TAG, it becomes clear from the results that the TAG position, by varying both h and d, directly influences the MOD for a specific power value. This information is given by the manufacturer, but the conditions for obtaining a specific MOD are not specified. This is also clearly observable for lower power values, where it is not possible to read the EPC from the RFID TAGs for higher d values.

4   Conclusion and Future Work

This work presents the experimental evaluation of the maximum operating distance (MOD) regarding 16 distinct commercial off-the-shelf (COTS) RFID tags in a real-world environment. The experimental procedure consisted in obtaining a valid MOD, for each test position (d, h) when more than 98% of RFID TAG readings have been successfully made. Based on the obtained results, and considering the specifications provided by the RFID TAG suppliers, it is not straightforward to design an RFID-based system to be directly scaled and deployed in a complex environment, based only on the RFID TAG datasheet. The properties of RFID TAGs, such as size and encapsulation type, are determinants in a longer range and optimal EPC code detection performance. In terms of distance to the antenna, it is shown that varying the alignment to the antenna's centroid is one of the parameters that most influence the range of RFID TAGs. This is directly related to both intervening RF devices, namely, the radiation pattern of the RFID reader antenna, and the radiation pattern of the RFID TAG antenna, which operates in backscatter mode.

Future work includes the implementation of the same experimental procedure in distinct, controlled, and real-world environments. Firstly, at an anechoic controlled environment to minimize the impact of interference generated by external RF sources. Secondly, using the previous setup, but using well-defined and known RF interference signals, thus allowing a broader evaluation. Thirdly, understanding the true influence of different real-world industrial environments, and effectively evaluate what are the most significant parameters that impact MOD, would allow optimal system calibration for the identification, sequencing, and traceability of products using UHF RFID technology.

Acknowledgements. This contribution has been done in collaboration with the Applied Digital Transformation Laboratory (ADiT-Lab), http://www.adit.ipvc.pt, and has been partially funded by the Polytechnic Institute of Viana do Castelo. A.P. and R.A have been supported by operation NORTE-06-3559-FSE-000226, funded by Norte Portugal Regional Operational Program (NORTE 2020), under the PORTUGAL 2020 Partnership Agreement, through the European Social Fund (ESF).

References

1. Weinstein, R.: RFID: a technical overview and its application to the enterprise. IT Prof. **7**(3), 27–33 (2005). https://doi.org/10.1109/MITP.2005.69
2. Pereira, H., Carreira, R., Pinto, P., Lopes, S.I.: Hacking the RFID-based authentication system of a University Campus on a budget. In: 2020 15th Iberian Conference on Information Systems and Technologies (CISTI), Sevilla, Spain, pp. 1–5 (2020). https://doi.org/10.23919/CISTI49556.2020.9140943
3. Curralo, A., Lopes, S.I., Mendes, J., Curado, A.: Joining sustainable design and Internet of Things technologies on Campus: the IPVC Smartbottle practical case. Sustainability **14**, 5922 (2022). https://doi.org/10.3390/su14105922
4. Amato, F., Torun, H.M., Durgin, G.D.: RFID backscattering in long-range scenarios. IEEE Trans. Wireless Commun. **17**(4), 2718–2725 (2018). https://doi.org/10.1109/TWC.2018.2801803
5. Dobrykh, D., et al.: Long-range miniaturized ceramic RFID tags. IEEE Trans. Antennas Propag. **69**(6), 3125–3131 (2021). https://doi.org/10.1109/TAP.2020.3037663
6. Chen, Z., Deng, F., He, Y., Liang, Z., Fu, Z., Zhang, C.: A self-powered RFID sensor tag for long-term temperature monitoring in substation. J. Electr. Eng. Technol. **13**(1), 501–512 (2018). https://doi.org/10.5370/JEET.2017.13.1.501
7. Klapf, C., Missoni, A., Pribyl, W., Hofer, G., Holweg, G., Kargl, W.: Improvements in operational distance in passive HF RFID transponder systems. In: IEEE International Conference on RFID 2008, pp. 250–257 (2008). https://doi.org/10.1109/RFID.2008.4519347
8. De Vita, G., Iannaccone, G.: Design criteria for the RF section of UHF and microwave passive RFID transponders. IEEE Trans. Microw. Theory Tech. **53**(9), 2978–2990 (2005). https://doi.org/10.1109/TMTT.2005.854229
9. Zhi-yuan, Z., He, R., Jie, T.: A method for optimizing the position of passive UHF RFID tags. In: IEEE International Conference on RFID-Technology and Applications 2010, pp. 92–95 (2010). https://doi.org/10.1109/RFID-TA.2010.5529867
10. Marrocco, G., Di Giampaolo, E., Aliberti, R.: Estimation of UHF RFID reading regions in real environments. IEEE Antennas Propag. Mag. **51**(6), 44–57 (2009). https://doi.org/10.1109/MAP.2009.5433096
11. Hodges, S., Thorne, A., Mallinson, H., Floerkemeier, C.: Assessing and optimizing the range of UHF RFID to enable real-world pervasive computing applications. In: LaMarca, A., Langheinrich, M., Truong, K.N. (eds.) Pervasive Computing, pp. 280–297. Springer, Cham (2007). https://doi.org/10.1007/978-3-540-72037-9_17

12. Nikitin, P., Rao, K.V.S., Lam, S.: UHF RFID tag characterization: overview and state-of-the-art. In: Antenna Measurement Techniques Association Symposium (AMTA) (2012). 10.1.1.362.2900
13. SB Components, UHF HAT for Raspberry Pi. shop.sb-components.co.uk/products/uhf-hat-for-raspberry-pi. Accessed 1 Sept 2022
14. Atlas RFID Store, Impinj UHF RAIN RFID Sample Pack. www.atlasrfidstore.com/impinj-uhf-rain-rfid-sample-pack/. Accessed 1 Sept 2022

IoT Architectures, Forecasting
and Adversarial Training

Philippine Stock Direction Forecasting Utilizing Technical, Fundamental, and News Sentiment Data

Sean Arthur E. Sombrito, Kenneth John G. Gonzales,
Jan Kyle Lewis T. Nolasco, and Nestor Michael C. Tiglao[✉]

Electrical and Electronics Engineering Institute, Velasquez St.,
University of the Philippines Diliman, 1101 Quezon City, Philippines
{sean.arthur.sombrito,kenneth.john.gonzales,jan.kyle.nolasco,
nestor.tiglao}@eee.upd.edu.ph

Abstract. Stock direction forecasting is a complex process and requires careful analysis of stock data. Past studies have implemented various machine and deep learning models to forecast stock directions with varying levels of success. In this capstone project, the proponents created long short-term memory (LSTM) neural network models that utilized a combination of technical, fundamental, and news sentiment stock data. Compared to previous work, input features were selected through forward stepwise selection, instead of using a fixed set. Furthermore, each model created was tuned for a specific stock and has a unique set of hyperparameters and input features. The models were capable of forecasting the future daily directions of the closing prices of stocks traded in the Philippine Stock Exchange (PSE) with an average directional accuracy of 57.38%, upward directional accuracy of 61.47%, and a downward directional accuracy of 54.72%, which are statistically significantly better than the naïve baselines. When compared to the models in previous work adapted to predicting Philippine stocks, our model achieved the highest performance among different accuracy measures. The results of the study suggest that indiscriminately adding indicators as input features would lower the accuracy of the model, and that the PSE may be more difficult to predict than other stock exchanges. Future work can focus on improving the accuracy of our models.

Keywords: Stock direction forecasting · PSE · LSTM

1 Introduction

The prediction of stock prices has always been a difficult task. One has to first learn fundamental and technical analysis which takes a lot of time and effort.

The authors acknowledge the financial support provided by the UP Engineering Research and Development Foundation, Inc. (UPERDFI).

© ICST Institute for Computer Sciences, Social Informatics and Telecommunications Engineering 2023
Published by Springer Nature Switzerland AG 2023. All Rights Reserved
S. I. Lopes et al. (Eds.): Edge-IoT 2022/SmartGov 2022, LNICST 510, pp. 43–58, 2023.
https://doi.org/10.1007/978-3-031-35982-8_4

Moreover, the process of analyzing stocks itself is time consuming since new information must be analyzed daily. Through the use of neural networks, specifically long-short term memory (LSTM) networks, one could potentially forecast stock prices without going through the effort of learning stock analysis techniques.

Multiple works on financial time series prediction using machine and deep learning techniques have already been conducted in the past. Works such as [11,13] tested multiple techniques and have found success with LSTM networks which is further supported by [10]. The main reason for this is that LSTM models are capable of storing both short and long term dependencies in data [2, p. 25], which other techniques lack. Furthermore, works such as [8,12,13] also utilized sentimental analysis and saw an increase in the accuracy of the prediction when compared to using technical analysis and/or fundamental analysis alone. Lastly, due to the difficulty of predicting the stock prices directly, works such as [4,6,13] sought to predict only the direction of the price itself, whether it will increase or decrease.

The goal of this work was to create an end user program that forecasts stock direction utilizing technical, fundamental, and sentimental analysis. To this end, the researchers implemented an LSTM model that used these indicators as its input features to accurately predict stock direction.

The contributions of this paper are as follows: (1) use of technical, fundamental, and sentiment indicators for stock direction forecasting in the Philippine setting, (2) creation of unique models for each stock through the use of feature selection and hyperparameter optimization, and (3) adoption of models used in foreign stock exchanges to the Philippine Stock Exchange (PSE).

2   Related Work

2.1   Traditional Approaches to Stock Forecasting

Traditional stock forecasting often takes two approaches: fundamental analysis and technical analysis. Sometimes, both are used at the same time. These approaches presume that the future state of the market can be predicted. Fundamental analysis mainly utilizes economic data for stock forecasting. These economic data, such as production, consumption and exports, is often used to analyze a company's performance and profitability [3, p.16]. On the other hand, technical analysis uses non-economic data to forecast stock prices. The data often used here are the stock price itself, volume, and open interest [3, p. 16]. Using current and past price data, statistics is employed to find trends and patterns that will help the investor to predict future stock prices [1]. There are also some theories that state that the stock market is unpredictable. These are the Random Walk, which states that the stock market is completely random [3, p. 29], and the Efficient Market Hypothesis, which states that to predict the future price of the stock, one must obtain future information on the said stock [3, p. 428], which is impossible.

2.2 Previous Machine/Deep Learning Techniques and Models in Stock Forecasting

A majority of previously developed direction forecasting models use historical price data of stocks and commonly-used technical indicators to predict stock trends. In [4], the author implemented LSTM models based on daily stock return data and achieved a statistically significant accuracy of 55.30% in predicting price directions of the OMX (Swedish Stock Exchange) index. However, only predicting directions and not returns themselves were possible; model-predicted returns only operated around the mean of actual returns. In [6], different technical indicators were used in artificial neural networks (ANN) and support vector machines (SVM) and have found success in predicting an index in the Istanbul Stock Exchange, achieving accuracies of 75.74% and 71.52%, respectively. Other deep learning approaches were tested in [11], where LSTM, SVM, eXtreme gradient boosting (XGBoost), and gated recurrent units (GRU) utilizing stock returns and widely used technical indicators were used to predict directions of several United States stocks. Similar to [4], the models were partly based on stock return data rather than closing price data as returns could be considered pseudo-stationary in time and minimizes variations in stock prices [11,13]. From the various model results, the author concluded that recurrent neural network (RNN) models such as LSTM and GRU may be more suited in time series related prediction applications as they achieved the best accuracies of 64.25% and 64.33% in the study.

Though not as common, researchers have also found success in utilizing other types of inputs, specifically fundamental indicators and even textual news data. In [5], fundamental indicators were used in SVM and achieved 70% accuracy during testing. Other authors focused on finding ways to further improve performance especially in terms of accuracy with the most common approach being combining different types of inputs. In [7], using a combination of technical and fundamental indicators in Multilayer Perceptron (MLP) achieved an average directional accuracy of 65.87%. This was higher compared to the 62.85% when using technical indicators alone and 64.28% when using fundamental indicators alone. As for [8,12], both combined LSTM for technical indicators and Convolution Neural Network (CNN) for textual news data to form a hybrid model. Both of their results showed that the use of technical indicators and textual news data in combination outperforms the use of only one type of input. The best performing model in [8,12] achieved an accuracy of 56.84% and 69.86%, respectively. Finally, one research that utilizes the combination of technical, fundamental, and sentiment indicators is [13]. The researchers implemented ARIMA, Linear Regression, Random Forest, Feed Forward Neural Network, and LSTM models for comparison. Results showed that machine learning models performed better than statistical models, with the LSTM model achieving the highest average directional accuracy at 61.69%.

Currently, although various deep learning techniques have been used in the field of stock direction forecasting, studies combining the three indicators were very limited, with none tackling the applicability of deep learning in forecasting directions of stocks specific to the Philippine Stock Exchange. Aside from that, it was also observed that LSTMs were the most prevalent model when performing stock price and trend forecasting. This is supported by [10] which performed a comprehensive literature review and is due to a number of reasons. First, they are more preferred as they are easier to implement and adapt to many time series forecasting problems. Moreover, they resulted in having higher performances, thus considered to be the optimal model for time series prediction and classification. This conclusion is consistent with the majority of the reviewed literature.

3   Methodology

3.1   Overview

The implemented system used two APIs, namely EOD (End-Of-Day) Historical Data API to extract daily stock data and fundamental data and News API to extract news headlines. Additional steps were first performed on the technical and fundamental data to obtain the necessary indicators while news headlines were scored by the sentiment model built by the proponents. These indicators were then processed before being used as input features to the direction forecasting model. The output of this model were predicted stock returns which forecasted the direction of a given stock. The system's operation is summarized in Fig. 1.

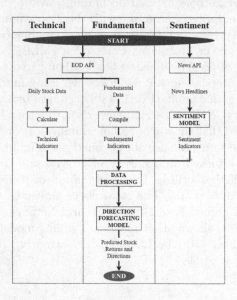

Fig. 1. System Operation

3.2   Sentiment Model

For the sentiment model, a convolutional neural network (CNN) model was built using TensorFlow 2 with Keras interface. To train the model, the annotated data set, Financial Phrase Bank, used in [13] was utilized. This was processed using *Tokenizer* from *keras.preprocessing* to convert the contained sentences into their numerical representations. The model itself had four types of layers with the first being the embedding layer, *keras.layers.Embedding*, which produces word embeddings or real valued vector representations of each word. Aside from training their own embedding layer, the proponents also used pre-trained word embeddings, specifically GloVe and word2vec, and determined which offered the best performance. The other three layers represent CNN itself: *keras.layers.Conv1D*, *keras.layers.GlobalMaxPooling1D*, and the final output layer *keras.layers.Dense*. The loss function used was Sparse Categorical Cross Entropy while the optimization algorithm was Adam, an adaptive learning rate method that generally yields better model performance and is most commonly used in practice [2].

In total, four model hyperparameters were tuned: the number of epochs for training, the number of filters and the kernel size of the convolutional layer, and the dropout probability for the dropout layer added before the final output layer. An early stopping callback function was implemented to tune the number of epochs while a *keras_tuner.Hyperband* tuner was utilized to tune the remaining three. The obtained best-performing model in terms of accuracy was used to score headlines extracted using News API. Other verb tenses were considered for those not in the vocabulary while converting them into their numerical representations. The final scores, which served as additional input to the direction forecasting model, were obtained by adapting the scoring in [13].

3.3   Data Processing

Data Set. The data set spanning April 2017 to April 2022 was prepared by gathering the necessary indicators. Technical and fundamental indicators were taken from EOD (End-Of-Day) Historical API, while sentiment indicators were taken from the sentiment model. The selection of indicators came from previous works, such as [8,11,13], and what was available form EOD Historical Data. The selected technical indicators, with their periods, and fundamental indicators are shown in Table 1.

Preparing the Data. In this work, the variable to be predicted was the log return format of the adjusted closing prices. Unlike the adjusted closing price, this format can be considered stationary in time and it makes it easier to compare stocks from different companies [13].

$$R_t = log(P_t) - log(P_{t-1}) \tag{1}$$

$$R_t = log(\frac{P_t}{P_{t-1}}) \tag{2}$$

Table 1. Chosen Technical and Fundamental Indicators

Technical Indicators	Fundamental Indicators
A/D (1)	P/E Ratio
CMF (5)	EPS
ATR (5)	ROE
RSI (5)	GDP
WR (5)	Interest Rate
CCI (5)	Inflation Rate
ADX (5)	PSEi Returns
Slope (5)	
%K (3)	
%D (3)	
MACD (4, 22)	
Signal Line (3)	
Divergence (1)	

After compiling the indicators into a single data set, the data was split into training (60%), validation (20%), and test (20%) sets. The training set was used to train the LSTM model, while the validation set was used for early stopping and tuning of hyperparameters, and lastly, the test set was used to check the accuracy of the trained model. The data was then preprocessed. The data was first cleaned by removing entries that are incomplete. For example, if an entry did not contain the CMF feature (technical indicator) and it can not be computed from the available data, then that entry was discarded from the data set. Afterwhich, the data was transformed using Yeo-Johnson Power Transformation similar to [13]. Lastly, outliers were removed by setting feature values below −4.5 and above 4.5 to −4.5 and 4.5, respectively. Finally, the data was grouped into timestep windows before it is fed into the model.

3.4   Direction Forecasting Model

For the direction forecasting models, LSTM neural networks were used and built using the aforementioned Tensorflow 2 library with Keras interface. Separate LSTM models were created, tuned, and tested for each of eight selected PSE stocks: {ALI, AP, BPI, JFC, MER, PGOLD, SM, TEL}. The models consisted of a variable number of LSTM layers with the *return_sequences* argument set to True and a single Dense output layer to capture the output labels of the LSTM layers. The input features to the models were the different technical, fundamental, and sentiment indicators, whereas the target output labels were the stock returns. Similar to the previous studies, the sign of the predicted stock returns of the models in this study determined the final predicted direction of stock price movement. The loss function used in training the models was mean squared error (MSE) while the optimization algorithm was Adam, which was shown to be the best optimizer for stock price prediction LSTM models in [9].

The proponents implemented forward stepwise feature selection to determine optimal input features to the models. Each feature was sequentially added and the mean directional accuracy (DA) of fifteen subsequent models was checked for improvement which determined whether a feature is selected or not. The testing order of the features was decided by grouping the indicator by their type: technical, fundamental, and sentimental.

After feature selection, there were five model hyperparameters tuned: the number of epochs for training, the number of hidden units in each LSTM layer, the number of LSTM layers in the model, the recurrent dropout probabilities of each LSTM layer, and the size of the input data windows to the model. The number of epochs was tuned through the implementation of an early stopping callback function, whereas the other hyperparameters except for window size were tuned using the Hyperband algorithm implemented in the KerasTuner library. Finally, proponents measured the DAs of tuned models of varying window sizes to determine the optimal window size. Tables 2 and 3 summarizes the implemented model tuning methods and search spaces, respectively.

Table 2. Model Tuning Methods for Direction Forecasting Model

Model Hyperparameter	Tuning Method
Number of Epochs	Early Stopping Callback Function
Number of Hidden Units in LSTM Layer/s	Hyperband Tuning
Number of LSTM Layers	Hyperband Tuning
Recurrent Dropout Probability	Hyperband Tuning
Input Data Window Size	Manual Search
Input Features	Forward Stepwise Selection

Table 3. Model Tuning Search Spaces for Direction Forecasting Model

Model Hyperparameter	Search Space
Number of Epochs	$\{x \mid x \in \mathbb{N}, x \leq 100\}$
Number of Hidden Units in LSTM Layer/s	$\{32, 64, 128, 256\}$
Number of LSTM Layers	$\{1, 2, 3, 4, 5\}$
Recurrent Dropout Probability	$\{\frac{x}{10} \mid x \in \mathbb{W}, x \leq 9\}$
Input Data Window Size	$\{1, 5, 10, 15, 20\}$
Input Features	All available indicators

The DA of the tuned models were measured, alongside the upward directional accuracy (UDA), and downward directional accuracy (DDA) to determine if forecasting performance was better for certain directions. These performance measures are based on the confusion matrix values of the models and their equations are listed below. For a model with a test data set of n samples, stock return R_t and model-predicted stock return $\hat{R}_t$ at time t:

$$f(R_t) = \begin{cases} 1 & \text{if } R_t \geq 0 \\ 0 & \text{if } R_t < 0 \end{cases} \tag{3}$$

$$TP = \sum_{t=0}^{n-1} \begin{cases} 1 & \text{if } f(R_t) = f(\hat{R}_t) = 1 \\ 0 & \text{otherwise} \end{cases} \tag{4}$$

$$TN = \sum_{t=0}^{n-1} \begin{cases} 1 & \text{if } f(R_t) = f(\hat{R}_t) = 0 \\ 0 & \text{otherwise} \end{cases} \tag{5}$$

$$FP = \sum_{t=0}^{n-1} \begin{cases} 1 & \text{if } (f(R_t) = 0) \wedge (f(\hat{R}_t) = 1) \\ 0 & \text{otherwise} \end{cases} \tag{6}$$

$$FN = \sum_{t=0}^{n-1} \begin{cases} 1 & \text{if } (f(R_t) = 1) \wedge (f(\hat{R}_t) = 0) \\ 0 & \text{otherwise} \end{cases} \tag{7}$$

$$DA = \frac{TP + TN}{TP + TN + FP + FN} \tag{8}$$

$$UDA = \begin{cases} \frac{TP}{TP+FP} & \text{if } (TP + FP) > 0 \\ 1 & \text{otherwise} \end{cases} \tag{9}$$

$$DDA = \begin{cases} \frac{TN}{TN+FN} & \text{if } (TN + FN) > 0 \\ 1 & \text{otherwise} \end{cases} \tag{10}$$

To evaluate the models, performance measures of naive optimistic and pessimistic direction forecasting models that always predict an upward and downward direction for stock price movements were used as baselines for comparison. The aforementioned measures were used as data in three separate one-tailed Wilcoxon signed-rank tests with a significance level of 0.05. In the tests, the DA measures of the LSTM models were paired with the baseline model with the higher mean DA, whereas the UDA and DDA measures of the LSTM models were paired with those from their corresponding baseline models.

4   Results and Analysis

4.1   Sentiment Model

Three models, each with a different embedding layer, were built using the default hyperparameters: one convolutional layer, 128 filters, a kernel size of 3, and a dropout probability of 0.5. The resulting untuned accuracies for one execution, five models were built every execution with their accuracies averaged, are shown in Table 4 below.

Since there was a chance that the untuned hyperparameters were affecting the performance of each model, hyperparameter optimization was performed for

Table 4. Summary of Accuracies & Optimal Hyperparameters

Model	Untuned Accuracy	Filters	Kernel Size	Dropout Probability	Tuned Accuracy
Preliminary	0.777113	128	4	0.2	0.784124
GloVe	0.789485	128	3	0.4	0.795670
word2vec	0.800865	256	3	0.3	0.809371

all three. The optimal hyperparameters for each model are presented in the same table together with the resulting tuned accuracies for one execution. It may be observed that there was only a slight improvement in accuracy for all three models since the default hyperparameters were already almost the same with the obtained optimal hyperparameters. Moreover, the use of pre-trained word embeddings, especially word2vec, resulted in better performances since they were trained on much larger data sets enabling them to better capture and represent the relationship between words.

After numerous testing, the obtained best-performing word2vec model had an accuracy of 0.828866. To show its usage, three random headlines were scored as shown in Fig. 2.

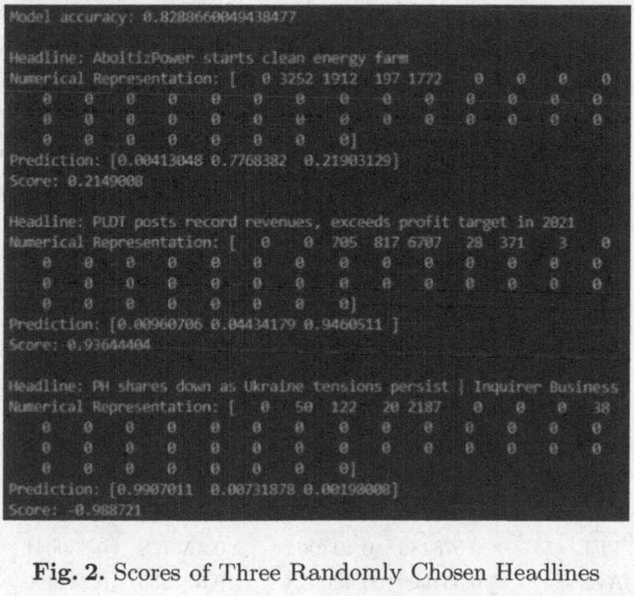

Fig. 2. Scores of Three Randomly Chosen Headlines

However, there were times that the model was not able to score properly since some of the important words, specifically verbs, were set to zero as they were not part of the vocabulary. To reduce this occurrence, the conversion method was modified so that other verb tenses were considered. A sample comparison is shown in Fig. 3.

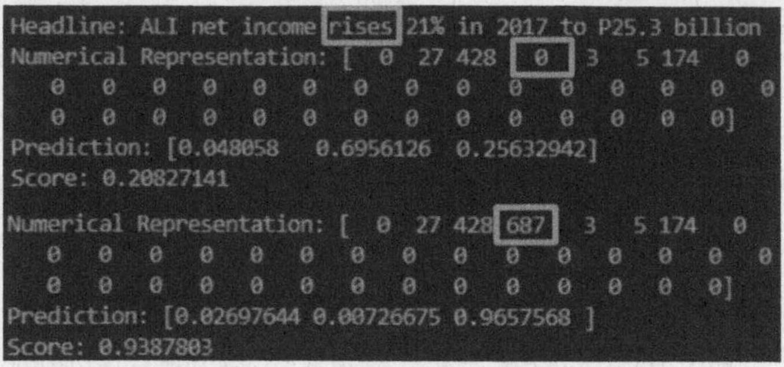

Fig. 3. Score Comparison (First Score Without Verb Tense Consideration)

Reevaluating the model on the test set also showed a slight improvement in performance, from 0.828866 to 0.831959, which shows that there is really a need to consider other verb tenses.

4.2   Direction Forecasting Models Using Various Indicators

Shown in Table 5 are the mean DAs for the evaluated stocks for each indicator type: technical, fundamental, and sentiment, and for models using all indicators. All the models shared the same default hyperparameters: 3 LSTM layers, 64 hidden units per layer, 0.6 recurrent dropout probability, and 1 timestep window size.

Table 5. Mean DA of the Evaluated Stocks Using Technical, Fundamental, Sentiment, and all Indicator Types

Stock Ticker	Technical	Fundamental	Sentiment	All
ALI	0.567490	0.551029	0.530864	0.564198
AP	0.585185	0.562963	0.523045	0.579012
BPI	0.512346	0.473251	0.484362	0.524691
JFC	0.504115	0.480247	0.496708	0.488066
MER	0.577366	0.552675	0.585185	0.545267
PGOLD	0.516049	0.492181	0.482716	0.525926
SM	0.599177	0.559671	0.562140	0.582716
TEL	0.578189	0.493004	0.477778	0.530041
Average	0.554990	0.520628	0.517850	0.542490

The models using only technical indicators have the highest average mean DA among the indicator types at 55.5%. Models utilizing only fundamental indicators were second at 52.06%, and models using only sentiment indicators were last at 51.79%. The average mean DA of the models using a specific indicator type determined the order in which feature selection was done. The order of indicators was technical, fundamental, then sentiment. Notably, the model using all indicators had an average mean DA of 54.25%, which was higher than the models using fundamental indicators only (52.06%) and sentiment indicators only (51.79%). However, it was lower than the average mean DA of the models using only technical indicators (55.5%). This implied that using technical indicators only produced better results than using all indicators.

4.3   Tuned Direction Forecasting Models

After conducting hyperparameter optimization and feature selection on the direction forecasting models, the optimal hyperparameters and features for the models of different Philippine stocks were determined and are presented below in Table 6.

Table 6. Summary of Optimal Hyperparameters & Selected Features

Stock Ticker	Hidden Units	LSTM Layers	Dropout	Window Size	Selected Features
ALI	32	1	0.7	1	{Stock Returns, A/D, CMF, ATR, PSEi Returns}
AP	256	5	0	1	{Stock Returns, A/D, ATR, ADX, Slope, %K}
BPI	64	2	0.7	1	{Stock Returns, A/D, WR, RSI, ADX, Inflation, P/E Ratio, PSEi Returns, Sentiment}
JFC	256	1	0.6	20	{Stock Returns, ATR, RSI, ADX, EPS, PSEi Returns, Sentiment}
MER	256	1	0.7	15	{Stock Returns, A/D, WR, CCI, Slope, MACD, Sentiment}
PGOLD	32	2	0.4	20	{Stock Returns, CMF}
SM	64	1	0.7	15	{Stock Returns, A/D, WR, CCI}
TEL	32	3	0.6	1	{Stock Returns, A/D, %K}

As seen from the listed hyperparameters, there does not appear to be any universal set of best values. The researchers note, however, that nearly all of the tuned models implemented recurrent dropout (with a majority having dropout probabilities of 0.6 or 0.7), supporting the idea that recurrent dropout as a form of LSTM regularization is beneficial for stock direction forecasting. For the selected features, the addition of only a few indicators improved model performance on the validation data sets of the different stocks. Furthermore, the selected indicators in the tuned models were mainly technical (A/D indicator being the most prominent), with only a few models having selected fundamental or sentiment indicators. This suggested that fundamental and news data are less important in predicting daily stock price directions as compared to the shorter-term technical data.

Table 7. Performance of Tuned Direction Forecasting Models

Stock	DA		UDA		DDA		Opt. Baseline	Pess. Baseline
	Mean	Std Dev	Mean	Std Dev	Mean	Std Dev		
ALI	0.564198	0.014831	0.566811	0.010553	0.559898	0.027762	0.526749	0.473251
AP	0.597531	0.013827	0.676849	0.012660	0.552971	0.012537	0.530864	0.469136
BPI	0.553086	0.006492	0.597806	0.011227	0.522332	0.005320	0.526749	0.473251
JFC	0.541975	0.015766	0.549906	0.014680	0.532424	0.024480	0.518519	0.481481
MER	0.595473	0.013996	0.713102	0.036108	0.516458	0.012444	0.576132	0.423868
PGOLD	0.552263	0.014876	0.604792	0.022700	0.512709	0.012546	0.539095	0.460905
SM	0.611523	0.009344	0.591026	0.008141	0.636166	0.016912	0.485597	0.514403
TEL	0.574074	0.013335	0.617321	0.011171	0.544853	0.014954	0.522634	0.477366
Average	0.573765	0.012808	0.614702	0.015905	0.547226	0.015869	0.528292	0.471708

In Table 7, the performance of the models with optimized hyperparameters and feature selection can be seen. The models achieved an average mean DA of 57.38%. Compared to the different models using various types of indicators, this model has the highest average mean DA, beating the model using only technical indicators by 1.88%. This indicated that in addition to technical indicators, fundamental and sentiment indicators can also increase accuracy if the said indicators undergo feature selection.

Table 8. Wilcoxon Signed-rank Test for General, Upward, and Downward Accuracies Against the Naive Baselines

Accuracy	Test Statistic	Critical Value	Result
General	0	5	significant difference
Upward	0	5	significant difference
Downward	0	5	significant difference

In Table 8, the results of the Wilcoxon signed-rank tests of the model performances against the optimistic (opt.) and pessimistic (pess.) baselines are shown. The null hypotheses for the three tests were that the medians of the samples were equal. At N=8 and $\alpha = 0.05$, the critical value was 5. For all the tests, the test statistic was found to be 0 and was less than the critical value. Therefore, the null hypotheses were rejected. This implied that the model's performance in terms of general, upward, and downward accuracy was superior to that of the naive baselines.

4.4 Performance Comparison with Previous Models

As evident in the performance metrics presented in the previous sections, the performance of the tuned direction forecasting models could be considered underwhelming when compared to the model performances recorded in foreign stock exchanges in the previously reviewed literature. As such, the proponents rebuilt several best performing models from other researches (i.e., [6, 11, 12]) and retested them to determine whether or not they continued to perform better than the tuned direction forecasting models on the selected Philippine stocks. Shown in Tables 9 and 10 are the mean model performances of the tuned models and the rebuilt models. From the results, the tuned models outperformed all of the rebuilt models, achieving respectable gains in average performance in all three performance measures, especially in the UDA performance. This behavior suggests that previous deep learning techniques are less effective on forecasting Philippine stocks and that the implementation of LSTM models utilizing various types of indicators, hyperparameter tuning, and feature selection are useful in improving direction forecasting performance in the Philippine setting.

Table 9. Performances of Previous Models

Stock Ticker	ANN Models from [6]			LSTM Models from [11]		
	DA	UDA	DDA	DA	UDA	DDA
ALI	0.521429	0.673528	0.488937	0.523392	0.537525	0.518419
AP	0.571429	0.598053	0.563451	0.550585	0.59605	0.514414
BPI	0.430952	0.505397	0.419505	0.518713	0.51804	0.519184
JFC	0.519048	0.73358	0.505657	0.509064	0.601728	0.498527
MER	0.497619	0.600319	0.416366	0.522807	0.567399	0.486641
PGOLD	0.528571	0.521789	0.540981	0.484211	0.497144	0.447071
SM	0.538889	0.530139	0.556642	0.54883	0.554948	0.54693
TEL	0.52381	0.539959	0.544132	0.533333	0.557399	0.53601
Average	0.516468	0.587846	0.504459	0.523867	0.553779	0.5084

Table 10. Performances of Previous Models (*Continued*)

Stock Ticker	CNN-LSTM Models from [12]			Final Tuned Models		
	DA	UDA	DDA	DA	UDA	DDA
ALI	0.522857	0.60027	0.267138	0.564198	0.566811	0.559898
AP	0.597436	0.586679	0.610208	0.597531	0.676849	0.552971
BPI	0.503226	0.582362	0.448768	0.553086	0.597806	0.522332
JFC	0.50687	0.47916	0.567302	0.541975	0.549906	0.532424
MER	0.50411	0.601115	0.429123	0.595473	0.713102	0.516458
PGOLD	0.502941	0.49898	0.610789	0.552263	0.604792	0.512709
SM	0.561818	0.56545	0.652863	0.611523	0.591026	0.636166
TEL	0.521019	0.55644	0.60407	0.574074	0.617321	0.544853
Average	0.527535	0.558807	0.523783	0.57377	0.61470	0.54723

4.5   User Application and Functionality

PyQt5 toolkit was used to create the end user interface of the stock direction forecasting application. Within the application window, there are two main tabs, the *Predict* and *Models* tab. Under the former, the user can generate models and direction forecasts for a publicly-traded Philippine company. Performance metrics were also shown in every prediction. A majority-vote system was utilized for the five models to ensure the consistency of the accuracy of the final direction forecast with the reported performance metrics of the models. As for the latter, the user can do two things, namely view relevant model information and perform model tuning. Relevant model information includes its last tuning date and hyperparameters. On the other hand, tuning processes include obtaining the optimal set of features and hyperparameters which are then saved in a parameters database. A sample use of the application to make a direction forecast is shown in Fig. 4.

Fig. 4. Sample Direction Forecast in the User Application

5   Conclusion

The tuned LSTM-based stock direction forecasting models were the first to consider technical, fundamental, and sentiment indicators in a deep learning model built for the PSE. They proved to be sufficiently able to predict stock price movement directions for Philippine stocks, achieving mean accuracies of 57.38%, 61.47%, and 54.72% in predicting general, upward, and downward stock price movements, respectively. However, in contrast to previous studies which used a fixed set, the optimal set of model features for each test stock was also determined during tuning through forward stepwise selection. From this, the proponents concluded that incorporating various indicators, primarily technical indicators, did improve model performance but the optimal model features will vary per stock; indiscriminately adding indicators will likely degrade model performance rather than improve it. The achieved accuracies were statistically significant and the LSTM models could be said to outperform an optimistic or pessimistic baseline model in stock direction forecasting. By extent, this proves that the movement of the Philippine stock market is not completely random and predictable to a certain degree.

Several best-performing models from previous studies that achieved high accuracies in stock direction forecasting in foreign exchanges were also rebuilt and tested on Philippine stocks. However, results show that the adapted models from previous studies achieved largely worse accuracies and did not outperform the created and tuned LSTM models. This would suggest that the Philippine stock market is governed by a stronger version of the efficient market hypothesis compared to foreign stock markets and as such, harder to use previous deep learning techniques and make predictions therein. In the end, the proponents recommend that stock traders use the direction forecasts by the user application as an additional tool in guiding them in making trading-related decisions rather than solely relying on them. Considering that the LSTM models were most suited in making upward stock price movement predictions, effective stock trading strategies may be developed and centered on the generated upward direction forecasts of the user application.

6   Recommendations for Future Work

The proponents recommend the following for future work.

- Try utilizing other model architectures (e.g., Transformers, MLP, combinational models, etc.) to empirically determine optimal model architecture for Philippine stock direction forecasting.
- Consider other loss functions, optimization algorithms, search spaces for hyperparameter optimization.
- Investigate effects of using technical and fundamental indicators not used in this study. Sentiment indicators based on other text sources such as social media websites could be considered as well.
- Develop and evaluate trading strategies based on the stock direction forecasting models.
- Apply models in predicting stock price movements for different time periods. (e.g., intraday, weekly, monthly, etc.)
- Utilize the techniques used in this study for other investment instruments such as cryptocurrencies.
- Try applying the feature selection approaches used in this study in other time series problems like weather forecasting.

References

1. Agrawal, J.G., Chourasia, D.V.S., Mittra, D.A.K.: State-of-the-art in stock prediction techniques. Int. J. Adv. Res. Electr. Electron. Instrument. Eng. **2**, 1360–1366 (2013). https://www.researchgate.net/publication/287653271
2. Bianchi, F.M., Maiorino, E., Kampffmeyer, M.C., Rizzi, A., Jenssen, R.: Recurrent Neural Networks for Short-Term Load Forecasting: A Review and Comparative Analysis. SCS, Springer, Cham (2017). https://doi.org/10.1007/978-3-319-70338-1
3. Etzkorn, M., Schwager, J.D.: A Complete Guide to the Futures Market: Technical Analysis and Trading Systems, Fundamental Analysis, Options, Spreads, and Trading Principles, 2 edn. Wiley trading series, John Wiley & Sons, Hoboken (2017)
4. Hansson, M.: On stock return prediction with LSTM networks (2017). https://www.lunduniversity.lu.se/lup/publication/8911069
5. Hu, Z., Zhu, J., Tse, K.: Stocks market prediction using Support Vector Machine. In: 2013 6th International Conference on Information Management, Innovation Management and Industrial Engineering, vol. 2, pp. 115–118 (2013). https://doi.org/10.1109/ICIII.2013.6703096
6. Kara, Y., Boyacioglu, M.A., Baykan, Ö.K.: Predicting direction of stock price index movement using artificial neural networks and support vector machines: the sample of the Istanbul Stock Exchange. Expert Syst. Appl. **38**(5), 5311–5319 (2011). https://doi.org/10.1016/j.eswa.2010.10.027, https://www.sciencedirect.com/science/article/pii/S0957417410011711
7. Namdari, A., Li, Z.S.: Integrating fundamental and technical analysis of stock market through multi-layer perceptron. In: 2018 IEEE Technology and Engineering Management Conference (TEMSCON), pp. 1–6 (2018). https://doi.org/10.1109/TEMSCON.2018.8488440
8. Oncharoen, P., Vateekul, P.: Deep learning for stock market prediction using event embedding and technical indicators. In: 2018 5th International Conference on Advanced Informatics: Concept Theory and Applications (ICAICTA), pp. 19–24 (2018). https://doi.org/10.1109/ICAICTA.2018.8541310
9. Saurabh, N.: LSTM-RNN model to predict future stock prices using an efficient optimizer. Int. Res. J. Eng. Technol. (IRJET) **7**(11) (2020). https://www.irjet.net/archives/V7/i11/IRJET-V7I11111.pdf
10. Sezer, O.B., Gudelek, M.U., Ozbayoglu, A.M.: Financial time series forecasting with deep learning: a systematic literature review: 2005–2019. Appl. Soft Comput. **90**, 106181 (2020). https://doi.org/10.1016/j.asoc.2020.106181, https://www.sciencedirect.com/science/article/pii/S1568494620301216
11. Song, Y.: Stock Trend Prediction: Based on Machine Learning Methods. Ph.D. thesis (2018). https://escholarship.org/uc/item/0cp1x8th
12. Vargas, M.R., dos Anjos, C.E.M., Bichara, G.L.G., Evsukoff, A.G.: Deep learning for stock market prediction using technical indicators and financial news articles. In: 2018 International Joint Conference on Neural Networks (IJCNN), pp. 1–8 (2018). https://doi.org/10.1109/IJCNN.2018.8489208
13. Zhong, S., Hitchcock, D.B.: S&P 500 Stock Price Prediction Using Technical, Fundamental and Text Data (2021)

IoT Architectures for Indoor Radon Management: A Prospective Analysis

Oscar Blanco-Novoa[1,2(✉)], Paulo Barros[3], Paula Fraga-Lamas[1,2],
Sérgio Ivan Lopes[3,4,5], and Tiago M. Fernández-Caramés[1,2]

[1] Department of Computer Engineering, Faculty of Computer Science,
Universidade da Coruña, 15071 A Coruña, Spain
{o.blanco,paula.fraga,tiago.fernandez}@udc.es
[2] Centro de Investigación CITIC, Universidade da Coruña, 15071 A Coruña, Spain
[3] ADiT-Lab, Instituto Politécnico de Viana do Castelo,
4900-348 Viana do Castelo, Portugal
paulobs@ipvc.pt, sil@estg.ipvc.pt
[4] CiTin - Centro de Interface Tecnológico Industrial,
4970-786 Arcos de Valdevez, Portugal
[5] IT - Instituto de Telecomunicações, Campus Universitário de Santiago,
3810-193 Aveiro, Portugal

Abstract. The demand for real-time Indoor Air Quality (IAQ) management has increased recently, since low-cost and modern sensors such as Particulate Matter (PM), Volatile Organic Compounds (VOCs), Carbon Monoxide (CO), Carbon Dioxide (CO_2), Radon (Rn), among others, have been put forward with considerable accuracy. Although these low-cost sensors cannot be considered measurement instruments, they are very useful for a vast number of application domains, such as home automation, smart building management, IAQ management, risk exposure assessment, to name a few. This paper presents a literature review and a prospective analysis and discussion regarding Internet of Things (IoT) technologies adopted to deal with scenarios that present known indoor Radon gas problems. Specifically, the main requirements for developing IoT-enabled radon management solutions are reviewed. Thus, a traditional IoT architecture is described, its main components are analyzed and some of the most recent academic solutions are reviewed. Finally, novel approaches for deploying IoT radon management architectures are presented together with the most relevant open challenges. In this way, this article presents a holistic review of the past, present, and future of indoor radon management in order to provide guidelines for future designers and developers.

Keywords: Internet of Things · IoT · Radon · Reference Architectures

1 Introduction

As humans spend more time indoors, it becomes more important to monitor Indoor Air Quality (IAQ) and manage the indoor environment. Clinical patholo-

© ICST Institute for Computer Sciences, Social Informatics and Telecommunications Engineering 2023
Published by Springer Nature Switzerland AG 2023. All Rights Reserved
S. I. Lopes et al. (Eds.): Edge-IoT 2022/SmartGov 2022, LNICST 510, pp. 59–74, 2023.
https://doi.org/10.1007/978-3-031-35982-8_5

gies such as asthma and chronic obstructive pulmonary disease (COPD) are two respiratory conditions that have recently emerged as widespread illnesses with a known relation to poor IAQ performances. In addition, improving IAQ has proven to be an effective measure for reducing the aerosol transmission of COVID-19.

The use of low-cost sensor-based Internet of Things (IoT) technologies not only promotes real-time and distributed indoor pollution monitoring, but also fosters novel paradigms for managing IAQ on indoor environments. This allows building managers to mitigate exposure risks.

Low-cost and modern IAQ commercial sensor systems show high availability and an accuracy that may not make them measurement instruments, but which make them useful for a vast number of application domains [1], such as home automation, smart building management or risk exposure assessment, among others.

Radon gas is a radioactive element that cannot be detected by the human senses. It has been proven that it is a carcinogen and is a common air pollutant inside buildings that can be reduced via IAQ solutions.

As it is indicated at the bottom of Fig. 1, multiple radon gas sources can exist in a building, although such a gas usually comes from the soil through cracks and ventilation areas in the building or through its piping. Prospective radon management solutions have been gradually making their way, especially in the last decade, where many innovative scientific works related to indoor radon monitoring and mitigation have been presented. On an economic and political level, the European Union (EU) has also carried out its work with the publication of the Council Directive 2013/59/EURATOM. As a consequence, most EU member states have transposed such a directive to national regulations and have defined radon action plans to support policy decisions in this matter [2].

This article presents a prospective analysis of IoT architectures that can be adopted to deal with indoor scenarios with known indoor radon issues. Specifically, Sect. 2 analyzes the state of the art on the latest IoT technologies for indoor radon management. Section 3 describes the traditional IoT architectures for indoor radon management. Section 4 describes the latest architectures and points out the most relevant future directions for indoor radon management. Finally, Sect. 5 is dedicated to the conclusions.

2   Related Works

This section reviews the state-of-the-art and related work on IoT technologies for indoor radon management. The performed analysis is focused on articles and publications with integrated radon monitoring and mitigation systems that include active detection, data communications networks, cloud-based architectures, along with clear and concise descriptions of the techniques and technologies that were used.

In November 2021, Barros et al. [2] presented a literature review that compiles and compares the most relevant features of recent IoT technologies for

Fig. 1. Traditional cloud communications architecture for radon gas monitoring.

indoor radon gas exposure management (i.e., for monitoring, assessment, and mitigation). This review also summarizes the main challenges and opportunities in the topic. All selected works included a cloud-based computing approach that follows the general architecture of IoT systems detailed in ITU-T Recommendation Y.4113 [3], which is composed of 3 blocks:

- **IoT Area Network**: It includes all sensors, actuators, and microcontroller units (MCUs) with storage and bidirectional communication capabilities.
- **Access network**: It includes the communication systems that allow IoT devices and gateways to connect with core networks through different technologies like optical fiber or radio access technologies (e.g., Wi-Fi, LoRa, BLE, ZigBee, 4G/LTE).
- **Core network**: It includes the physical infrastructure that is responsible for interconnecting the access network with service providers. It provides connectivity to web servers (for data processing and local or online storage), it allows for the visualization of the received data, it analyzes the impact of pollutants on target facilities, and it indicates end users radon gas levels and IAQ in general, among other information.

Table 1 identifies six different types of radon sensors presented by Barros et al. in [2], which use different radon gas detection techniques. Three of them are commercial sensors, while the other three are academic prototypes.

Table 1. Radon gas detection techniques and sensors.

Radon detection technique	Radon sensor	Reference
Current or pulse ionization chambers	Radon FTLab RD200M	[4–10]
	Radon sensor from MidDec Scandinavia AB	[11]
Photodiode detection of alpha particles	Safety Siren Pro Series 3	[12]
	Algade ÆR Plus	[13]
	Teviso RN53 (PIN diode)	[14]
	SARAD Radon Scout sensor	[15]

The preferred architectures for connecting sensors include different MCUs and interfaces, being one of the most popular the ones from Espressif, Arduino and Raspberry Pi solutions, as it can be observed in Table 2.

Table 2. Hardware development kit.

Brand	IoT DevKit	Reference
Espressif Systems	ESP8266	[4–7]
	WeMos Mini D1 ESP8266Wi-Fi ESP-12F	[12]
Arduino	Arduino MKR	[8,9]
	Arduino UNO Rev3	[10]
Raspberry Pi	Raspberry Pi 3 A +	[11]
	Raspberry Pi 3 Model B v1.2	[15]

The adopted communication technologies for real-time data collection are shown in Table 3. The most popular are SigFox, LoRaWAN and Wi-Fi, being the latter widely preferred.

Table 3. Communication technologies.

Wireless Protocols (available)	Wireless Communications (used)	Reference
Wi-Fi	Wi-Fi (license-free 2.4 GHz and 5 GHz)	[10–12,14,15]
Wi-Fi and LoRaWAN	LoRaWAN (licence-free sub-1 GHz)	[4–7]
Sigfox and Wi-Fi	Sigfox (licence-free sub-1 GHz: 868 MHz)	[8,9]
LoRaWAN	LoRaWAN (licence-free sub-1 GHz)	[13]

Table 4. Summary of the most relevant features.

Feature	Reference
Monitors radon concentration	[4–15]
Monitors hygrometric variables	[4–11,13,14]
Monitors other IAQ pollutants (CO_2, TVOC, etc.)	[4–9]
Sends alerts based on a pre-defined threshold	[4–10,12,13]
Includes risk prediction model and/or radon risk predictive algorithms	[9]
Includes a holistic risk prediction model and/or predictive algorithms (considering thermal comfort, energy efficiency, etc.)	none
Includes risk mitigation through human intervention	[4–8,11–15]
Includes active risk mitigation through actuator devices	[9–11,14]
Includes autonomous ventilation system	[9,10]

Table 4 summarizes the most important characteristics of the analyzed systems. Most studies follow a non-mechanical approach to IAQ monitoring. Mitigation actions are mostly taken by human operators after receiving alert messages, except for the study carried out by Alvarellos et al. [9], which already considers active mitigation and predictive risk prevention models.

These works show that, currently, IoT technologies are essential to improve IAQ, and can contribute to the so-called cognitive or intelligent buildings, where human intervention is no longer necessary, being replaced by autonomous building management systems. This paves the way for a holistic vision of the future, boosting critical factors, such as IAQ, energy efficiency and thermal comfort, which must be aligned with the use of indoor spaces (occupied rooms versus empty rooms). By considering these factors together, it is possible to improve the health and quality of life of buildings' residents.

The main challenges and opportunities of the previously mentioned technologies are related to the way they operate, the type of detection mechanisms they use, the type of system architecture, and the auxiliary communication components and technologies. Practical implementations require careful planning and an extensive list of requirements. These implementations should perform a meticulous selection of development kits that guarantee accuracy (for MCUs, sensors, and actuators), and consider the choice of secure wireless communication protocols (for data transmission and firmware updates). Moreover, recursive testing should be performed in experimental scenarios that are representative of the various dimensions for a healthy life indoors. The primary goal with this testing is to reach an ideal equilibrium point between IAQ, energy efficiency and thermal comfort.

3   Traditional IoT Architectures for Radon Management

This section analyzes traditional IoT technologies for radon gas management to perceive the convergence of the various scientific studies towards the compatibility of their architectures and among the involved different systems, in a medium and long-term vision. Figure 1 depicts a traditional Cloud Computing based communications architecture for radon gas monitoring, which is divided into two main layers:

- **IoT device layer**: it is composed of the different IoT radon gas monitoring sensors and IoT mitigation actuators like fans. Such sensors and actuators are deployed throughout the building and transmit data to a wireless communications router that is connected to the Internet (in Fig. 1, it is assumed that IoT nodes make use of Wi-Fi).
- **Cloud**: it collects data through a backend from the deployed IoT sensors/actuators, and processes and stores them in a Cloud database. Such data are then used for making decisions on the mitigation measures and are shown to remote users through an interface like a web-based frontend.

The focus of this work is on prospective analysis, where to anticipate is to act. It is based on uncertainties and on the anticipation of logical scenarios and future events, considering the existence of possible ruptures that can help to dispel doubts regarding the way forward. It is not intended to evaluate quantitative and qualitative factors, but rather to study the risks from a holistic perspective. The prospective strategy is, perhaps, the most important element of this analysis since it allows for taking strategic decisions as an anticipated response to future events. In this way, the prospective analysis will be divided into 2 types of uncertainties:

- **Structural uncertainties**: Based on the cause-effect principle.
- **Unpredictable uncertainties**: Based on the anticipation of sequential chains of events that can turn into disruptive future events. The narrative of future events is extremely difficult to conceive, and it starts with the origin of the idea, always based on scientific credibility, coherence of facts, probability of occurrence, pertinence, and transparency.

3.1   Structural Uncertainties

Cloud-based communications architectures are currently very popular for deploying IoT applications, but they have a number of drawbacks:

- **Saturation**: As the number of IoT communications grows, the Cloud can become saturated and its performance may decrease dramatically and even stop working at certain moments if mitigation measures are not taken.
- **Scalability**: To address IoT device growth, a Cloud should be scaled, which is not always straightforward, since it requires adding computer servers to already crowded physical spaces and rack servers that cannot be uploaded easily.

- **Internet connectivity dependence**: Internet connectivity is essential to connect IoT radon gas monitoring nodes to the cloud. Therefore, if no Internet connectivity is available (e.g., due to the lack of Wi-Fi coverage in a building), IoT nodes cannot communicate with the Cloud.
- **Single point of failure**: If the Cloud stops working (e.g., due to an internal malfunction, a power outage, a cyberattack, or due to being maintained), the whole IoT system cannot be accessed.

3.2   Unpredictable Uncertainties

As exploration scenarios that depart from present situations to the future, those related to Cloud-based communications architectures stand out, but it should be noted that they have the following disadvantages:

- **Data privacy and management**: Cloud servers are usually managed by third parties, so data leaks can occur. In addition, many Cloud servers are deployed in foreign countries, whose laws may not guarantee data privacy.
- **Deployment and maintenance cost**: Many Cloud-based solutions are based on third-party services (e.g., Amazon Web Services, Microsoft Azure), which require paying periodic fees. It is possible to deploy private Clouds, but for certain applications, such a deployment and its periodic maintenance may be too expensive.

It is worth considering a fact that is evident: Information and Communication Technology (ICT) industries, building owners, and governments are embracing the concept of smart buildings as a new standard in the world of commercial construction these days. Thus, the future integration of IoT solutions for indoor radon management with Building Automation and Control Systems (BACS) will be feasible. This anticipates the practical implementation of the revision operated by European Directive 2018/844, where the European Union reaffirms its commitment to the development of a sustainable, safe and decarbonized energy system by 2050.

Directive 2018/844 aims to ensure that measures to improve the energy performance of buildings do not focus only on the building envelope but also include all relevant technical elements and systems of a building, which are aimed at reducing energy needs for heating, cooling, lighting, and ventilation. These measures are focused on improving the IAQ and the levels of comfort and well-being of the occupants of the building. In practical terms, it is assumed that this legal framework will be combined with the growing adoption of IP-connected IoT devices to automate unique tasks in smart buildings, which will certainly enhance IAQ-related aspects in future building automation systems, including radon gas mitigation.

Currently, traditional BACS encompasses fully self-contained and largely automated buildings, managed in an integrated manner with the support of Supervisory Control and Data Acquisition (SCADA) systems or specialized industry standards such as LonWorks, BACnet, or KNX. If the paradigm shifts in today's building automation systems to include a permanent interconnection with the building Local Area Network (LAN) or even with the Internet, the cost will be a wider exposure to cyberattacks, which can start inside the building or be initiated anywhere on the Internet.

Therefore, several technical challenges are foreseen for the main players in this area, such as:

– **IP network interconnection with building automation protocols**: Current BACS include a variety of choices for installation, either wired, wireless, or both. There are several popular connectivity protocols and communication technologies such as GSM, Bluetooth, Wi-Fi, ZigBee, Z-Wave, and KNX. Less popular alternatives include EnOcean, Insteon, LoRaWAN, Sig-Fox, 6LowPAN, Thread and DASH7 [16]. The variety of choices can confuse stakeholders and difficult the right choice, as each of these technologies has some advantages and disadvantages with various technology maturity levels. Yet, it is possible that two or more of these technologies can co-exist in the same building. So, the big challenge will be to converge towards an architecture of compatibility of different building automation protocols with IoT devices, where all protocols can communicate through a common gateway.

– **Smart buildings require security**: Communication networks and transmitted/received data must be completely secure, to prevent unauthorized access and sophisticated cyberattacks that could compromise or disable operations and functionality of smart buildings.

– **Smart buildings require a low-latency communication infrastructure** (like, for instance, the one based on 5G technologies) to enable the simultaneous interconnection of numerous IoT devices and reconcile the combined computation of sensory technologies, analytical data, Machine Learning (ML), Artificial Intelligence (AI) and Machine-to-Machine (M2M) communication.

– **High-volume data processing**: If the amount of collected and processed data for a given building is very large, it may be necessary to resort to a Big Data system to optimize the computation, which will necessarily increase the cost of the solution in the medium and long term.

– **Standards and certifications**: The establishment of technological standards and certifications must increase feasibility, interoperability, security, privacy, data confidentiality (no one should have access to data without proper authorization), integrity (ensuring that data will not be unduly modified), availability, scalability, and performance to IoT applications, among others.

– **Quality of Service**: It is necessary to define and follow the criteria that guarantee rapid recovery in cases of failures or attacks, protection of communications with redundancy, and rigorous audit protocols and processes.

Considering all these aspects is far from being a trivial task. In addition to the technological challenges, it is essential that all points are treated and shared transparently among the various actors and take into account the global conventions and legislation of each country.

4 Novel Approaches and Future Directions

4.1 Edge Computing Architectures

Due to the aforementioned restrictions and risks, new architectures have been recently proposed. Such new architectures are focused on offloading the cloud from the tasks that can be performed in a distributed manner at the network edge. This type of approach is generally called Edge Computing and allows many of the tasks to be carried out on devices close to the end nodes that embed radon gas monitoring sensors.

There are different ways of implementing Edge Computing architectures. When the architecture makes use of devices with significantly high computational power, the devices on the network edge (usually high-performance computers) are called cloudlets [17]. Thus, cloudlets are located close to the end nodes and can process the information received from them [18,19]. In contrast, when the devices on the network edge have low computing power (e.g., when using Raspberry Pis or other types of Single-Board Computers (SBCs)), the paradigm is called Fog Computing, which was proposed by Cisco in 2012 [20].

Figure 2 shows an example of Edge Computing based architecture for radon gas monitoring through IoT nodes. Three different layers can be distinguished:

- **IoT Device Layer**: It works as in a Cloud-based architecture, but its data are forwarded to the Edge Computing Layer.
- **Edge Computing Layer**: It collects, processes, and stores the information from the IoT Device Layer. In Fig. 2, heavy data processing is carried out employing a Cloudlet, while low computing workloads can be handled by Fog Computing gateways. Such gateways can respond fast to the deployed IoT devices and act rapidly on the actuators. Moreover, several gateways can collaborate to perform complex computational tasks.
- **Cloud**: It carries out the tasks that cannot be performed by the Edge Computing Layer and also provides access to remote users through a frontend.

This kind of architecture has contributed to the development of modern IoT systems, but they also suffer from certain drawbacks. Foremost, the deployment of Cloudlets and other Edge Layer gateways in different locations incur additional equipment costs. Also, their maintenance can be complex and expensive. In addition, Edge Layer devices are usually less robust than the cloud and, since they are installed in less controlled environments than a big datacenter, they are exposed to external factors such as changes in temperature or weather conditions that negatively affect their availability. This sort of impact can be a major problem for the performance of the overall system since the Edge Layer is a single point of failure for the area that is being managed. This can lead to connection losses that in IAQ management systems can result in the potential loss of relevant data for an entire area.

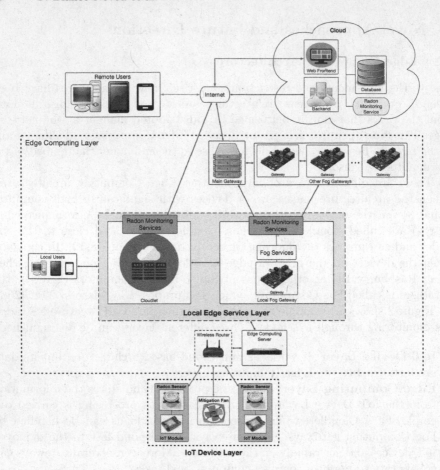

Fig. 2. Example of Edge-based computing and communications architecture for indoor radon management.

4.2 Mist Computing and Decentralized Architectures

Another type of architecture relies on offloading network computational capacity directly to the IoT end nodes. Such a computation is usually performed by the microcontrollers or System-on-Chips (SoCs) that collect the information from the deployed sensors [21,22]. This type of architecture is commonly termed as Mist Computing [23] and allows complex tasks to be performed without the need for delegating them to higher layers thanks to the ability of the mist devices to communicate and coordinate with each other.

Mist Computing systems, thanks to their capacity for not depending on higher layers, reduce significantly the amount of hardware required to deploy the architecture, which often implies lower costs and less energy consumption. In addition, by reducing the number of nodes that the requests have to go through to reach the end devices, latency time is also reduced.

Since in this type of architecture, nodes have greater autonomy for data processing and decision-making, the system can continue to operate even if some nodes are out of service. In addition, the opportunity of communicating from node to node makes it possible for communications to occur through the shortest paths or through alternative paths in case of failures.

Figure 3 illustrates a Mist-based computing architecture for indoor radon management that uses IoT nodes with limited computing capabilities that can communicate with each other. As it can be observed in Fig. 3, each IoT device has networking capabilities that allow them to exchange information with other IoT devices and to send and receive data directly to and from the cloud through a communications gateway.

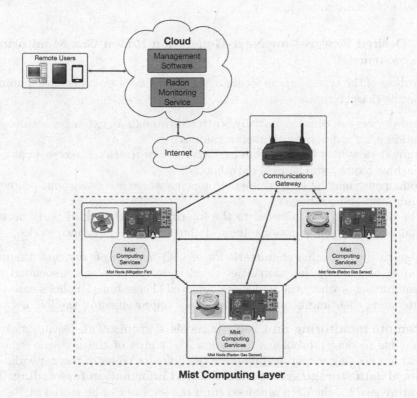

Fig. 3. Example of Mist-based computing and communications architecture for Radon gas monitoring.

Mist-based architectures can be considered decentralized, as most of the computational load is distributed across different devices and end nodes have great autonomy to perform complex tasks. However, most mist architecture still has a centralized element that is often a service running in the cloud that performs coordination tasks and provides access to external applications or user interfaces. To avoid this limitation, recently novel completely decentralized architectures are emerging. In these architectures all nodes perform their role in accordance with a decentralized protocol. Such architectures seek to eliminate as much as possible the dependency on external services so that no network node is absolutely necessary and all of them cooperate to achieve the same purpose making use of specialized protocols to achieve decentralized networking, computing, and/or storage [24]. This allows decentralized networks to have a very high availability without significantly increasing the material cost.

Typically, the different types of edge architectures are not mutually exclusive, and, depending on the specific application, different types can be used together to obtain the required features [25]. Thus, a system can make use of both Fog Computing devices and Cloudlets, which handle the most complex computational processes, and a Mist Computing layer that is able to manage the collected data autonomously.

4.3   Desired Features for Next-Generation Radon Gas Monitoring Systems

Regardless of the type of architecture, IAQ management systems have a number of specific characteristics:

- End devices are usually spatially scattered through an extensive area (e.g., a building, an industrial complex, a campus).
- Some devices may be located in hard-to-reach or restricted access areas (e.g., machine rooms, warehouses, datacenters).
- Some nodes may be located in environments where access without protective equipment is discouraged.
- The nodes may be connected to the Internet through a third-party network that may suffer interruptions due to failures or to maintenance works.

Due to these specific characteristics of IAQ monitoring systems, there are a number of desirable functionalities to mitigate the problems associated with the environments where the nodes are deployed. These functionalities ease their maintenance, their audits, and the continuous improvement of the IoT network:

- **Remote monitoring and self-diagnosis systems**: This feature makes it possible to detect problems and know the status of the network remotely without needing to physically access the different nodes of the network.
- **Local data storage system and delayed information forwarding**: This feature enables the data obtained from the sensors can be stored at the end node itself to prevent losses of information in the event of network interruptions.
- **Remote update system**: This system allows for performing firmware updates of the nodes through the network in order to improve and to keep the system up to date without the need for physically visiting or replacing all the deployed nodes, which would have a high cost.
- **System reaction to planned events**: The deployed radon gas monitoring nodes must be programmed to react to certain planned events and to be able to make simple decisions without relying on third parties to mitigate a possible network outage.

Finally, it is worth mentioning that there are a number of research lines on radon gas and IAQ management systems that are currently gaining interest:

- **Full decentralization**: Fully decentralized IoT systems are being proposed to provide decentralized data sharing systems and consensus protocols for the network [26,27].
- **Energy consumption optimization**: Each node in an IoT system usually consumes an almost negligible amount of power, but the deployment of thousands of IoT nodes globally has a considerable impact on energy consumption and resource management. Thus, energy awareness is a topic that is gaining more and more interest, as well as the creation of more efficient and sustainable IoT networks [28,29].
- **Energy harvesting systems**: Along with efficient use of resources, harvesting energy from alternative sources is a topic that is gaining more and more interest to power devices in remote areas for long periods of time or to facilitate energy supply to low-power devices using sources available in their environment (e.g., piezoelectric, thermal, RF) [30].
- **Digital Twin integrations**: The standardization of data format protocols is enabling the integration of multiple sensors into complex systems that enable advanced data analysis in what is known as digital twins. This term is being widely studied in Industry 4.0 [31], but recently it is also gaining interest in home automation environments.

5   Conclusions

This article reviewed the evolution of IoT architectures for indoor radon gas management (which includes both monitoring and mitigation) by providing a holistic approach to the topic. The main characteristics of IoT technologies for indoor radon management were described, and the most relevant subsystems were detailed, as well as their main communications architectures. In addition, the most relevant academic works related to indoor radon management solutions have been analyzed, showing the potential of such IoT-enabled systems. Furthermore, after describing traditional IoT architectures, novel approaches like Edge, Mist, and decentralized computing paradigms, have also been analyzed in order to emphasize their potential for creating next-generation indoor radon management solutions. Finally, the main open challenges and future directions for the development of such solutions have been enumerated. As a result, this article provided useful guidelines for the IoT designers and developers of future indoor radon management systems.

Acknowledgments. This work is a result of the project TECH-Technology, Environment, Creativity and Health, Norte-01-0145-FEDER-000043, supported by Norte Portugal Regional Operational Program (NORTE 2020), under the PORTUGAL 2020 Partnership Agreement, through the European Regional Development Fund (ERDF). The authors would like to thank CITIC for its support for the research stay that led to this article. CITIC, as Research Center accredited by Galician University System, is funded by "Consellería de Cultura, Educación e Universidades from Xunta de Galicia", supported in an 80% through ERDF Funds, ERDF Operational Programme Galicia 2014–2020, and the remaining 20% by "Secretaría Xeral de Universidades" (Grant ED431G 2019/01). This work has also been funded by the Xunta de Galicia (by grant ED431C 2020/15), the Agencia Estatal de Investigación of Spain, MCIN/AEI/10.13039/501100011033 (by grant PID2020-118857RA-I00 (ORBALLO)) and ERDF funds of the EU (FEDER Galicia 2014–2020 & AEI/FEDER Programs, UE).

References

1. García, M.R., et al.: Review of low-cost sensors for indoor air quality: features and applications. Appl. Spectrosc. Rev., 1–33 (2022). https://doi.org/10.1080/05704928.2022.2085734
2. Barros, P., Curado, A., Lopes, S.I.: Internet of Things (IoT) technologies for managing indoor radon risk exposure: applications, opportunities, and future challenges. Appl. Sci. **11**(22), 11064 (2021). https://doi.org/10.3390/app112211064
3. Recommendation Y.4113 (09/16): Requirements of the Network for the Internet of Things. International Telecommunication Union. https://www.itu.int/rec/T-REC-Y.4113-201609-I. Accessed 15 July 2022
4. Pereira, F., Lopes, S.I., Carvalho, N.B., Curado, A.: RnProbe: a LoRa-enabled iot edge device for integrated radon risk management. IEEE Access **8**, 203488–203502 (2020). https://doi.org/10.1109/ACCESS.2020.3036980
5. Lopes, S.I., et al.: On the design of a human-in-the-loop cyber-physical system for online monitoring and active mitigation of indoor Radon gas concentration. In: Proceedings of the 2018 IEEE International Smart Cities Conference (ISC2), Kansas City, MO, USA, 16–19 September 2018, pp. 1–8 (2018). https://doi.org/10.1109/ISC2.2018.8656777
6. Lopes, S.I., Moreira, P.M., da Cruz, A.M.R., Martins, P., Pereira, F., Curado, A.: RnMonitor: a WebGIS-based platform for expedite. In situ deployment of IoT edge devices and effective Radon Risk Management. In Proceedings of the 2019 IEEE International Smart Cities Conference (ISC2), Casablanca, Morocco, 14–17 October 2019, pp. 451–457 (2019). https://doi.org/10.1109/ISC246665.2019.9071789
7. Martins, P., Lopes, S.I., Pereira, F., Curado, A.: RnMonitor: an IoT-enabled platform for radon risk management in public buildings. In: Santos, H., Pereira, G.V., Budde, M., Lopes, S.F., Nikolic, P. (eds.) SmartCity 360 2019. LNICST, vol. 323, pp. 49–55. Springer, Cham (2020). https://doi.org/10.1007/978-3-030-51005-3_6
8. Alvarellos, A., Gestal, M., Dorado, J., Rabuñal, J.R.: Developing a secure low-cost radon monitoring system. Sensors **20**(3), 752 (2020). https://doi.org/10.3390/s20030752
9. Alvarellos, A., Chao, A.L., Rabuñal, J.R., García-Vidaurrázaga, M.D., Pazos, A.: Development of an automatic low-cost air quality control system: a radon application. Appl. Sci. **11**(5), 2169 (2021). https://doi.org/10.3390/app11052169
10. Moreira, S.M.: An Internet of Things (IoT) Ecosystem for Detection and Removal of Radon Gas, Universidade da Beira Interior, Portugal. Dissertation (2020). https://hdl.handle.net/10400.6/10818

11. Forsström, S., Jennehag U., Guan, X.: A plain low threshold IoT platform for enabling new IoT products from SMEs. In: 2020 IEEE International Workshop on Metrology for Industry 4.0 & IoT, pp. 390–394 (2020). https://doi.org/10.1109/MetroInd4.0IoT48571.2020.9138303

12. Blanco-Novoa, Ó., Fernández-Caramés, T.M., Fraga-Lamas, P., Castedo, L.: A cost-effective IoT system for monitoring indoor radon gas concentration. Sensors **18**(7), 2198 (2018). https://doi.org/10.3390/s18072198

13. Terray, L., et al.: From sensor to cloud: an IoT network of radon outdoor probes to monitor active volcanoes. Sensors **20**(10), 2755 (2020). https://doi.org/10.3390/s20102755

14. Amato, A., et al.: A new cyber physical system for gas radon monitoring and controlling. In: Proceedings of the 2020 IEEE International Symposium on Medical Measurements and Applications (MeMeA), Bari, Italy, 1 June–1 July 2020, pp. 1–6 (2020). https://doi.org/10.1109/MeMeA49120.2020.9137176

15. Medina-Pérez, A., Sánchez-Rodríguez, D., Alonso-González, I.: An internet of thing architecture based on message queuing telemetry transport protocol and node-RED: a case study for monitoring radon gas. Smart Cities **4**(2), 803–818 (2021). https://doi.org/10.3390/smartcities4020041

16. Orfanos, V., Kaminaris, S.D., Piromalis, D., Papageorgas, P.: Trends in home automation systems and protocols. In: AIP Conference Proceedings, vol. 2190, p. 020049 (2019). https://doi.org/10.1063/1.5138535

17. Dolui, K., Datta, S.K.: Comparison of edge computing implementations: fog computing, cloudlet and mobile edge computing. In: 2017 Global Internet of Things Summit (GIoTS), pp. 1–6. IEEE (2017)

18. Fraga-Lamas, P., Fernández-Caramés, T.M., Blanco-Novoa, O., Vilar-Montesinos, M.A.: A review on industrial augmented reality systems for the Industry 4.0 shipyard. IEEE Access **6**, 13358–13375 (2018)

19. Suárez-Albela, M., Fernández-Caramés, T.M., Fraga-Lamas, P., Castedo, L.: A practical evaluation of a high-security energy-efficient gateway for IoT fog computing applications. Sensors **17**(9), 1978 (2017)

20. Bonomi, F., Milito, R., Zhu, J., Addepalli, S.: Fog computing and its role in the Internet of Things. In: Proceedings of the First Edition of the MCC Workshop on Mobile Cloud Computing, pp. 13–16 (2012)

21. Froiz-Míguez, I., et al.: Design, implementation, and empirical validation of an IoT smart irrigation system for fog computing applications based on LoRa and LoRaWAN sensor nodes. Sensors **20**(23), 6865 (2020)

22. Fraga-Lamas, P., et al.: Design and empirical validation of a Bluetooth 5 fog computing based industrial CPS architecture for intelligent Industry 4.0 shipyard workshops. IEEE Access **8**, 45496–45511 (2020). https://doi.org/10.1109/ACCESS.2020.2978291

23. Preden, J.S., Tammemäe, K., Jantsch, A., Leier, M., Riid, A., Calis, E.: The benefits of self-awareness and attention in fog and mist computing. Computer **48**(7), 37–45 (2015)

24. Oktian, Y.E., Witanto, E.N., Lee, S.G.: A conceptual architecture in decentralizing computing, storage, and networking aspect of IoT infrastructure. IoT **2**(2), 205–221 (2021)

25. Ketu, S., Mishra, P.K.: Cloud, fog and mist computing in IoT: an indication of emerging opportunities. IETE Tech. Rev. **39**, 1–12 (2021)

26. Song, J.C., Demir, M.A., Prevost, J.J., Rad, P.: Blockchain design for trusted decentralized IoT networks. In: 2018 13th Annual Conference on System of Systems Engineering (SoSE), pp. 169–174. IEEE (2018)

27. Sun, M., Tay, W.P.: On the relationship between inference and data privacy in decentralized IoT networks. IEEE Trans. Inf. Forensics Secur. **15**, 852–866 (2019)
28. Albreem, M.A., Sheikh, A.M., Alsharif, M.H., Jusoh, M., Yasin, M.N.M.: Green internet of things (GIoT): applications, practices, awareness, and challenges. IEEE Access **9**, 38833–38858 (2021)
29. Fraga-Lamas, P., Lopes, S.I., Fernández-Caramés, T.M.: Green IoT and edge AI as key technological enablers for a sustainable digital transition towards a smart circular economy: an industry 5.0 use case. Sensors **21**(17), 5745 (2021)
30. Gilbert, J.M., Balouchi, F.: Comparison of energy harvesting systems for wireless sensor networks. Int. J. Autom. Comput. **5**(4), 334–347 (2008)
31. Fuller, A., Fan, Z., Day, C., Barlow, C.: Digital twin: enabling technologies, challenges and open research. IEEE Access **8**, 108952–108971 (2020)

Adversarial Training for Better Robustness

Houze Cao[1] and Meng Xue[2(✉)]

[1] School of Cyber Science and Engineering, Wuhan University, Wuhan, China
harrycao@whu.edu.cn
[2] School of Computer Science, Wuhan University, Wuhan, China
xuemeng@whu.edu.cn

Abstract. As the vulnerabilities of neural networks are gradually exposed, the security of deep learning attracts the thoughtful attention of researchers. Adversarial training is a promising way to enhance the robustness of deep learning models, which can defend against white-box targeted attacks by learning from the dedicated designed adversarial samples. In recent years, researchers have proposed many algorithms to promote the security of learning models, such as training effectiveness and decreasing limitations. In this survey, we propose a novel taxonomy to categorize the progress of adversarial training and analyze current constraints. Apart from introducing an overall picture of adversarial training in terms of adversarial attack/robustness, we make a conclusion and prospect of this area.

Keywords: Adversarial training · Adversarial robustness · Adversarial example

1 Introduction

With a more profound and comprehensive analysis and evaluation of the neural network model, its weakness against targeted attacks with slight perturbation draws more attention, threatening the confidence of massive application of deep learning, especially for those security-critical situations [4,7–10]. From this perspective, robustness becomes more vital and is emphasized by researchers and engineers.

The malicious inputs with elaborately modified perturbation are generally considered adversarial examples, which are unable to recognize from the clean dataset for humans in most circumstances and can fool a model to a false output [23]. Therefore, researchers propose adversarial training (AT) mechanism to improve the robustness of a deep learning model [11,13], which trains the model again with adversarial samples. In the following period, advanced approaches were introduced, enhancing the robustness of the re-trained deep learning model, while the attack side (adversarial example) developed at the same time, a vivid interpretation of the meaning of 'adversary' with both sides became more advanced.

© ICST Institute for Computer Sciences, Social Informatics and Telecommunications Engineering 2023
Published by Springer Nature Switzerland AG 2023. All Rights Reserved
S. I. Lopes et al. (Eds.): Edge-IoT 2022/SmartGov 2022, LNICST 510, pp. 75–84, 2023.
https://doi.org/10.1007/978-3-031-35982-8_6

In this survey, we aim to present a general summary of adversarial training in three parts: background, progress, and limitation. We will select the most typical terms or methods for detailed analysis for each part. Finally, we propose a novel taxonomy for current progress, present the latest breakthrough in this field, and conclude the potential directions.

2 Background

In this section, we will introduce the three fundamentals in the field of adversarial training, briefly explaining its concept, notion, and theory. Notably, We only focus on the training set and the testing set follows the same distribution $\mathcal{D}$.

2.1 Adversarial Attack

Adversarial attack in adversarial training denotes finding the imperceptible perturbation on input that can most effectively mislead the model to have an incorrect output [6,19]. Moreover, as [21] illustrated, the critical problem of adversarial training is finding the worse adversarial example. Hence, how to find the most potent adversarial attack has been explored over time.

For a model $f(x, \theta)$, x and y refer to the input sample and the corresponding true label, respectively, while θ denotes the parameter of the neural network model f. Moreover, the adversarial example for clean input x is defined as x' or x_{adv} specifically. In this way, adversarial perturbation δ follows the formulation.

$$\delta = x' - x \tag{1}$$

Given the perturbation budget ϵ, the magnitude of adversarial perturbation is constrained by ϵ, formulated as $\|\delta\|_p \leq \epsilon$. In different cases, p represents different values, such as ∞, 1 and 2. To get the worst case for the attack, we need to maximize the loss function for model $f_\theta.$, such as cross-entropy loss.

$$\delta^* = \arg\max_{\|\delta\|_p \leq \epsilon} \mathcal{L}(f_\theta(x + \delta), y) \tag{2}$$

After the iteration, δ iterates to δ^*, making the adversarial attack more malicious. In the following parts, we will introduce two categories for adversarial example generation: gradient-based (FGSM, PGD) and optimization-based (C&W). For the gradient-based method, the *Loss* function is approximated as a linear function whose gradient direction can be utilized to find the worst direction. In contrast, the worst perturbation is found by optimizing the *Loss* function in the neighborhood of the original sample for optimization approaches.

Fast Sign Gradient Method (FGSM). FGSM is initially proposed by [11], whose main idea is to iterate δ only for one time based on classic gradient, which means that the speed is accelerated but the attack is weaker compared to more times of iteration. Based on the early idea of adversarial regularization in [11], FGSM includes another regularization term in function $\mathcal{L}$, where $\delta = \epsilon \, \mathrm{sign}\,(\nabla_x \mathcal{L}(f_\theta(x + \delta), y))$.

Projected Gradient Descent (PGD). [15] was the first to introduce Projected Gradient Descent (PGD), which was later implemented by adding a random index in [20]. Similar to FGSM, PGD is also a gradient-based method. PGD utilizes several rounds of iteration, while starting from a random step, to find the worse case as the following formulation:

$$x^{t+1} = \prod_{x+B(\varepsilon)} \left(x^t + \alpha \cdot \text{sign} \left(\nabla_x \mathcal{L}(f_\theta(x + \delta), y) \right) \right) \tag{3}$$

where $\prod_{x+B(\varepsilon)}$ means that the x follows the perturbation set $B(\varepsilon)$ that constraints both $x + \delta \in \mathbb{R}^m$ and $\|\delta\|_p \leq \varepsilon$. α denotes the step size of each iteration. Due to different sets of iterations, the time cost for PGD is 3–30 times longer than that of FGSM to generate adversarial examples, as multiple forward and backpropagation are required during batch training. But at the same time, its efficiency is much better with lower accuracy for the model before adversarial training, which is a coin from both sides.

Carlini & Wagner Attacks (C&W). C&W is a typical method that employs an optimization approach to generate adversary examples, proposed in [3]. Generally speaking, the optimization method is formulated as follows:

$$\min \ \mathcal{D}(x, x + \delta) \ \ while \ C(x + \delta) = t \ and \ x + \delta \in [0, 1]^n \tag{4}$$

$\mathcal{D}$ refers to the distance matrix between x and $x+\delta$ and $C(x+\delta)$ denotes that the classification for $x + delta$ is t. It does not mean that C&W sets the expectation for the output for a certain adversary example but sets a constraint that the adversary example must be valid. Hence, the $C(x+\delta)$ is highly non-linear. Using an alternative function f to replace C, the objective can be formulated as:

$$\min \|\delta\|_p + c \cdot f(x + \delta) \ \ while \ x + \delta \in [0, 1]^n \tag{5}$$

where $f(x + \delta) \leq 0$ if and only if $C(x + \delta) = t$. In this way, C&W could find a small perturbation that can fool the model to the worst.

2.2 Adversarial Training

Adversarial training (AT)) aims at enabling the target model to operate well against malicious adversary attacks, or more specifically, adversarial examples (AEs), which have been explained above. With this aim, AT trains the pretrained model (usually PreAct ResNet-18 [12] or Wide-ResNet [28], practically) to perform best with minimized risk under the worst adversarial example input, which is generally abstracted as a min-max problem [21]. The general process of adversarial training is presented in Fig. 1.

The mathematical formulation for AT is as follows.

$$\min_\theta \mathbb{E}_{(Z,y) \sim \mathcal{D}} \left[\max_{\|\delta\|_p \leq \epsilon} \mathcal{L} \left(f_\theta(\boldsymbol{X} + \delta), y \right) \right] \tag{6}$$

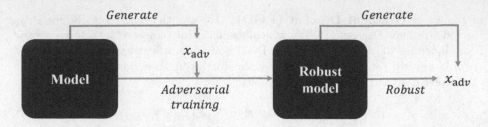

Fig. 1. General process of adversarial training

As Eq. 6 shows, the inner equation is to maximize the maliciousness of adversarial example $x + \delta$. At the same time, the outer loop is the minimization part of training the model to better learn from the perturbation.

This direct and intuitive idea of training erases the dense mixture accumulated in the hidden weights during the training process of a neural network on the clean dataset, which enables AT to boost the robustness of the model [1].

2.3   Adversarial Robustness

Adversary robustness is defined in the face of adversary examples (i.e., the test accuracy by a dataset with targeted generated perturbation). In different domains, adversary robustness is represented by different evaluations (accuracy for image classification, NLP, voice recognition, etc.) on the trained model. Currently, PGD (explained in Sect. 2.1) has been the primary evaluation method to compare the robustness of different models, such as PGD, with 50 iterations and ten restarts.

3   Progress in Adversarial Training

As illustrated before, the critical part of adversary training is the generation of adversary examples. Therefore, we propose a novel taxonomy to categorize different AT methods. This section will introduce each category and highlight some representative progress, such as FAST-AT, GradAlign, and Sub-AT.

We set our taxonomy referring to the MIN-MAX problem of adversarial training, based on where the most significant innovation lays for each progress. For those highlights in the inner max loop for adversarial training mechanism, we categorize them as the MAX ones, further dividing them into Mid MAX and Whole MAX. From this perspective, we conclude three categories, namely Mid MAX, Whole MIN, and Mid MIN, as shown in the following Table 1.

Table 1. A summary of different AT methods

Taxonomy	Name	Method	Robustness
Whole MAX	FGSM-AT [11]	Generation of AEs	0.00%(PGD-50)
Whole MAX	PGD-10-AT [15, 20]	Generation of AEs	50.79%(PGD-50)
Mid MAX	FGSM-AT-GradAlign [2]	Regularization of AEs	47.58%(PGD-50)
Mid MAX	FW-ADAPT [24]	Regularization of AEs	49.67%(PGD-50)
Whole MIN	TRADE [29]	Principle of AT	56.61%(PGD-20)
Mid MIN	Fast-AT [26]	Strategy of AT	46.06%(PGD-50)
Mid MIN	SADS [25]	Strategy of AT	45.66%(PGD-7)
Mid MIN	Sub-Fast-AT [18]	Regularization of AT	48.22%(PGD-50)
Mid MIN	AVmixup [16]	Data process of AT	58.23%(PGD-20)

3.1 Whole MAX

Whole MAX refers to the fundamental changes in the generation of adversarial examples, including FGSM-AT ([11]) and PGD-AT ([15,20]). As explained in Sect. 2.1, FGSM, representative of single-step attack, and PGD, representative of multi-step attack, feature in the ways to generate adversarial examples. The corresponding adversarial training methods that utilize adversarial example generation methods are FGSM-AT and PGD-AT.

3.2 Mid MAX

Mid MAX refers to some modification in the MAX loop, the generation of adversarial examples, such as the setting of the iteration process and regularization of adversarial examples. For instance, frank-Wolfe Adversarial Training (FW-ADAPT) in [24] utilizes Frank-Wolfe to adapt the number of iterations in adversarial example generation dynamically, dramatically cutting the time cost for multi-step AT while keeping the performance stable.

GradAlign. [2] introduces GradAlign based on Fast-AT to act as a novel regularization to explicitly maximize the *gradient alignment* in the generation of adversary examples, overcoming catastrophic overfitting phenomenon and leading to higher robustness of trained model even for large ℓ_∞-perturbations. The novel regularization can be formulated as follows.

$$\Omega(x,y,\theta) = \mathbb{E}_{(x,y)\sim D, \delta\sim\mathcal{U}([-\varepsilon,\varepsilon]^d)}\left[1 - \cos\left(\nabla_x\mathcal{L}(f_\theta(x),y), \nabla_x\mathcal{L}(f_\theta(x+\delta),y)\right)\right] \tag{7}$$

where $\Omega(x,y,\theta)$ is the GradAlign, which aim to maximize the *gradient alignment* part $\mathbb{E}_{(x,y)\sim D, \delta\sim\mathcal{U}([-\varepsilon,\varepsilon]^d)}\left[\cos\left(\nabla_x\mathcal{L}(f_\theta(x),y), \nabla_x\mathcal{L}(f_\theta(x+\delta),y)\right)\right]$. It calculates the local linearity metric of the loss function $\mathcal{L}$ between the gradients at point x and at a randomly perturbed point $x+\delta$ inside the ℓ_∞-ball around x. In this way, the perturbation generated avoids the condition that input gradients are nearly orthogonal to each other, avoiding catastrophic overfitting.

3.3   Whole MIN

Whole MIN means the big picture of training parts from theory, training process arrangement, etc. The representative for that is Tradeoff-inspired Adversarial Defense via Surrogate-loss minimization (TRADE) in [29].

TRADE. TRADE ([29]) comes from the intuition of trading-off between robustness and standard accuracy, hence adding the loss for the standard dataset without any perturbation. It explains the three errors: robust, natural, and boundary errors, and proposes the following principle for TRADE.

$$\min_f \mathbb{E}\{\ \underbrace{\phi(f(\boldsymbol{X})Y)}_{\text{for natural accuracy}}\ +\ \underbrace{\max_{\boldsymbol{X}'\in\mathbb{B}(\boldsymbol{X},\epsilon)} \phi\left(f(\boldsymbol{X})f\left(\boldsymbol{X}'\right)/\lambda\right)}_{\text{for robust accuracy}}\} \tag{8}$$

where the MAX part is the same as the PGD attack, while the MIN part includes the loss function $\phi(f(\boldsymbol{X})Y$ to reduce the degradation of natural accuracy.

3.4   Mid MIN

Mid MIN denotes methods that change or replace the parameters or regularization of the training part. SADS in [25] is a single-step adversarial training method with dropout scheduling, introducing the dropout layer and decaying the dropout probability. AVmixup is proposed in [16] to introduce a data augment approach in the training part on the generated adversarial example, boosting the robustness.

Fast-AT. Based on the FGSM-AT proposed in [11], Fast Adversarial Training (Fast-AT in [26]) features in its random initialization, cyclic learning rate, and mixed-precision arithmetic, which are inspired by the DAWNBench competition in [5].

More specifically, Fast-AT uses a cyclic learning rate increased linearly from 0 to λ over the first $N/2$ epochs, then decreases linearly from λ to 0 for the second half number of epochs, where λ, the maximum learning rate, usually equals to 0.1. As for mixed-precision arithmetic, [26] employs it to fully use the GPU resources and reduce memory utilization, speeding the training period, corresponding to the word "fast."

Sub-AT. Subspace Adversarial Training (Sub-AT) is proposed in [18] to deal with catastrophic overfitting. It applies the DLDR algorithm in [17] to extract the subspace of the dataset to regularize the change of parameters of the model during the training process, inspired by the application of DLDR in subspace training.

Take Sub-PGD-AT, for instance. First, PGD-AT trains a model like PreAct Resnet-18 ([12]) for over 100 epochs with standard settings, saving the model after each epoch. Then apply DLDR to reduce the dimension of the matrix extracted from the parameters of models after 0 epoch to 100 epochs to 80 rows. The size of the matrix A is $100 \times n$ where n is the total number of parameters, which means that $A[i]$ represents the model trained for i epochs. The matrix after DLDR is used as a regularization each time for parameters update.

4   Limitations for Adversarial Training

Although adversarial training is generally reckoned more effective in the robustness of the trained model compared to several other approaches designed to strengthen robustness [22], adversary training also has its limitations, which have been under the spotlight of researchers. Given that some solutions emerged to deal with the limits, but regretfully, none of them solve perfectly.

4.1   Catastrophic Overfitting

Similar to the training of deep learning networks, it is easy for the network trained by AT to be over-parameterized, resulting in overfitting. But overfitting is catastrophic for adversarial training, especially for single-step adversary training (typically FGSM-AT). At the same time, multi-step adversary training (typically PGD-AT) also has the problem of catastrophic overfitting. Details for that would be analyzed as follows.

For Single-Step AT. As demonstrated in [26], for a model trained by ℓ_{∞} single-step AT (Fast-AT), the robust accuracy against PGD attack will drop dramatically to approximately zero with train processing, even in a single epoch. More specifically, the model trained by Fast-AT with step size $\alpha > 12/255$, cyclic learning rate, random initialization, and 30 epochs will be significantly vulnerable against a PGD adversarial. Admittedly, the model trained by FGSM-AT behaves weaker compared to PGD-AT, but this does not mean it could collapse when confronted with a PGD attack.

For Multi-step AT. Multi-step AT does not survive the overfitting problem. A model trained behaves differently from the tested for its robustness, which indicates the gap between the best robust accuracy and the final robust accuracy. But this problem is off the spotlight with the serious overfitting for single-step AT still the focus.

Current Countermeasures. Through the years, many works have focused on this problem; we will select some specific measures but not cover the details of new methods, which will be introduced in the following section.

   In [26], this phenomenon is recognized as the lack of diversity in adversary examples generated by FGSM. Hence it could be buffered by an "early stop" in the training period by regularly checking the test accuracy on a mini-batch of training data. GradAlign is proposed with the discovery of the connection behind catastrophic overfitting and *local linearity* in a deep-learning network to regularize inside the perturbation part in [2]. Moreover, [14] holds that decision boundary distortion in single-step AT leads to overfitting and designs an algorithm to determine the appropriate magnitude of the perturbation for each image. [18] discover the connection between catastrophic overfitting and fast-growing gradient, hence applying the DLDR algorithm ([17]) to control the rapid explosion of average gradient norm.

4.2 Trade-Off Between Robust and Standard Accuracy

With many approaches aiming to lift the robustness of the model and handle the existing limitations, the natural accuracy (or standard accuracy) truly decreases compared with the model without AT. More specifically, standard accuracy under a clean dataset after adversarial training generally falls for 10% from the original performance of PreAct Resnet ([12]) without it.

As analyzed theoretically in [29], the robust error is decomposed as the sum of the natural and boundary errors. A differentiable upper bound is provided using the theory of classification-calibrated loss, which is shown to be the tightest possible upper bound with uniform overall probability distributions and measurable predictors. It is held in [27] that the trade-off might not be inherent but a consequence of current adversarial training methods. New methods are still emerging, considering that robust accuracy should not be at the cost of natural accuracy.

5 Conclusion

In this paper, we introduce the basic notions of some related terms concerning adversarial training, review representative progress, and analysis current limitations in this field, especially for the latest methods, aiming to provide a precise yet comprehensive picture of adversary training. Although adversarial training is an effective way to enhance the robustness of deep learning models, the model's vulnerability is not solved completely, and the limitations are still outstanding issues.

From the innovation side, many methods get inspiration from other fields. Sub-AT ([18]) introduces subspace training to AT, and FW-AT employs recently proposed Frank-Wolfe (FW) optimization, while Fast-AT learns from DAWN-Bench competition ([5]). At the same time, some methods come from reflections on current limitations. A typical instance is a TRADE, which concentrates on decreased natural accuracy.

As for the potential direction, some problems are still waiting to be solved. Firstly, the MIN-MAX problem has been the center of much progress with limited implementation. It could be further modified to improve its effectiveness. Or even jump out of the box of AT to exploit more effective ways for robustness. Moreover, catastrophic overfitting remains a limitation. Although many methods focus on it and have valid progress, the theoretical explanation and low-cost countermeasures are still open to researchers.

References

1. Allen-Zhu, Z., Li, Y.: Feature purification: How adversarial training performs robust deep learning. CoRR abs/2005.10190 (2020). https://arxiv.org/abs/2005.10190

2. Andriushchenko, M., Flammarion, N.: Understanding and improving fast adversarial training. In: Advances in Neural Information Processing Systems, vol. 33, pp. 16048–16059 (2020)

3. Carlini, N., Wagner, D.: Towards evaluating the robustness of neural networks. In: 2017 IEEE Symposium on Security and Privacy (SP), pp. 39–57. IEEE (2017)

4. Chen, Y., Gong, X., Wang, Q., Di, X., Huang, H.: Backdoor attacks and defenses for deep neural networks in outsourced cloud environments. IEEE Network $34(5)$, 141–147 (2020)

5. Coleman, C., et al.: DAWNBench: an end-to-end deep learning benchmark and competition. Training $100(101)$, 102 (2017)

6. Dong, J., Gong, X., Xue, M.: Adversarial examples in wireless networks: a comprehensive survey. In: Wu, K., Wang, L., Chen, Y. (eds.) International Conference on Edge Computing and IoT, pp. 92–97. Springer, Cham (2022). https://doi.org/10.1007/978-3-031-04231-7_8

7. Gong, X., Chen, Y., Huang, H., Liao, Y., Wang, S., Wang, Q.: Coordinated backdoor attacks against federated learning with model-dependent triggers. IEEE Network $36(1)$, 84–90 (2022)

8. Gong, X., et al.: Defense-resistant backdoor attacks against deep neural networks in outsourced cloud environment. IEEE J. Sel. Areas Commun. $39(8)$, 2617–2631 (2021)

9. Gong, X., Chen, Y., Wang, Q., Wang, M., Li, S.: Private data inference attacks against cloud: model, technologies, and research directions. IEEE Commun. Mag. (2022)

10. Gong, X., Wang, Q., Chen, Y., Yang, W., Jiang, X.: Model extraction attacks and defenses on cloud-based machine learning models. IEEE Commun. Mag. $58(12)$, 83–89 (2020)

11. Goodfellow, I.J., Shlens, J., Szegedy, C.: Explaining and harnessing adversarial examples (2014). https://doi.org/10.48550/ARXIV.1412.6572. https://arxiv.org/abs/1412.6572

12. He, K., Zhang, X., Ren, S., Sun, J.: Deep residual learning for image recognition. In: Proceedings of the IEEE Conference on Computer Vision and Pattern Recognition, pp. 770–778 (2016)

13. Huang, R., Xu, B., Schuurmans, D., Szepesvari, C.: Learning with a strong adversary (2015). https://doi.org/10.48550/ARXIV.1511.03034. https://arxiv.org/abs/1511.03034

14. Kim, H., Lee, W., Lee, J.: Understanding catastrophic overfitting in single-step adversarial training. In: Proceedings of the AAAI Conference on Artificial Intelligence, vol. 35, pp. 8119–8127 (2021)

15. Kurakin, A., Goodfellow, I., Bengio, S.: Adversarial machine learning at scale. arXiv preprint arXiv:1611.01236 (2016)

16. Lee, S., Lee, H., Yoon, S.: Adversarial vertex Mixup: toward better adversarially robust generalization. In: Proceedings of the IEEE/CVF Conference on Computer Vision and Pattern Recognition, pp. 272–281 (2020)

17. Li, T., Tan, L., Tao, Q., Liu, Y., Huang, X.: Low dimensional landscape hypothesis is true: DNNs can be trained in tiny subspaces. arXiv e-prints pp. arXiv-2103 (2021)

18. Li, T., Wu, Y., Chen, S., Fang, K., Huang, X.: Subspace adversarial training. In: Proceedings of the IEEE/CVF Conference on Computer Vision and Pattern Recognition, pp. 13409–13418 (2022)
19. Luo, X., Qin, Q., Gong, X., Xue, M.: A survey of adversarial attacks on wireless communications. In: Wu, K., Wang, L., Chen, Y. (eds.) International Conference on Edge Computing and IoT. pp. 83–91. Springer, Cham (2022). https://doi.org/10.1007/978-3-031-04231-7_7
20. Madry, A., Makelov, A., Schmidt, L., Tsipras, D., Vladu, A.: Towards deep learning models resistant to adversarial attacks. In: International Conference on Learning Representations (2018)
21. Shaham, U., Yamada, Y., Negahban, S.: Understanding adversarial training: increasing local stability of supervised models through robust optimization. Neurocomputing **307**, 195–204 (2018)
22. Silva, S.H., Najafirad, P.: Opportunities and challenges in deep learning adversarial robustness: a survey. arXiv preprint arXiv:2007.00753 (2020)
23. Szegedy, C., et al.: Intriguing properties of neural networks. In: 2nd International Conference on Learning Representations, ICLR 2014 (2014)
24. Tsiligkaridis, T., Roberts, J.: Understanding and increasing efficiency of Frank-Wolfe adversarial training. In: Proceedings of the IEEE/CVF Conference on Computer Vision and Pattern Recognition, pp. 50–59 (2022)
25. Vivek, B., Babu, R.V.: Single-step adversarial training with dropout scheduling. In: 2020 IEEE/CVF Conference on Computer Vision and Pattern Recognition (CVPR), pp. 947–956. IEEE (2020)
26. Wong, E., Rice, L., Kolter, J.Z.: Fast is better than free: revisiting adversarial training. In: International Conference on Learning Representations (2019)
27. Yang, Y.Y., Rashtchian, C., Zhang, H., Salakhutdinov, R.R., Chaudhuri, K.: A closer look at accuracy vs. robustness. In: Advances in Neural Information Processing Systems, vol. 33, pp. 8588–8601 (2020)
28. Zagoruyko, S., Komodakis, N.: Wide residual networks. arXiv preprint arXiv:1605.07146 (2016)
29. Zhang, H., Yu, Y., Jiao, J., Xing, E., El Ghaoui, L., Jordan, M.: Theoretically principled trade-off between robustness and accuracy. In: International Conference on Machine Learning, pp. 7472–7482. PMLR (2019)

Artificial Intelligence and Machine Learning for Smart Governance

Integrating Computer Vision and Crowd Sourcing to Infer Drug Use on Streets: A Case Study with 311 Data in San Francisco

Hye Seon Yi[✉], Tanvir Bhuiyan, and Sriram Chellappan

University of South Florida, Tampa, FL 33620, USA
{hsyi,bhuiyan,sriramc}@usf.edu

Abstract. Use of illegal drugs has been a bane of society for decades, and the problem is only increasing globally. Billions of dollars, time, effort and expertise among various stakeholders are being invested to combat this problem, but novel approaches are still needed. In this paper, we investigate the exciting possibility of leveraging big-data provided by the crowd to detect illegal drug use on streets. Our discussions with stakeholders revealed that drug use can be inferred via detection of any of the following components - syringes (including barrels and plungers), needles, needle caps, vials and tourniquets. We also learnt that in localities, where drug is common, these items are casually discarded on streets. Motivated by these, we conducted an investigation centered around San Francisco. We collected images from their SF311 platform where the public can actually upload their observations in the city for service. From more than 5 million images uploaded, we extracted $1,759$ images that contained one or more of drug use components mentioned above. We designed and validated state of the art Computer Vision techniques to both detect and localize components of interest with an uploaded image. Results demonstrate high utility, as we report later in the paper. To the best of our knowledge, our study is amongst the first to tackle the problem of detecting drug use automatically via AI techniques from crowd uploaded images. We believe that our study has practical impact.

Keywords: Object Detection · Drug Detection · Needle · Public Health · Smart Governance · Transfer Learning · Computer Vision · AI

1 Introduction

According to the CDC, in the US alone, drug overdose was the primary reason for $71,000$ deaths in 2019, and $94,000$ deaths in 2020 [7], [9]. A critical challenge in the war against drugs stems from users discarding needles, syringes (and related drug use components) in public. It is obvious to infer how discarded syringes will enable drug use among others should they discover them on streets. In fact, the problems emanating from the use of discarded syringes is well studied in

© ICST Institute for Computer Sciences, Social Informatics and Telecommunications Engineering 2023
Published by Springer Nature Switzerland AG 2023. All Rights Reserved
S. I. Lopes et al. (Eds.): Edge-IoT 2022/SmartGov 2022, LNICST 510, pp. 87–101, 2023.
https://doi.org/10.1007/978-3-031-35982-8_7

other contexts also, beyond just drug use. Many past studies have investigated how discarded syringes (and their components) on streets can disrupt local communities via encouraging more drug use, create environmental harm, spread of many diseases, and also enable injuries to children on streets [21, 29].

Our objective in this paper is geared towards detecting discarded drug usage components (needles, vials, caps etc) on streets. To do so however, we investigate an innovative source of big-data that is getting increasingly popular today, namely image observations uploaded by the public for community services. Such systems now are very popular in advanced societies. In the US alone, many big cities like San Francisco, Atlanta, Boston, Chicago, Denver, Houston and more have dedicated online platforms where public can upload images indicating problems that they believe need intervention from city officials.

Let us consider San Francisco (a city with serious drug use problems [18, 20]). San Francisco has a dedicated system called SF311 [4], that also has a mobile version for public uploads. The system has been in operation for more than ten years now, and at the time of writing this paper, more than 5 million observations (some descriptive, while others not) have been posted by local residents. Fortunately, all image uploads are publicly available. We downloaded the dataset, and filtered out 1, 759 images that contained one or more of drug use components (syringes, barrels, plungers, needles, needle caps, vials and tourniquets). Each component of interest is shown in Table 1 for clarity. The table also contains the number of images of each component in our dataset, split into training, testing and validation for AI model development. Note that in many public-uploaded images, multiple drug use components appear (in a single image).

Using this dataset of 1, 759 images uploaded by the public (within which 10, 676 images of multiple drug use components are present), we designed and validated state of the art computer vision algorithms, namely EfficientDet, Faster R-CNN and YOLO v5, to detect objects of drug use if present in any image, and furthermore, also localize where they are within the image (via a bounding box), since some objects may appear too small to the naked eye, and a clear box may help the operator to focus on the drug-use component within the image. Our accuracies of detecting and localizing drug use objects is quite high, with particularly high accuracies for larger objects like biohazard boxes and syringes.

To the best of our knowledge, our work is unique in utilizing images generated by public and computer vision techniques to automatically infer drug usage on streets. We believe that our work thus provides innovative tools for officials to detect and combat the usage of illegal drugs in our cities.

2   Related Work

We now highlight peer literature where drug abuse detection is made via novel data sources - specifically from the web and from social media platforms.

Perdue et al. [22] examined if internet search trends can be used to predict the use of novel psychoactive drugs (NPD) across the US. They leveraged Google Trends to find the internet search trends of NPDs. Note that Google Trends is a free service from Google showing interests or popularity of specific terms or

Table 1. Counts for labeled objects in Train/Validation/Test datasets

#	Class	Examples	Training	Validation	Test
1	**biohazard_box** - container for discarded syringes and other syringe related items		144	14	15
2	**cooker** - apparatus to mix a drug		309	25	16
3	**plunger** - component of a syringe to eject the liquid through the needle		461	52	47
4	**syringe** - one whole or main part of the syringe also called as a barrel		3,995	551	503
5	**syringe_packaging** - plastic wrapper or paper boxes for packaging syringes		163	19	18
6	**orange_cap** - cap for storing syringes		1,764	241	196
7	**tourniquet** - long elastic strip to tie a body part for injection		128	14	14
8	**vial** - container of liquid (usually sterile water) to mix a drug		679	82	36
9	**white_cap** - cap for storing syringes		986	124	80
	Total		8,629	1,122	925

expressions in a given time range. The authors correlated Google Trends data on five NPDs (Adderall, Salvia divinorum, Snus, Synthetic marijuana and Bath salts) with reports of drug use from *Monitoring the Future (MTF)*, a highly respected source of data since 1975 that has measured drug and alcohol use and related attitudes among adolescent students across the US. Using statistical methods, the authors identified strong positive correlations among the two data sources. In another study, Phan et al. [23] designed machine learning techniques to detect drug use from tweets. The method entailed: collecting tweets with names of illegal or prescription drugs; generating training data by labeling tweets as indicative of drug abuse or not; designing algorithms to classify tweets; and evaluation. The authors used methods such as random forests, decision tree (J48), SVM and Naive Bayes and were able to achieve good accuracy in detection. In another study, Kim et al. [19] investigated issues related to drug use, humans and social media platforms. The authors claimed that different types of users (adolescents, tech savvy users, social media users) have different motivations and means for drug use and suggest tailor made social media interventions for specific groups. While these studies are relevant and important, we are not aware of studies that design AI techniques to detect drug-use on streets using images uploaded by the general public, which is our focus in this paper.

3   Data Collection

For this study, we collected drug usage related images from SF311. SF311 is "the primary customer service center for the City of San Francisco". The service is accessible using phone, web, mobile and Twitter. Fortunately, and since this is for the general public in San Francisco, SF311 requests are publicly available through DataSF [2], the data portal for the City of San Francisco. DataSF provides APIs which allow to manage and share datasets for the City of San Francisco including SF311 dataset.

Using available APIs, we downloaded 4,954,128 SF311 requests from July 1, 2008 to July 31, 2021. Out of nearly 5 million SF311 requests by the public, 44,475 requests were categorized as needles - about 1% of the of total requests. From this, we identified 24,698 requests that contained images within them, which formed our dataset for descriptive analysis in Sect. 4. We selected and labeled 1,759 images from these for training and testing of our object detection models, described in Sect. 5. Note that a total of 10,676 drug use components were within these 1,759 images, as presented in Table 1, and this is because a single image contained multiple drug use components in our dataset.

4   Descriptive Analysis

This section is to assist readers with an overall descriptive analysis on the 44,475 requests categorized as needles in the SF311 dataset. This section is brief, and basically provides background information related to tangible increase in needle

related service requests in San Francisco over the last few years, and also highlights in which locations most needle related requests are coming from. Please
note that when we say *"request"*, we mean that a public person is requesting
service from city official pertinent to his or her upload to the SF311 platform.
To be more specific, when a person has uploaded something related to needle
usage on streets to SF311, we term that as a needle-related request.

4.1 SF311 Requests by Month

At the outset, Fig. 1 compares counts of total SF311 requests, and those pertinent
to needles, since 2008. Figure 1a plots overall counts of all SF311 requests across
six months duration, while Fig. 1b does the same for SF311 requests categorized
as needles. Then, in order to compare trends of needle related requests w.r.t.
overall requests for services, we scaled these counts with log base 2 function and
plotted them in Fig. 1c. We see that in recent years, the rate of needle related
requests is sharply increasing compared to overall requests. This basically reflects
the explosion in drug related activity over the past few years in San Francisco
[12,28], and most importantly demonstrates the importance of public efforts,
and automated detection of needle/drug use activity (using AI) in fighting this
problem.

(a) All Requests   (b) Needle requests   (c) All vs Needle (scaled)

Fig. 1. SF311 requests by month

4.2 SF311 Requests by Location

Figure 2a displays locations of all SF311 service requests, and Fig. 2b displays
those specific to needles only. As we see, SF311 requests in general are spread
all over San Francisco, but those specific to needles are heavily concentrated
in the Upper Eastern side of San Francisco. To better understand this, we
plot the same results over defined neighborhoods in Figs. 3a and 3b. To do so,
we downloaded the neighborhood map from DataSF contributed by the San
Francisco Association of Realtors. The shape file of the neighborhood map can
be accessed at https://data.sfgov.org/Geographic-Locations-and-Boundaries/
Realtor-Neighborhoods/5gzd-g9ns. Then, we plotted the choropleths maps to

show distribution of SF311 requests over different neighborhoods in San Francisco. Figure 3a is the choropleths map for all SF311 requests and Fig. 3b is the same for needle SF311 requests. The actual numbers are shown in Table 2 and Table 3, ranked in decreasing order of requests.

What is interesting is that neighborhoods like Market Street and Inner Mission (top two rows in Table 2 and Table 3) are extensively identified in peer research (including recent studies, since 2021) as being hotbeds of drug activity in San Francisco [14,17]. This means that SF311 service requests related to needle usage are indeed correlating with current trends in drug use across San Francisco, and hence, our AI approaches for automated detection of needles can serve as indicators of drug activity. With rapid detection, targeted and more effective control programs can be generated, which increases the practical impact of our work in this paper.

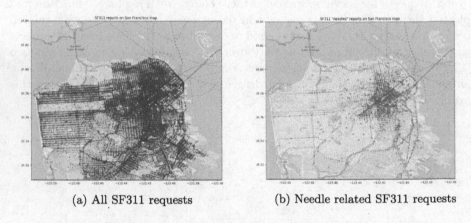

(a) All SF311 requests   (b) Needle related SF311 requests

Fig. 2. SF311 requests on San Francisco map

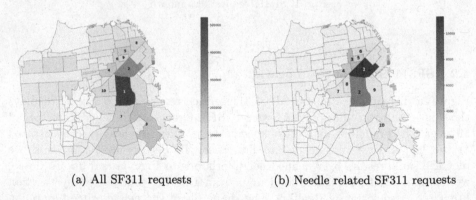

(a) All SF311 requests   (b) Needle related SF311 requests

Fig. 3. SF311 requests on San Francisco neighborhood map

Table 2. Top 10 neighborhoods with most SF311 requests on San Francisco neighborhood map

Neighborhood name	All requests	Percent
Inner Mission	527,655	10.7%
Market Street	297,592	6.0%
Bayview	166,103	3.4%
Hayes Valley	158,856	3.2%
Downtown	152,838	3.1%
Van Ness/Civic Center	137,575	2.8%
Bernal Heights	133,713	2.7%
Financial District/Barbary Coast	121,023	2.4%
Tenderloin	116,476	2.4%
Eureka Valley/Dolores Heights	113,237	2.3%
Total	1,925,068	38.9%

Table 3. Top 10 neighborhoods with most needle related SF311 requests on San Francisco neighborhood map

Neighborhood name	Needle requests	Percent
Market Street	11,299	25.4%
Inner Mission	6,642	14.9%
Van Ness/Civic Center	3,502	7.9%
Hayes Valley	2,622	5.9%
Tenderloin	2,184	4.9%
Downtown	1,712	3.8%
Eureka Valley/Dolores Heights	1,405	3.2%
Mission Dolores	1,203	2.7%
Potrero Hill	1,134	2.5%
Bayview	1,093	2.5%
Total	32,796	73.7%

5 Methodology

Recall that our objective is to detect indication drug usage if any in an image, and also localize (via a bounding box) where the object of interest appears within that image. The latter is particularly important since components of drug use (e.g., needles) are sometimes tiny, and informing humans the exact location of a tiny object within an image is much more practically useful than merely detecting that the tiny object is present "somewhere" in an image.

To do so, in this section, we first present discussions on what specific classes (i.e., components) were identified to detect drug usage in our image dataset, followed by how we labeled them for ground-truthing. Then, we discuss how we fine-tuned state of the art AI architectures in drug-use detection and localization.

5.1   Classes for Drug Usage Detection

Prior to deciding on the classes to detect for drug use, we carefully investigated the mechanisms of how addicts inject drugs, so that we can learn about the specific components involved. From several related studies in peer literature [13, 15,16], and from our own visual inspection of images in our SF311 dataset, we identified *nine* components that were pertinent for detecting drug use on streets from the SF311 dataset. Table 1 presents each component along with a small description of its relevance to drug use. We also present the total number of images for each component in our dataset that we use for detection and localization (which forms our overall dataset of images). Once again, all of these images are uploaded by the general public in San Francisco, and clearly represent a great potential to detect and proactively combat drug use in urban cities today.

5.2   Image Labeling

Recall that our motivation in this paper is to detect whether or not a drug-usage related component (one of the nine in Table 1) is present in an uploaded images, and furthermore, we want to localize (via a bounding box) the specific component(s). The size of our dataset was each class was also presented in Table 1. Once the images in each class were confirmed, we label the specific components of interest within the image via a bounding box, which will serve as the ground-truth for training and validation of the localization phase of the proposed AI algorithm.

Fig. 4. LabelImg

For training and testing for this study, we manually labeled all drug-related images in our dataset in Table 1 using LabelImg, which is one of well known tools for annotating images [5]. The screenshot of LabelImg is Fig. 4 in which three syringes were identified and localized. The green dots in each box represent the four corners of our manual annotation for each drug use related component in our images. Within these boxes, our algorithm learns to detect the object of interest (if present) in an image, and also localizes it by emplacing similar bounding boxes during execution. In this manner, even minor components that indicate drug usage could not only be detected, but also localized within the image for easier visual validation.

5.3   Fine-Tuning Deep Neural Network Architectures

We now present technical details regarding fine-tuning of three established deep neural network architectures for our problem of drug usage detection and localization. The architectures are Faster R-CNN, EfficientDet and YOLO v5. These architectures are the state-of-the-art in the domain of object detection and localization. These architectures have been extensively trained, validated and tested on multiple state-of-the-art datasets, and have also been widely used via transfer learning techniques. Likewise, we employ the principle of Transfer Learning to save both time and cost of learning towards fine-tuning the architectures. These are elaborated upon below.

Principle of Transfer Learning. It is a fact that the state-of-the-art in AI algorithms are deep neural networks, and within deep neural networks, multiple models/architectures are published, and each of them has pros and cons for a problem of interest. It is also a standard practice today, to explore the notion of transfer learning, the goal of which is to already take advantage of an existing and validated model for a general range of classification problems, and adapt that model via fine-tuning to address classification in another (related) domain [26]. This is because, creating a new deep neural model from scratch can take significant time and resources to optimize, and instead if we can learn from an already optimized model trained and validated for a generic class of related problems, time and cost savings will be significant if that existing model can be only fine-tuned for another related classification problem, while still obtaining high accuracy. In this paper, we have utilized three pre-trained and well established object detection models, namely Faster R-CNN, EfficientDet and YOLO v5, and fine-tuned them for our drug usage classification problem, details of which are presented below.

Faster R-CNN. Faster R-CNN is an object detection model proposed by Ren, He, Girshick and Sun [25]. Faster R-CNN is a successor from Fast R-CNN [1]. Faster R-CNN utilizes Region Proposal Networks (RPNs) that take an image and returns an initially randomly computed set of rectangular region proposals called regions of interest (RoIs), or anchors. The goal here then is to determine which of these anchors or proposals within the larger image encompasses an object of interest. Doing so, is a two step process. First, features are computed for the image using a comprehensive CNN that can separate the foreground from the background. Then, features are computed for the images within each generated proposal, and compared against the features already computed (for separating the foreground from the background), and these are done using a simpler CNN to determine if the object of interest is within a proposal or not. Subsequently, the proposals are tightened using regression. The loss functions of Faster R-CNN are two: the classification loss and regression loss. The classification loss is a logarithmic loss while the regression loss is the smoothed L1 loss [10]. In the base architecture, "proposals" are used to detect objects with various sizes and shapes. These proposals are pre-defined with multiple scales and aspect ratios. The original architecture in [25] used nine anchors with a combination of three scales and three aspect ratios. For our study in this paper, the codebase for Faster R-CNN pre-trained model is from Tensorflow Object Detection API which is available on GitHub [6], and is the one we fine-tuned for our classification problem of detecting drug-usage components.

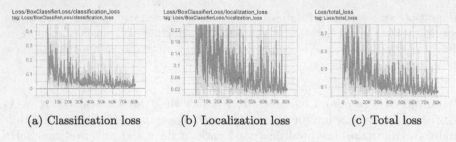

(a) Classification loss   (b) Localization loss   (c) Total loss

Fig. 5. Training loss for Faster R-CNN

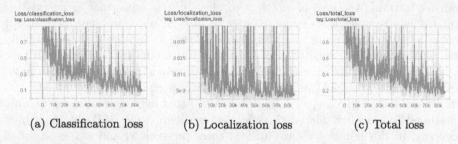

(a) Classification loss   (b) Localization loss   (c) Total loss

Fig. 6. Training loss for EfficientDet

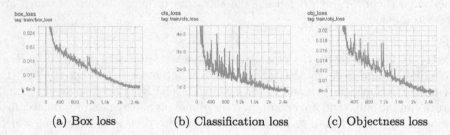

(a) Box loss   (b) Classification loss   (c) Objectness loss

Fig. 7. Training loss for YOLO v5

EfficientDet. EfficientDet is another deep neural network architecture proposed by Tan, Pang and Le in 2020 [27]. EfficientDet's main goal is to improve computational efficiency while enhancing the accuracy of the object detection model because many high performing object detection models require heavy computational load. One improvement of EfficientDet is using EfficientNet as its backbone network. EfficientNet is a very successful convolutional neural network proposed by Tan and Le [27] and it has achieved state-of-the-art accuracy on ImageNet (0.84), CIFAR-100 (0.92) and Flowers (0.99) datasets. Building off this, EfficientDet introduces BiFPN (bidirectional feature pyramid network) for efficient multi-scale feature fusion. Lastly, it proposes a novel scaling method called compound scaling that scales up the combination of backbone, feature network and prediction network for higher accuracy and performance. The overall architecture has three core components: EfficientNet backbone network, BiFPN network, and box/class prediction network. To elaborate, EfficientNet backbone network performs feature extraction in images [11]. Then, the detected features are passed to BiFPN network where feature fusion is performed. BiFPN contains cross-scale connections for more flexible information flow and performs weighted feature fusion so that features with different resolutions can have different importance. Lastly, these fused features are fed to the box/class prediction network for classification and regression of output bounding boxes. As a loss function, EfficientDet uses Focal loss with $\alpha = 0.25$ and $\gamma = 1.5$ [27]. With these improvements, EfficientDet has outperformed many object detection models in accuracy and also reducing number of parameters and computational cost on Imagenet dataset. For our paper, the codebase for EfficientDet pre-trained model is from Tensorflow Object Detection API which is available on GitHub [6].

YOLO V5. YOLO is short for You Only Look Once and it is an one-stage object detection model, first proposed by Redmon, Divvala, Girshick and Farhadi [24] in 2015. YOLO has been very successful and received much attention. Basically, YOLO divides images into a grid system, and each cell in the grid is responsible for detecting objects within itself. To do so, first, the image is divided into an $S \times S$ grid. Then, each grid proposes a number of bounding boxes and their respective confidence score which is a score how likely and accurately a bounding box will contain an object. Also, each grid cell calculates its conditional class probabilities which represent how likely each grid cell contains an object. With these predictions and scores, final predictions are made. The loss function for YOLO v5 is combined with regression loss (mean squared error), objectness loss (binary cross entropy loss) and classification loss (cross entropy loss) [8]. For our paper, the codebase for YOLO v5 pre-trained model is provided by Ultralytics which is available on GitHub [3].

6   Results

6.1   Evaluation Metrics

To evaluate classification and localization performance of our AI algorithms, we use multiple critical metrics: Precision, Recall, Intersection over Union (IoU) and mean average precision (mAP). Precision is the fraction of relevant instances (which in this case is a correct classification) among those instances that are retrieved. Recall is the fraction of the relevant instances that were actually retrieved. IoU is a metric that assesses the ratio of areas of the intersection over the union among the predicted bounding boxes and the ground truth. A higher IoU means more overlap between predictions and the ground-truth, and so better localization. An Iou of 0.5 is considered very good for state of the art AI models. The last metric is Mean Average Precision (mAP). Before defining this, we define another metric called Average Precision (AP), which is the average of all the Precision values for a range of Recall (0 to 1 for our problem) at a certain preset IoU threshold for a particular class among the nine (in Table 1) for our problem. This metric essentially balances both Precision and Recall for a particular value of IoU for one class. Finally, the Mean Average Precision (mAP) is the average of AP values among all our nine classes.

6.2   Training Loss

Training loss is a critical component of AI model development. The loss function must decrease during training in order for the model to learn correctly. Figures 5, 6 and 7, show the loss functions during training for both classification loss and localization loss, along with the total loss for our three architectures that we fine-tuned. As we can see, the loss functions progressively decrease, and reach stability, at which point the training completes.

Table 4. APs and mAPs for Validation and Test datasets with different object detection models

Model	EfficientDet		Faster R-CNN		Yolo v5	
Dataset	Validation	Test	Validation	Test	Validation	Test
AP - biohazard_box	0.00	0.00	0.00	0.00	0.72	0.80
AP - cooker	0.10	0.29	0.31	0.16	0.29	0.56
AP - orange_cap	0.58	0.52	0.55	0.63	0.63	0.80
AP - plunger	0.31	0.46	0.46	0.40	0.41	0.67
AP - syringe	0.73	0.68	0.69	0.70	0.83	0.85
AP - syringe_packaging	0.21	0.07	0.55	0.28	0.44	0.36
AP - tourniquet	0.06	0.08	0.58	0.42	0.40	0.43
AP - vial	0.48	0.44	0.59	0.56	0.64	0.70
AP - white_cap	0.23	0.18	0.20	0.41	0.45	0.63
mAP	0.30	0.30	0.44	0.40	**0.53**	**0.64**

6.3   mAP on Validation and Test Dataset for All AI Models

Table 4 shows evaluation results on validation and the test datasets for our AI models. Overall, YOLO v5 performed the best with a mAP of 0.64 on the test dataset (and hence we highlight that in the paper). Figure 8 plots the precision-recall curves of Yolo v5 model on the test dataset. The dark blue line is the precision-recall curve of all classes while the others represent the precision-recall curves of each class. Table 5 shows examples of ground-truth data on the test dataset and their corresponding predictions from YOLO v5 pre-trained model.

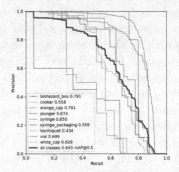

Fig. 8. Precision-recall curve of Yolo v5 on the test dataset

Table 5. Comparisons between ground-truth data vs YOLO v5 predictions for some drug usage objects of interest in our dataset

ground-truth (boxes were emplaced manually)				
YOLO v5 prediction (boxes were emplaced automatically)				
ground-truth (boxes were emplaced manually)				
YOLO v5 prediction (boxes were emplaced automatically)				
ground-truth (boxes were emplaced manually)				
YOLO v5 prediction (boxes were emplaced automatically)				

7   Conclusion

There is now an urgent need for new approaches to combat drug use. In this paper, our contribution is to focus on using massive-scale and freely available images uploaded by the public to detect drug use on streets in a major city in the US, namely San Francisco. We downloaded images from the SF311 platform that the public widely uses in San Francisco to report civic problems. We identified that these images posted by the general public do contain components that indicate drug use on streets. We then leveraged state of the art AI models and fine-tuned them for detecting drug usage on streets. Our accuracy results are favorable, suggesting that our contributions in this paper integrating AI and crowd-provided images can be excellent resources to detect drug use on streets in urban America and across the world, too. In terms of limitations, our accuracy can be improved with more data, and we could also explore explainability to our AI models. Furthermore, processing data from social media platforms for drug use detection is also a possible avenue we will explore in the future.

References

1. Computer vision | learning machine learning. https://learningmachinelearning.org/computer-vision. Accessed 26 July 2022
2. Datasf | office of the chief data officer | city and county of San Francisco. https://datasf.org. Accessed 31 July 2021
3. Github − ultralytics/YOLOv5: YOLOv5 in PyTorch > ONNX > coreml > Tflite. https://github.com/ultralytics/yolov5. Accessed 22 Sept. 2021
4. Home | SF311. https://sf311.org. Accessed 28 June 2022
5. Labelimg · PyPI. https://pypi.org/project/labelImg. Accessed 13 July 2022
6. models/research/object_detection at master · tensorflow/models · github. https://github.com/tensorflow/models/tree/master/research/object_detection. Accessed 30 Oct 2021
7. Opioids | CDC. https://www.cdc.gov/opioids/index.html. Accessed 12 Aug 2021
8. The practical guide for object detection with YOLOv5 algorithm | by Lihi Gur Arie, PHD | towards data science. https://towardsdatascience.com/the-practical-guide-for-object-detection-with-yolov5-algorithm-74c04aac4843. Accessed 13 July 2022
9. Products - vital statistics rapid release - provisional drug overdose data. https://www.cdc.gov/nchs/nvss/vsrr/drug-overdose-data.htm. Accessed 12 Aug 2021
10. SAS help center: object detection: faster R-CNN. http://go.documentation.sas.com/doc/en/pgmcdc/8.11/casdlpg/p1np8zbnoyd0brn1dhehthuuxj4q.htm#p01r9nxiv9wu0in150lnlp23bfwb. Accessed 13 July 2022
11. Understanding google EfficientDet, BiFPN for object detection | jarvislabs.ai. https://jarvislabs.ai/blogs/efficientdet, last accessed 28 July 2022
12. Appa, A., et al.: Drug overdose deaths before and after shelter-in-place orders during the COVID-19 pandemic in San Francisco. JAMA Netw. Open **4**(5), e2110452–e2110452 (2021)
13. Brothers, T.D., Mosseler, K., Kirkland, S., Melanson, P., Barrett, L., Webster, D.: Unequal access to opioid agonist treatment and sterile injecting equipment among hospitalized patients with injection drug use-associated infective endocarditis. PLoS ONE **17**(1), e0263156 (2022)

14. Cosma, A.: New York, San Francisco and Los Angeles: a cultural map of the beat generation. Linguaculture **12**(2), 19–31 (2021)
15. Goldstein, D.A., Harvey, R.D., Chan, K.K.: Enabling the sharing of single-dose vials through risk mitigation to decrease financial toxicity. JAMA Oncol. (2022)
16. Hrycko, A., Mateu-Gelabert, P., Ciervo, C., Linn-Walton, R., Eckhardt, B.: Severe bacterial infections in people who inject drugs: the role of injection-related tissue damage. Harm Reduct. J. **19**(1), 1–13 (2022)
17. Jonas, S., Rodríguez, N.: Contradictions of the San Francisco area. In: Guatemala-US Migration, pp. 156–199. University of Texas Press (2021)
18. Kim, K., Oh, H., Miller, D., Veloso, D., Lin, J., McFarland, W.: Prevalence and disparities in opioid overdose response training among people who inject drugs, San Francisco: Naloxone training among injectors in San Francisco. Int. J. Drug Policy **90**, 102778 (2021)
19. Kim, S.J., Marsch, L.A., Hancock, J.T., Das, A.K.: Scaling up research on drug abuse and addiction through social media big data. J. Med. Internet Res. **19**(10), e6426 (2017)
20. Mirzazadeh, A., et al.: Progress toward closing gaps in the hepatitis C virus cascade of care for people who inject drugs in San Francisco. PLoS ONE **16**(4), e0249585 (2021)
21. Papenburg, J., et al.: Pediatric injuries from needles discarded in the community: epidemiology and risk of seroconversion. Pediatrics **122**(2), e487–e492 (2008)
22. Perdue, R.T., Hawdon, J., Thames, K.M.: Can big data predict the rise of novel drug abuse? J. Drug Issues **48**(4), 508–518 (2018)
23. Phan, N., Chun, S.A., Bhole, M., Geller, J.: Enabling real-time drug abuse detection in tweets. In: 2017 IEEE 33rd International Conference on Data Engineering (ICDE), pp. 1510–1514. IEEE (2017)
24. Redmon, J., Divvala, S., Girshick, R., Farhadi, A.: You only look once: unified, real-time object detection. In: Proceedings of the IEEE Conference on Computer Vision and Pattern Recognition, pp. 779–788 (2016)
25. Ren, S., He, K., Girshick, R., Sun, J.: Faster R-CNN: towards real-time object detection with region proposal networks. In: Advances in Neural Information Processing Systems, vol. 28 (2015)
26. Sarkar, D., Bali, R., Ghosh, T.: Hands-On Transfer Learning with Python: Implement Advanced Deep Learning and Neural Network Models Using TensorFlow and Keras. Packt Publishing Ltd. (2018)
27. Tan, M., Pang, R., Le, Q.V.: EfficientDet: scalable and efficient object detection. In: Proceedings of the IEEE/CVF Conference on Computer Vision and Pattern Recognition, pp. 10781–10790 (2020)
28. Valdez, A., Cepeda, A., Frankeberger, J., Nowotny, K.M.: The opioid epidemic among the Latino population in California. Drug Alcohol Depend. Rep. **2**, 100029 (2022)
29. Wenger, L.D., Martinez, A.N., Carpenter, L., Geckeler, D., Colfax, G., Kral, A.H.: Syringe disposal among injection drug users in San Francisco. Am. J. Public Health **101**(3), 484–486 (2011)

Machine Learning Approach to Crisis Management Exercise Analysis: A Case Study in SURE Project

Henry Joutsijoki[1]([✉]), Sari Mäenpää[1], Ilari Karppi[2], and Iina Sankala[2]

[1] Insta Advance Oy, Sarankulmankatu 20, 33900 Tampere, Finland
{henry.joutsijoki,sari.maenpaa}@insta.fi
[2] Faculty of Management and Business, Tampere University, Kanslerinrinne 1, 33014 Tampere, Finland
{ilari.karppi,iina.sankala}@tuni.fi

Abstract. Crisis management exercises play a key role in preparation for different scenarios such as natural disasters, or large crowd events. Moreover, they act as a platform for testing new technologies and finding common practices between different actors. In this preliminary paper, we apply a collection of machine learning methods to a questionnaire data to find factors, where authorities' and non-authorities' perspectives differ when a large number of questions are covered simultaneously. Such factors may be focal elements in hindering the co-operation between different actors in a real-world case. Therefore factors are essential to be revealed. Feedback data was collected from a multi-organizational crisis management exercise that was organized as part of an EU funded Smart Urban Security and Event Resilience (SURE) project. Dataset was examined in four question set scenarios and in each case we obtained around 80% accuracy when classifying authorities and non-authorities. This indicates that parties' perspectives differ about the crisis management exercise and it strengthens the idea of recognizing the possible obstacles of co-operation. Although crisis management exercises are relatively well researched area in the literature, the use of machine learning methods in this context gives a novel approach for analyzing the results. Machine learning based analysis of results enables improving crisis management exercises in the future.

Keywords: Crisis management exercise · Machine learning · Classification

1 Introduction

Management of crisis situations typically takes place in a multi-actor setting due to the division of labor among different safety and law enforcement agencies. Actors' prompt, correctly resourced and well-timed response to any situation requires joint action that, in turn is conditioned by their shared ability to process information, communicate and, generally, consider themselves as a team even if

© ICST Institute for Computer Sciences, Social Informatics and Telecommunications Engineering 2023
Published by Springer Nature Switzerland AG 2023. All Rights Reserved
S. I. Lopes et al. (Eds.): Edge-IoT 2022/SmartGov 2022, LNICST 510, pp. 102–116, 2023.
https://doi.org/10.1007/978-3-031-35982-8_8

some of the organization-specific tasks might first appear as counterproductive to each other. This process requires a great deal of interorganizational trust, the embodiments of which are individual functionaries of safety and security agencies in joint command centers or situation rooms. In research literature individuals that actually make the joint action happen are sometimes referred to as "boundary spanners" [13].

Digitalization, particularly the fusion of extensive datasets and machine learning, has the capacity to endow the situation room boundary spanners with new tools, services and practices that help them to act promptly and command the necessary resources in right measures and in a timely manner. This requires both clarity of responsibilities among all parties involved and shared situational understanding as concerns the unfolding of the crisis. To enable the actors' best possible individual and joint performance in situations with the above parameters, crisis management exercises are needed.

Authorities often have their internal exercises as well as rehearsals with some other authority. The technological tools used in these exercises are mostly the official tools and authority-specific systems. However, joint crisis management exercises are not common where also non-authorities, like local red cross actors or event safety organizations, are involved and where light, user-friendly technological solutions are available. Technology can be one of the key enablers, among authorities and non-authorities alike, for improved communication, enriched and shared situational awareness, and collaboration. Co-operation does not take place automatically and common "language" or vocabulary as well as different tools and enablers are needed for successful and efficient co-operation, so that correct information can be shared in challenging and rapidly changing situations.

A multi-organizational crisis management exercise was held in Tampere, Finland as a part of ongoing SURE project. Feedback data was collected from participants and was examined in four scenarios with machine learning methods. In this paper, we bring a machine learning perspective into an analysis of crisis management exercises. Machine learning methods can be used to find novel relationships from multi-dimensional data that could not be found with traditional statistical methods and observed questionwise. The main idea is to examine the differences between authorities' and non-authorities' answers in these scenarios. Findings may help to improve the quality and usefulness of crisis management exercises and to advance interorganizational collaboration by revealing the existing obstacles between the collaboration of authorities and non-authorities.

The use of machine learning in feedback data analysis has been examined before. For example, in [12] feedback data was examined to determine the effectiveness of teaching and learning activities, whereas in [6] authors performed opinion mining to the student feedback data to identify polarities in the data. Gamon [7] investigated sentiment analysis on customer feedback data. Khanbhai et al. [11] instead examined patient experience data, which has a free-text format and includes essential information that can be analyzed with machine learning and NLP methods.

If we consider crisis management exercises, the situation is different. Scott et al. [15] collected three types of data from the crisis management exercise, but the data analysis did not include the use of machine learning. Zagorecki et al. [20] reviewed extensively possibilities and challenges of data mining and machine learning in disaster and crisis management, but the concrete usage of machine learning was missing. AL-Ma'aitah [2] investigated the impact of big data and predictive analytics capabilities on crisis management and performed a questionnaire to which 140 participants answered. However, the analysis of data was restricted to statistical analysis.

The paper is organized as follows. In Sect. 2, we give a short description about SURE project, Insta Advance's technological solutions, and the executed crisis management exercise. Section 3 covers the technical aspects of the paper. Section 4 includes the results and in Sect. 5 conclusions are given.

2   SURE Project

2.1   SURE in General

European Union has highlighted safety as one of the focal themes and this emphasis can also be seen in EU's funding instruments such as Horizon 2020 programme. SURE [17] is an EU UIA funded project led by the City of Tampere. The participating organizations in the project are Insta, Tampere University, Tampere University of Applied Sciences, Business Tampere, Nokia Solutions & Networks and Securitas.

SURE project has three main objectives:

1. Improving the citizens' and tourists' sense of everyday safety and security by developing and piloting intelligent technology solutions for urban security.
2. Enhancing the preparedness for smooth and seamless coordination and collaboration between different safety and security actors, emergency medical service and event organizers.
3. Providing the local companies opportunities to develop and pilot innovations, services and products concerning urban security.

In addition to technological tests and pilots enabled by SURE partners, there were altogether six agile experiments during the project. Four of these experiments were implemented by crisis management exercise in June 2021. The needs for agile experiments were gathered during workshops and conversations with Särkänniemi Amusement Park, Tampere Hall and representatives of Tampere city's school network as well as local authorities. The agile experiments were put out to tender for companies willing to experiment and pilot their sensor or AI analytics solutions within city and event context. The sensor data, e.g., sensor locations, alarms of anomalies or gas leaks, analytical outcomes such as gas spread prognosis or detected targets, was integrated into Insta Blue Aware (IBA) platform to enhance situation awareness.

2.2   Insta's Technologies

Insta provides technological solutions that can be tested during the project in order to receive feedback, development ideas and experiences about the use of solutions in various situations. The provided technologies cover three alternatives called IBA, IBT and info link.

IBA (Insta Blue Aware) is a map-based situation awareness platform that enables simple integration of various actors' sensors and data sources. By using IBA, situation awareness can be shown and shared between authorities and it also enables collaboration towards civilians and volunteers. IBA is a versatile technology that can be used via mobile phone, tablet or desktop. This again broadens its usefulness among civilians, authorities and volunteers.

IBT (Insta Blue Tracker) is a mobile app for sharing the situation picture as well as for collaboration between team members. It is used for sharing pictures, videos and location data from the field. IBT enables collaboration between field operators and those forming an overall situation awareness picture. Third technology is the so called info link, or citizen link. It is a link between non-authority representative's mobile phone and IBA platform in authority's situation awareness room. Info link is activated by sending an SMS from IBA and by using it a citizen can share both picture or video and location data from the field. Info link is valid for only a definite period of time.

2.3   Crisis Management Exercise in SURE

Simulation exercises are a focal part of SURE development as they will allow for real-life co-operation with the target beneficiaries in Tampere. When thinking about alignment of key stakeholders, the biggest challenge is to succeed in creating a "common language" between otherwise very divergent sectors such as the police, private event organizers and the social services department of a municipality. To tackle this, light and user-friendly technological solutions together with common crisis management exercises can be the solution.

The first large-scale multi-actor (both authorities and non-authorities) crises management exercise was arranged within the SURE project on the 10th June 2021. There were more than 50 participants from Central Police Finland Department, Pirkanmaa Rescue Department, Pirkanmaa Hospital District Emergency Services, Emergency Response Centre Agency, Finnish Red Cross, City of Tampere Social and crisis stand-by service, and event security actor.

The objective of the exercise was to train multi authority collaboration and to discuss technological opportunities. The general objective of SURE project is to support authorities and event organizers in planning, anticipating and testing different scenarios for big events. The focal scenario (fire during a stadium concert) for the exercise was divided and scheduled into three separate parts to enable the focusing on specific actors and activities. The exercise was managed by using technological solutions, situation awareness platform enriched with simulated events. Due to COVID-19 situation the participants of the exercise were divided into different rooms and Teams was used for conversation between rooms. The crisis management exercise lasted for four hours.

3   Technical Description

3.1   Questionnaire Design

In the end of the crisis management exercise, participants were asked to fill up a web-based questionnaire regarding the exercise. No time limit was given for answering. The questionnaire was compiled by the Tampere University researchers in SURE project. Questionnaire was divided into four parts: general, exercise, technology and agile experiments. All Likert-scale questions were used in this paper and can be seen in Table 1. Questions were originally in Finnish, but in Table 1 an English translation is given. Answers included seven possible alternatives and the following list represents them together with the original Finnish form in the parenthesis.

- Totally disagree (Täysin eri mieltä)
- Partially disagree (Osittain eri mieltä)
- Not agree or disagree (Ei samaa eikä eri mieltä)
- Partially agree (Osittain samaa mieltä)
- Totally agree (Täysin samaa mieltä)
- Cannot say (EOS)
- Missing value

Questionnaire included open questions regarding the exercise, technology and agile experiments but these were not utilized in this paper as well as two binary questions. Participant's organization was asked so that the labeling to authorities/non-authorities was possible to make. In the data, starting and end time of answering the questionnaire were recorded but not used. No names or email addresses were asked from the participants, but an ID number was saved for the answers.

3.2   Dataset and Preprocessing

Altogether, 39 participants answered to the questionnaire and only Likert-scale questions given in Table 1 were taken into account. As a first preprocessing step, we label participants' original organization into authority/non-authority. If we would use the original organizations as a class label, the number of different classes would be too large compared to dataset's size. Label 'authority' was given for Pirkanmaa Rescue Department, Pirkanmaa Hospital District Emergency Services, City of Tampere Social and crisis stand-by service, Central Police Finland Department and Emergency Response Centre Agency. Otherwise, label 'non-authority' was given. Hence, the class sizes of non-authorities and authorities were 14 and 25.

After labeling, the textual Likert-scale was transformed into numeric scale such that totally disagree equals 1 and totally agree equals 5. Options 'Cannot say' and missing value had to be handled differently since they are not part of natural Likert-scale. Firstly, 'Cannot say' and missing values were mapped to a value 3. Secondly, we constructed a separate binary variable for each question,

Table 1. Likert-scale questions in the questionnaire with English translation.

Section	Question
Exercise	Exercise was important for developing my own expertise
Exercise	Exercise was important for developing the operation of my organization
Exercise	Exercise was important for developing participants' (authorities and others) co-operation
Exercise	Exercise was well organized
Exercise	Issues covered during the exercise can really happen in practice
Exercise	I had enough information about the purpose of the exercise
Exercise	I performed well at the exercise
Exercise	I knew what was expected from me in the exercise
Technology	In this exercise IBA was useful for taking care of my own duty
Technology	I received via IBA a good perspective about the work of other participants (authorities and others)
Technology	I received a good perspective about the big picture of situations practiced via IBA
Technology	Via IBT received situational information is useful for me
Technology	Via IBT received situational information is useful with respect to co-operation (authorities and others)
Technology	Via citizen link received situational information was useful for me
Technology	Via citizen link received situational information is useful with respect to co-operation (authorities and others)
Technology	Experience is a significant factor for mastering my task
Technology	In my task, technology is a significant factor for mastering the task
Technology	Technology what I use causes stress
Technology	Available technologies improve the safety of citizens and event visitors
Agile experiments	Presented solution is interesting with respect to my organization and its operation (agile experiment #1)
Agile experiments	Presented solution offers information that clarifies the situational understanding (agile experiment #1)
Agile experiments	Presented solution is interesting with respect to my organization and its operation (agile experiment #2)
Agile experiments	Presented solution offers information that clarifies the situational understanding (agile experiment #2)
Agile experiments	Presented solution is interesting with respect to my organization and its operation (agile experiment #3)
Agile experiments	Presented solution offers information that clarifies the situational understanding (agile experiment #3)
Agile experiments	Presented solution is interesting with respect to my organization and its operation (agile experiment #4)
Agile experiments	Presented solution offers information that clarifies the situational understanding (agile experiment #4)

which depicted whether or not the original value in the question was 'Cannot say' or a missing value. As a final preprocessing stage, dataset was normalized into $[0,1]$ range excluding class variable and generated binary variables. The normalization was performed using the formula $x' = \frac{x-1}{5-1}$, where x' is the new value and x is the original value. If some column does not include extreme values, columnwise min-max normalization would have led to a controversial situation where in one variable, for example, 'Partially disagree' would get different values in different variables. In order to avoid such discrepancy, aforementioned normalization was used.

3.3   Methods and Test Set-Up

Altogether eight machine learning methods (CART, k-means++, KNN, LDA, Logistic regression, Naïve Bayes, QDA, and SVM) were utilized in the analysis. We chose these methods since they are suitable with small datasets and present different characteristics giving new insights from the dataset.

K-Nearest Neighbor method (KNN) [5] is a machine learning algorithm where the selection of a proper k value, distance metric and distance weighting play a key role. In this study, we tested three distance metrics (Euclidean, Manhattan and Chebyshev) and $k \in \{1, 3, 5\}$. Distance weighting was kept equal for all examples. Besides KNN, we used two other parameter dependent classification algorithms. These were Support Vector Machine (SVM) [1] and Classification and Regression Trees (CART) [16]. SVM aims at finding a classes separating maximal margin classifier in the input space, but the use of SVM was extended with kernel trick to cover linearly non-separable cases. The performance of SVM is dependent on the selection of kernel and hyperparameter values. We examined the linear, the quadaratic and the Radial Basis Function (RBF) kernels. A common parameter for all kernels is a regularization parameter called boxconstraint (C). We chose that $C \in \{2^{-5}, 2^{-4}, \ldots, 2^5\}$. The RBF kernel includes a hyperparameter, $\gamma > 0$, and for it we tested same values as for boxconstraint.

CART includes several tunable parameters. In our study, we varied the tree depthness and the minimum number of examples required to be at a leaf node. For the depth parameter we examined values $\{None, 1, 2, 3, 4, 5, 6\}$, whereas for the second parameter we tested values $\{1, 2, 3, 4, 5, 6, 7\}$. In depth parameter, $None$ means that the tree is grown to the maximum size when other parameters are taken into account. From the parameter free methods, we applied Naïve Bayes (NB) [9], linear discriminant analysis (LDA) [19], quadratic discriminant analysis (QDA) [18] and logistic regression [14]. Furthermore, k-means++ algorithm [3] was used.

We have different test set-ups for classification and clustering. Due to dataset's size, we applied leave-one-out (LOO) method in classification whereas in clustering the whole dataset was clustered at the same time. With parameter dependent classification methods, we repeated LOO procedure with all parameter combinations examined. Then we selected the best parameter value combination based on the accuracy obtained. For parameter-free classification methods, we performed LOO procedure only once to the dataset. Besides parameter' tuning, we explored the impact of feature set selection in four different scenarios (all Likert-scale questions and sections presented in Table 1). In all cases, parameter tuning was repeated similarly.

3.4   Performance Measures

A great collection of performance measures exists for binary classification problems. The origin of performance measures is in confusion matrix [8, 10] and a general form of binary confusion matrix adjusted to the context of this paper is given in Table 2. In the table, TP (true positive), FN (false negative), TN (true negative), FP (false positive) represent how many non-authorities/authorities were classified correctly/wrongly.

Table 2. A general form of binary confusion matrix

		Predicted	
		Non-authorities	Authorities
True	Non-authorities	TP	FN
class	Authorities	FP	TN

True positive rate (TPR) describes the proportion of correctly predicted non-authorities compared to the total number non-authorities in a dataset [8, 10]. True negative rate (TNR) presents the proportion of correctly classified authorities [8]. Accuracy (ACC) depicts how many examples were classified correctly in total [8]. However, it can be a misleading performance measure when the classes are highly uneven. Thus, F1-score (F1) may give a better insight for the results, although it does not utilize TN value in calculation [10]. To overcome the limitation of F1-score, we also evaluate Matthews Correlation Coefficient (MCC) [4] in this paper.

4   Results

When in binary classification tasks the classes are equal size, 50% accuracy is a baseline for the results and it represents decision making by flipping a coin. In our case, the baseline for classification would be the accuracy when all examples are classified to the majority class. This again gives 64.1% accuracy as a baseline for comparison.

Table 3 shows the results when all features were used in classification. If we look at the accuracies, they have quite a big variance. The lowest accuracy, 35.9%, is obtained by KNN with the Chebyshev metric, whereas the highest accuracy (79.5%) is gained by the CART method. Besides the highest accuracy, F1 and MCC values were the best ones (71.4% and 0.6) by CART. For TP, FN and TPR, KNN with Chebyshev metric ($k = 3$ and $k = 5$) yielded the best result, although otherwise it did not achieve good results. A noticeable detail in KNN results is that when k value is increased, the KNN results get worsen. This means that with KNN, at least with large k values, we obtain inevitably also noise along. Topmost TN was achieved by SVM with the quadratic and the RBF kernels. In terms of accuracy, SVM with the quadratic kernel received the baseline result and the RBF kernel slightly above it. The reason why the quadratic kernel gave NaN for MCC is that TP and FP were both 0. Overall, the classification of non-authorities and authorities succeeded quite well and we can say that there is a difference between the responses of authorities and non-authorities when all variables are used in the classification.

Table 3. Classification results when using all variables.

Method	TP	FN	FP	TN	TPR (%)	TNR (%)	ACC (%)	F1 (%)	MCC
CART (depth=None, minleaf=7)	10	4	4	21	71.4	84.0	**79.5**	**71.4**	**0.6**
KNN Chebyshev, $k = 1$	2	12	4	21	14.3	84.0	59.0	20.0	0.0
KNN Chebyshev, $k = 3$	**11**	**3**	19	6	**78.6**	24.0	43.6	50.0	0.0
KNN Chebyshev, $k = 5$	**11**	**3**	22	3	**78.6**	12.0	35.9	46.8	−0.1
KNN Euclidean, $k = 1$	6	8	4	21	42.9	84.0	69.2	50.0	0.3
KNN Euclidean, $k = 3$	5	9	8	17	35.7	68.0	56.4	37.0	0.0
KNN Euclidean, $k = 5$	2	12	8	17	14.3	68.0	48.7	16.7	−0.2
KNN Manhattan, $k = 1$	4	10	6	19	28.6	76.0	59.0	33.3	0.1
KNN Manhattan, $k = 3$	5	9	8	17	35.7	68.0	56.4	37.0	0.0
KNN Manhattan, $k = 5$	2	12	12	13	14.3	52.0	38.5	14.3	−0.3
LDA	5	9	11	14	35.7	56.0	48.7	33.3	−0.1
Logistic Regression	5	9	6	19	35.7	76.0	61.5	40.0	0.1
Naïve Bayes	9	5	6	19	64.3	76.0	71.8	62.1	0.4
QDA	4	10	13	12	28.6	48.0	41.0	25.8	−0.2
SVM linear, $C = 2^{-5}$	5	9	1	24	35.7	96.0	74.4	50.0	0.4
SVM quadratic, $C = 2^{-5}$	0	14	**0**	**25**	0.0	**100.0**	64.1	0.0	NaN
SVM RBF, $C = 2^{1}$, $\gamma = 2^{-5}$	1	13	**0**	**25**	7.1	**100.0**	66.7	13.3	0.2

The second experiment was performed by using only exercise related variables and the results are given in Table 4. When considering the results, we notice that NB managed to classify almost all non-authorities (TP) correctly having TPR of 92.9%. Otherwise, NB did not succeed well from the classification task. Similar behavior is visible with the QDA. For classification of authorities, SVM with the RBF kernel performed well having TNR value of 88.0%. Besides high TNR, the RBF kernel had the highest accuracy together with CART. However, CART achieved still a little bit better F1 and MCC values than SVM RBF.

The general level of results in Table 4 is better than in Table 3 since many of the accuracies are higher than baseline. This may be a result of smaller number of variables and the suitability of them. Although CART and SVM RBF had the best accuracies, KNN with the Euclidean distance metric and SVM with the linear kernel obtained above 74% accuracy, that can be considered as a good result. Compared to Table 3, now in KNN results similar decrease of performance is not visible when k value is larger. This again shows what kind of influence selected variables may have to the classifier's performance.

Table 4. Classification results when using exercise related variables.

Method	TP	FN	FP	TN	TPR (%)	TNR (%)	ACC (%)	F1 (%)	MCC
CART (depth=None, minleaf=7)	10	4	4	21	71.4	84.0	**79.5**	**71.4**	**0.6**
KNN Chebyshev, $k = 1$	6	8	5	20	42.9	80.0	66.7	48.0	0.2
KNN Chebyshev, $k = 3$	10	4	13	12	71.4	48.0	56.4	54.1	0.2
KNN Chebyshev, $k = 5$	11	3	12	13	78.6	52.0	61.5	59.5	0.3
KNN Euclidean, $k = 1$	9	5	8	17	64.3	68.0	66.7	58.1	0.3
KNN Euclidean, $k = 3$	9	5	5	20	64.3	80.0	74.4	64.3	0.4
KNN Euclidean, $k = 5$	8	6	7	18	57.1	72.0	66.7	55.2	0.3
KNN Manhattan, $k = 1$	9	5	10	15	64.3	60.0	61.5	54.5	0.2
KNN Manhattan, $k = 3$	9	5	6	19	64.3	76.0	71.8	62.1	0.4
KNN Manhattan, $k = 5$	10	4	9	16	71.4	64.0	66.7	60.6	0.3
LDA	10	4	11	14	71.4	56.0	61.5	57.1	0.3
Logistic Regression	8	6	7	18	57.1	72.0	66.7	55.2	0.3
Naïve Bayes	**13**	**1**	19	6	**92.9**	24.0	48.7	56.5	0.2
QDA	**13**	**1**	25	0	**92.9**	0.0	33.3	50.0	−0.2
SVM linear, $C = 2^5$	9	5	4	21	64.3	84.0	76.9	66.7	0.5
SVM quadratic, $C = 2^2$	10	4	7	18	71.4	72.0	71.8	64.5	0.4
SVM RBF, $C = 2^3$, $\gamma = 2^1$	9	5	**3**	**22**	64.3	**88.0**	79.5	69.2	0.5

Next, we have the results in Table 5 when technology related variables are used in classification. Immediately, a noticeable detail is the decrease in results. Only six methods got accuracy above the baseline level. The reasons behind the results may be diverse. The role of technology in the actual crisis management exercise may have effected on the results and some participants may have had more experience on using different technologies in their work than others and this might cause difference in results. The design of technology related questions can also be one reason.

When looking more closely the results, we see that four methods obtained almost 77% accuracy. These methods were CART, NB and SVM with the quadratic and the RBF kernels. Respectively, these methods gained the best F1 and MCC results. Nevertheless, the best performance is explained with the perfect recognition of authorities. At the same time, these methods managed to identify non-authorities with TNR value below 40% that can be considered as low result. Non-authorities were recognized best using KNN with Chebyshev metric ($k = 3$, $k = 5$), but still the recognition rate was left to a modest 50% level. To the classification results effects the slight skewness in class sizes. Since the dataset is relatively small and non-authorities are in a minority position in a dataset, smaller classes are usually more difficult to recognize. Moreover, if we think about the authority class as a whole, authorities have similar operating principles whereas non-authorities can be more heterogeneous group with different backgrounds and educations.

Table 5. Classification results when using technology related variables.

Method	TP	FN	FP	TN	TPR (%)	TNR (%)	ACC (%)	F1 (%)	MCC
CART (depth=1, minleaf=1)	5	9	0	25	35.7	**100.0**	**76.9**	**52.6**	**0.5**
KNN Chebyshev, $k = 1$	3	11	8	17	21.4	68.0	51.3	24.0	-0.1
KNN Chebyshev, $k = 3$	**7**	**7**	20	5	**50.0**	20.0	30.8	34.1	-0.3
KNN Chebyshev, $k = 5$	**7**	**7**	20	5	**50.0**	20.0	30.8	34.1	-0.3
KNN Euclidean, $k = 1$	4	10	8	17	28.6	68.0	53.8	30.8	0.0
KNN Euclidean, $k = 3$	2	12	12	13	14.3	52.0	38.5	14.3	-0.3
KNN Euclidean, $k = 5$	3	11	10	15	21.4	60.0	46.2	22.2	-0.2
KNN Manhattan, $k = 1$	5	9	10	15	35.7	60.0	51.3	34.5	0.0
KNN Manhattan, $k = 3$	0	14	10	15	0.0	60.0	38.5	0.0	-0.4
KNN Manhattan, $k = 5$	3	11	12	13	21.4	52.0	41.0	20.7	-0.3
LDA	6	8	11	14	42.9	56.0	51.3	38.7	0.0
Logistic Regression	5	9	3	22	35.7	88.0	69.2	45.5	0.3
Naïve Bayes	5	9	0	25	35.7	**100.0**	**76.9**	**52.6**	**0.5**
QDA	0	14	0	25	0.0	**100.0**	64.1	0.0	NaN
SVM linear, $C = 2^{-4}$	4	10	1	24	28.6	96.0	71.8	42.1	0.4
SVM quadratic, $C = 2^{-3}$	5	9	0	25	35.7	**100.0**	**76.9**	**52.6**	**0.5**
SVM RBF, $C = 2^3$, $\gamma = 2^{-4}$	5	9	0	25	35.7	**100.0**	**76.9**	**52.6**	**0.5**

The last scenario was to use variables concerning agile experiments. In the crisis management exercise, four different solutions were introduced for participants and Table 6 shows the results when agile experiments related variables were used in classification. An eye-catching issue in Table 6 is that QDA again obtained a perfect 100% TNR result, but misclassified all the non-authorities. Same phenomenon can be seen in Table 5 results. CART performed again well and was able to classify non-authorities with above 70% level. Moreover, CART was the best method in terms of accuracy, F1 and MCC values. The accuracy of 82.1% was the best among all experiments in this paper. An interesting detail is that CART had only depth of 2, which means a very small tree in size.

Besides CART, SVM RBF was the only method to obtain above 70% accuracy. Otherwise, accuracies were around the baseline and the level of classification was modest. A reason behind this fact can be participants' lack of time to explore the possibilities of the different solutions presented. A bit surprising result, not only in Table 6, but also in other result tables is that KNN did not succeed very well in the classification. CART, SVM with the RBF kernel and NB were throughout the experiments the best methods. The goodness of SVM can be explained partly by its capabilities to handle nonlinear classification tasks and it suits well for the analysis of smaller datasets. In this last classification scenario, there was not any problem about the ratio of features and examples.

Table 6. Classification results when using agile experiments variables.

Method	TP	FN	FP	TN	TPR (%)	TNR (%)	ACC (%)	F1 (%)	MCC
CART (depth=2, minleaf=1)	**10**	**4**	3	22	**71.4**	88.0	**82.1**	**74.1**	**0.6**
KNN Chebyshev, $k = 1$	5	9	7	18	35.7	72.0	59.0	38.5	0.1
KNN Chebyshev, $k = 3$	9	5	17	8	64.3	32.0	43.6	45.0	0.0
KNN Chebyshev, $k = 5$	6	8	19	6	42.9	24.0	30.8	30.8	−0.3
KNN Euclidean, $k = 1$	7	7	10	15	50.0	60.0	56.4	45.2	0.1
KNN Euclidean, $k = 3$	6	8	5	20	42.9	80.0	66.7	48.0	0.2
KNN Euclidean, $k = 5$	3	11	5	20	21.4	80.0	59.0	27.3	0.0
KNN Manhattan, $k = 1$	7	7	10	15	50.0	60.0	56.4	45.2	0.1
KNN Manhattan, $k = 3$	7	7	5	20	50.0	80.0	69.2	53.8	0.3
KNN Manhattan, $k = 5$	4	10	7	18	28.6	72.0	56.4	32.0	0.0
LDA	8	6	8	17	57.1	68.0	64.1	53.3	0.2
Logistic Regression	2	12	5	20	14.3	80.0	56.4	19.0	−0.1
Naïve Bayes	9	5	9	16	64.3	64.0	64.1	56.3	0.3
QDA	0	14	**0**	**25**	0.0	**100.0**	64.1	0.0	NaN
SVM linear, $C = 2^2$	8	6	7	18	57.1	72.0	66.7	55.2	0.3
SVM quadratic, $C = 2^2$	6	8	6	19	42.9	76.0	64.1	46.2	0.2
SVM RBF, $C = 2^1$, $\gamma = 2^{-1}$	7	7	4	21	50.0	84.0	71.8	56.0	0.4

Tables 3-6 covered classification results in different scenarios but Table 7 shows how authorities and non-authorities can be separated by means of clustering. An ideal situation would be that each cluster would include examples only from one class. Results indicate that in majority of the cases clusters include quite evenly both classes. Exceptions are encountered in cluster 2 where in three cases non-authorities are a clear minority class, but at the same time in cluster 1 both classes are quite equally represented. Overall, we can say that authorities and non-authorities cannot be well separated at least with k-means++ clustering method.

Table 7. Clustering results using k-means++ algorithm and with different feature sets.

Feature set	Cluster 1 non-authorities	Cluster 1 authorities	Cluster 2 non-authorities	Cluster 2 authorities
All	12	17	2	8
Exercise	13	12	1	13
Technology	4	4	10	21
Agile experiments	12	17	2	8

5   Conclusions

This paper analyzed the differences between authorities' and non-authorities' answers by classifying them based on questionnaire data collected at a multi-organizational crisis management exercise that was part of SURE project. Crisis management exercises are not easy to organize and the first thing to raise up is the workload required for organizing this kind of event especially due to the special arrangements caused by COVID-19. It is not a trivial thing to summon a large number of safety and security actors from their tasks at respective organizations. Hence, it is necessary to keep in mind that the amount of work behind the data is significant even if the size of data is not large.

The idea of classifying authorities and non-authorities using machine learning methods in the crisis management exercise context is rarely examined. That their preferences and other observable markers enabled their identification is an outcome on its own right. Yet, this finding opens an operational question of a greater magnitude: what may follow from what was revealed? It is possible that some of the differences identified here are in areas that challenge the buildup of interorganizational trust among the different actors. The need to identify such factors was one of the main drivers for designing the exercise feedback data survey. Another outcome is that machine learning based analysis of feedback data may help to improve the crisis management exercises through identification of the most important factors.

The questionnaire was a web-based and answering to it was on a voluntarily basis. Altogether, there were over 50 participants in the exercise and 39 persons answered to the questionnaire. Traditionally, questionnaire data is analyzed by doing simple one-dimensional distribution examination from each question and then doing the inference from the results. However, this is not favorable for turning out the big picture of the data or for "seeing the wood for the trees". Machine learning methods enable multidimensional analysis and take complex relationships within the data into account. This would not be possible in one-dimensional distribution analysis.

Our analysis applied eight machine learning methods with some variants. The analysis was divided into four scenarios and by investigating these scenarios, we were able to obtain a good perspective on the separability of authorities' and non-authorities' answers. This gives insights as concerns the content and implementation of the crisis management exercise. By testing several machine learning methods with good results in each case, we were able to show that the selection of machine learning method is meaningful. Moreover, it points out that answers truly vary between different actors. A different situation would have been, if all methods tested would have given poor results.

CART and SVM-based solutions differed, generally speaking, from the rest of the methods results' point of view. CART obtained in all scenarios over 70% accuracy as well as SVM with the RBF kernel in three scenarios. NB had a good recognition rate in some of the cases well but not constantly. A slightly surprising result was the performance of KNN classifier. KNN usually gives good results with small datasets when parameters are appropriately chosen. However, the analysis showed that KNN did not achieve topmost result in any of the cases. The rest of the methods (discriminant analysis methods and logistic regression) did not perform well. The analysis shows that regardless of the feature set used, we were able to find a method that can classify authorities and non-authorities with a good level of accuracy. Nevertheless, we need to bear in mind the limitations regarding the data when doing any wider conclusions about the results. Feedback data includes always uncertainty and it is time and date dependent, but if similar questions are asked in several exercises and more data is collected, more general conclusions can be expected.

The results show that there are differences between authorities' and non-authorities' answers. This again emphasizes that when organizing, designing and interpreting the results of a multi-organizational crisis management exercise, the background of the participants need to be taken carefully into account. With the needs of the actual exercise as the top priority, the participants' institutional status as an independent variable may have a major effect on the analyzed survey outcomes. Event's main organizer's/organizers' fingerprint and own interests may be easily shown in the actual event, which may bias the actual implementation of the exercise and, thus, does not fully satisfy all participants' needs and expectations.

In practice, it is not possible to organize a multi-actor exercise that would satisfy all perfectly, but the machine learning oriented way of analyzing the feedback data can bring new perspectives and insights of how to improve exercises in the future. Moreover, feedback data thus operationalized may enable finding the critical points for building interorganizational trust in crisis management situations in a multi-actor setting. This paper was our first attempt to scrutinize the utilization of machine learning methods for feedback data gained from the crisis management exercise. The experiences and results obtained in this paper give a good starting point for improving machine learning based analysis for the crisis management exercises both in SURE project and in other future contexts.

Acknowledgements. Research was done in UIA104-158 SURE project funded by the EU UIA programme. Authors want to thank Chief Data Scientist Harri Kukkasniemi for the valuable comments regarding the manuscript.

References

1. Abe, S.: Support Vector Machines for Pattern Classification, 2nd edn. Springer, London (2010). https://doi.org/10.1007/978-1-84996-098-4
2. AL-Ma'aitah, M.A.: Utilizing big data and predictive analytics capability in crisis management. J. Comput. Sci. **16**(3), 295–304 (2020)
3. Arthur, D., Vassilvitskii S.: k-means++: the advantages of careful seeding. In: Proceedings of the Eighteenth Annual ACM-SIAM Symposium on Discrete Algorithms, ACM, New Orleans, USA, pp. 1027–1035 (2007)
4. Chicco, D., Jurman, G.: The advantages of the Matthews correlation coefficient (MCC) over F1 score and accuracy in binary classification evaluation. BMC Geno. **21**, Article number 6 (2020)

5. Chomboon, K., Chujai, P., Teerarassamee, P., Kerdprasop, K., Kerdprasop, N.: An empirical study of distance metrics for k-nearest neighbor algorithm. In: Proceedings of the 3rd International Conference on Industrial Application Engineering 2015, Kitakyushu, Japan, pp. 280–285 (2015)

6. Dhanalakshmi, V., Bino, D., Saravanan, A.M.: Opinion mining from student feedback data using supervised learning algorithms. In: Proceedings of the 2016 3rd MEC International Conference on Big Data and Smart City, pp. 1–5. IEEE, Muscat, Oman (2016)

7. Gamon, M.: Sentiment classification on customer feedback data: noisy data, large feature vectors, and the role of linguistic analysis. In: Proceedings of the 20th International Conference on Computational Linguistic (COLING 2004), pp. 841–848. ACL, Geneva, Switzerland (2004)

8. Han, J., Kamber, M., Pei, J.: Data Mining: Concepts and Techniques, 3rd edn. Morgan-Kaufmann, London (2012)

9. Jiang, L., Wang, D., Cai, Z., Yan, X.: Survey of improving naive bayes for classification. In: Alhajj, R., Gao, H., Li, J., Li, X., Zaïane, O.R. (eds.) ADMA 2007. LNCS (LNAI), vol. 4632, pp. 134–145. Springer, Heidelberg (2007). https://doi.org/10.1007/978-3-540-73871-8_14

10. Joutsijoki, H., Rasku, J., Pyykkö, I., Juhola, M.: Classification of patients and controls based on stabilogram signal data. Intell. Data Anal. **23**(1), 215–226 (2019)

11. Khanbhai, M., Anyadi, P., Symons, J., Flott, K., Darzi, A., Mayer, E.: Applying natural language processing and machine learning techniques to patient experience feedback: a systematic review. BMJ Health Care Inform. **28**(1), e100262 (2021)

12. Lwin, H.H., Oo, S., Ye, K.Z., Lin, K.K., Aung, W.P., Ko, P.P.: Feedback analysis in outcome base education using machine learning. In: Proceedings of the 2020 17th International Conference on Electrical Engineering/ Electronics, Computer, Telecommunications and Information Technology (ECTI-CON), pp. 767–770. IEEE, Virtual conference (2020)

13. Oomsels, P., Bouckaert, G.: Studying interorganizational trust in public administration. A conceptual and analytical framework for "administrational trust". Public Perform. Manag. Rev. **37**(4), 577–604 (2014)

14. Peng, C.-Y.J., Lee, K.L., Ingersoll, G.M.: An introduction to logistic regression analysis and reporting. J. Educ. Res. **96**(1), 3–14 (2002)

15. Scott, D., Brandow, C., Hobbins, J., Nilsson, S., Enander, A.: Capturing the citizen perspective in crisis management exercises: possibilities and challenges. Int. J. Emerg. Serv. **4**(1), 86–102 (2015)

16. Speybroeck, N.: Classification and regression trees. Int. J. Public Health **57**, 243–246 (2012)

17. City of Tampere, SURE. https://www.uia-initiative.eu/en/uia-cities/tampere. (Accessed 4 July 2022)

18. Tharwat, A.: Linear vs. quadratic discriminant analysis: a tutorial. Int. J. Appl. Patt. Recognit. **3**(2), 145–180 (2016)

19. Tharwat, A., Gaber, T., Ibrahim, A., Hassanien, A.E.: Linear discriminant analysis: A detailed tutorial. AI Commun. **30**(2), 169–190 (2017)

20. Zagorecki, A.T., Johnson, D.E.A., Ristvej, J.: Data mining and machine learning in the context of disaster and crisis management. Int. J. Emerg. Manag. **9**(4), 351–365 (2014)

Quantitative Evaluation of Saudi E-government Websites Using a Web Structure Mining Methodology

Tahani M. Alqurashi[1]([⊠]) [iD] and Zahyah H. Alharbi[2] [iD]

[1] Information System Department, Umm Al-Qura University, Mecca, Saudi Arabia
tmqurashi@uqu.edu
[2] Management Information Systems Department, King Saud University, Riyadh, Saudi Arabia
zalharbi@ksu.edu.sa

Abstract. E-government websites represent the main gateway for public services and play an important role in providing access to reliable and personalized information. This paper presents an initial study aiming to quantitatively assess the internal structure of Saudi e-government websites in terms of ease of navigation using a web structure mining methodology. For the purposes of the study, we selected four Saudi ministry websites. In the web network analysis and mining stages, we calculated seven graph property measures, including the average directed distance, the giant connective component, graph closeness centralization, and the average cluster coefficient (ACC). The analysis revealed a strong and statistically significant negative correlation between the average degree of nodes and the number of strongly connected components (SCCs). The ministry websites had an average directed distance of 2–5 and a relatively high number of SCCs with a low ACC.

Keywords: E-government · Quantitative Evaluation · Web Structure Mining · Internal Structure · Graph Theory

1 Introduction

Electronic government (e-government) represents more than an internet-based website and means of processing transactions whereby users can access information. It represents the gateway, as well as the entire structure, of government services. Besides services, e-government also provides information on regulations and policies to all citizens in a country. Therefore, it should provide users with easy access to information, while making a good impression on stakeholders through making the return on scale less significant and lowering the cost of interaction and collaboration. This means the process of government will become more accessible to more people at a lower cost in terms of time and money, and government does not need to expand to provide specific services [1].

Following the global trend, the Kingdom of Saudi Arabia (KSA) established its e-government web portal in 2003 to provide services and information on policies to

© ICST Institute for Computer Sciences, Social Informatics and Telecommunications Engineering 2023
Published by Springer Nature Switzerland AG 2023. All Rights Reserved
S. I. Lopes et al. (Eds.): Edge-IoT 2022/SmartGov 2022, LNICST 510, pp. 117–129, 2023.
https://doi.org/10.1007/978-3-031-35982-8_9

residents, visitors, and businesses. Its services were intended to improve communication between Saudi citizens, between the private sector and government organizations, as well as between government organizations themselves [2]. In line with Vision 2030, the KSA strongly supports digital transformation, which is based on three action plans. The first phase aimed to provide high-quality government services anywhere at any time though integrated, convenient, and safe electronic means by the end of 2010. The second phase aimed to enable people to use these services effectively through several electronic channels by 2016. The third stage aims to implement smart government by 2024 [3]. The Saudi e-government portal acts as a gateway to 24 ministry websites [4].

The quality of e-government websites plays an important role in providing reliable, centralized, and personalized information. Therefore, it is important to assess their ease of use. One approach has quantitatively assessed the internal structures of websites using web structure mining (WSM) [5, 6]. WSM investigates the hyperlink structure of web pages to determine how the structure of sets of pages is connected on a single website or between different websites [7]. Thus, WSM exploits hidden information contained in hypertext. The main contribution of this paper is to investigate the internal structures of Saudi e-government websites by using WSM. Specifically, we have assessed the internal structure of four Saudi ministries websites in terms of navigation ease for users.

The rest of this paper is organized as follows. Section 2 reviews related work that investigates the quality of Saudi e-government websites. Section 3 presents the WSM methodology used in this study. Section 4 reports the assessment results of the four ministry websites. Sections 5 presents the evaluation and discussion topics. Finally, the conclusion is presented in Sect. 6.

2   Related Work

In this section, we first provide an overview of e-government implementation in Saudi Arabia and then review the literature on the internal structure and accessibility of websites. Subsequently, we briefly present the graph properties used in the WSM methodology.

2.1   E-government in Saudi Arabia

The government of Saudi Arabia has massively invested in enhancing its e-government services [8]. "Yesser" was its first action plan, which was launched in 2005 [9]. The goal of this plan was to enable everyone in the country to access e-government services by the end of 2010 [10]. Since then, considerable research has been devoted to enhancing Saudi Arabia's e-government initiatives. Several studies have evaluated citizens' satisfaction and acceptance of e-government services [11], assessed the importance of integrating usability into e-government projects [12, 13] and enhancing the security of e-government transactions [14]. International best practices were studied to serve as guidelines for the successful development of Saudi e-government [15]. Other studies performed quantitative analyzes based on survey data and questionnaires regarding challenges to the adoption of e-government services [15], assessed government web portals [7, 8], evaluated the accessibility of Saudi ministry websites according to their frequency of use [16], and investigated the factors negatively affecting the implementation of Saudi Arabia's e-government [17].

Moreover, Al-Nuaim [20] conducted a study to assess the development and relevant issues of 21 Saudi ministry websites using a quantitative framework. The results showed that 41% of these websites did not employ the key standards of e-government websites. Moreover, 45.4% of websites were partially or entirely in the web presence stage (first stage), while 13.6% were in the one-way communication stage (second stage), and the remaining websites did not provide online services. The study found that the assessed ministries lacked citizen-centered e-government websites and thus transactional services, causing citizens to feel dissatisfaction and frustration. However, this study [20] was conducted at a time when Saudi ministry websites were in their initial stages of development.

In 2020, the Saudi government ranked 43rd in the E-Government Development Index (EGDI), a high rise from its 52nd place in 2018, according to the United Nations' annual report [18]. Nevertheless, it has only achieved 0.6882 in the Online Services Index, which is considered low. This disparity indicates that there is a need for continuous and extensive evaluation of its services [19].

2.2 Internal Website Structures

The internal structures of many domains have already been investigated. Thelwall [21] analyzed the internal structures of UK university websites using Alternative Document Models (ADM) to investigate their research productivity. The author found a strong association between research productivity and the number of university website's incoming links [21]. Also using ADM, Payne and Thelwall [22] examined the structures of UK university websites and found a positive association between site size and the quantity of target indexes. Alqurashi and Wang [6] proposed a WSM methodology that used several graph properties to investigate the structures of 110 UK university websites. They found that the average cluster coefficient (ACC) was the most important property for evaluating website structures in terms of ease of navigation. Petricek et al. [5] investigated e-government websites using graph properties to assess their internal and external structures. They found that assessing websites using graph properties was considerably less expensive than other evaluation methods, which normally involve website users in the assessment process, and that a site's structure could be constructed, and its properties determined and employed in the evaluation process [5].

To the best of our knowledge, no previous studies have used web mining to investigate the structure of Saudi e-government websites. In this study, graph properties are utilized. In the following sub-section, we explain the graph representation of a website's internal structure.

3 Graph Representations of Internal Website Structures

A graph representation can be used to construct the website structure, in which a web page is represented by a node and a hyperlink is represented as a link that pairs the nodes. It can represent the external structures, and local structures, which portray the internal structures. Each level has a variety of properties that can be analyzed. In this study, we considered only seven internal structure measurements, as proposed by Alqurashi and Wang [6]. These include graph size and graph density, as well as the giant connective component (GCC). The GCC includes strongly connected components (SCCs) and OUT components. Analyzing the GCC can help identify parts of a website that need improvement in terms of navigation.

The path in a graph is the set of linked nodes, which can help identify a potential navigation path from one page to another. The degree of a node is another graph property that indicates the number of neighbors of a given node. As this study focused on websites' internal structures, we constructed undirected graphs in which the direction of links was not considered. Another graph property is the cluster coefficient (CC). A cluster is a set of nodes that are tightly linked, and the cluster coefficient measures how interconnected the closest neighbors are. The CC ranges from 0 to 1 [23]. The CC of a node e is calculated as:

$$CC(x) = \frac{l}{k(k-1)}, \tag{1}$$

where k is the number of nearest neighbors, and l is the number of links between them.

The average cluster coefficient (ACC) of a graph is a measure of the cohesion of its local and internal structures and can be used to compare different graphs.

In a graph, closeness centrality C is a measure of the closeness between nodes and can be calculated as:

$$C(x) = \frac{1}{\sum_{y \in N} S(x, y)}, \tag{2}$$

where S denotes the shortest distance between nodes x and y.

4   Research Methodology

As mentioned in Sect. 2, various approaches have been used to investigate the quality of Saudi e-government websites. In this study, we adapted a previously developed web structure methodology that uses graph properties to assess the quality of websites in terms of their information accessibility and ease of navigation [6]. As shown in Fig. 1, the methodology consists of five main stages: link data collection, link data familiarization, link data pre-processing, web network analysis and mining, and web structure evaluation.

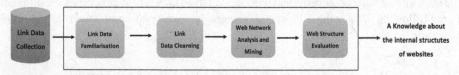

Fig. 1. Website structure mining methodology (adapted from [6])

In the first stage, the required link data are collected using a web crawler, or spider, which is a program designed to retrieve web pages and extract hyperlink data from them.

The second stage, link data familiarization, involves an initial investigation of the collected data to statistically consider its basic information. This helps to determine how to pre-process the data and other steps that may be required in the next stages.

The third stage, link data pre-processing, consists of two main steps. The first step is data cleansing, which includes a simple statistical analysis. The second step is data visualization, in which the graph topology of each website is constructed using special graph visualization software.

The fourth stage, web network analysis and mining, is the core element of the methodology. Its aim is to reveal hidden information in the link data by measuring seven graph properties of the studied websites.

Finally, in the web structure evaluation stage, the obtained results are evaluated, and a correlation test is performed to identify statistically significant relationships between graph measurements.

5 Assessment of Saudi E-government Websites

5.1 Link Data Collection

For this study, we selected the websites of four Saudi ministries: the Ministry of Health (moh), the Ministry of Municipal & Rural Affairs & Housing (housing), the Ministry of Human Resources and Social Development (hrsd), and the Ministry of Justice (moj). Table 1 shows the selected Saudi e-government websites. We collected the data using the Netpeak Spider crawler[1]. Its parameters were the maximum number of pages and the maximum depth to fetch links from the home page of each website. Due to time constraints, we set the parameters to 2,000 pages and unlimited depth for each website.

Table 1. The selected Saudi e-government websites

Ministry	Website
Ministry of Health	https://www.moh.gov.sa
Ministry of Human Resources and Social Development	https://www.hrsd.gov.sa
Ministry of Justice	https://www.moj.gov.sa
Ministry of Municipal, Rural Affairs and Housing	https://www.housing.gov.sa

5.2 Link Data Familiarization

In this stage, our main aim was to conduct a simple investigation to familiarize ourselves with the data. Firstly, we found that each website link file had a different size, which meant that the number of HTML pages differed, depending on their depths. The Ministry of Justice website had the highest number (1,869 links), while the Ministry of

---

[1] https://netpeaksoftware.com/spider#bonuses

Human Resources and Social Development website had the lowest number (733 links). The Ministry of Housing and Ministry of Health websites had 1,664 and 1,222 links, respectively.

Secondly, by examining the report of all the external links, we found that the ministries' domain was well linked to other websites in the same domain "gov.sa". Another interesting finding was that all websites were well linked to "Absher", which is the web portal of the Ministry of Interior. All websites were well connected to social media websites, such as Facebook, Twitter, and Instagram. Moreover, they were well linked to the websites of commercial companies in the same geographical locations as the ministries, such as bank websites, as well as to apps such as Sehaty, Moaed, and Absher. Most websites used Google as their main search engine.

Thirdly, the collected data included several duplicate links. This was mainly because some websites included links to social media websites on almost every page.

Finally, several documents (such as.pdf and.doc) were also crawled. These needed to be removed in the pre-processing stage where we performed data cleansing. The process is detailed in the following subsections.

5.3   Link Data Cleansing

Data cleansing makes data more reliable and ensures a more accurate evaluation. We took great care to collect data as clean as possible at the collection stage. Netpeak Spider allowed us to avoid duplicate and unwanted data in the dataset, for example, by defining the home page for each site and specifying the depth and number of links for the sample (2,000 links). However, to eliminate duplicate and unwanted link data, we performed the following additional steps:

- We removed the social media links, not only because of their large number, but also because such links contain no essential information. Thus, they were considered external links.
- We removed unwanted file extensions (Table 2).
- We removed external links and app links.
- We removed duplicate links.

Table 2. File extensions removed as undesirable data.

File type	File extension
Images	jpg, gif, png
Audio	wav, mp3, mp4
Video	mpg, mov, flv
Other	xls, pdf, doc, ppt

5.4 Web Network Analysis and Mining

This was the main stage of our methodology, which aimed to extract hidden information about the accessibility and ease of navigation of the websites. After visualizing the link data as graph topologies, we measured seven graph properties: graph sizes, GCC, average directed distance, graph diameters, average degree of nodes, ACC, and CC. These properties are detailed in the following sub-sections:

Graph Sizes. This was measured in terms of graph density and the total number of nodes, which ranged from 9,292 nodes (Ministry of Health website) to 12,894 nodes (Ministry of Human Resources and Social Development website). This range indicated that the graph sizes were large, with substantial numbers of nodes and links. Moreover, Fig. 2 shows that the density of all graphs was very low, indicating that all pages had a high degree of interconnection.

Giant Connective Component. There were pages with two GCC components: SCCs and OUT components. There were no pages with IN components because the crawler started from the home page of each website. SCCs represent the number of pages on a site that are strongly interconnected. We hypothesized that a higher number of SCCs would positively impact the website navigation. Figure 3 shows the total number of SCCs for each website. Three websites had more than 10,000 pages classified as SCC pages, suggesting they were more strongly interconnected and thus easier to navigate than other pages. The Ministry of Human Resources and Social Development website had the highest number of SCC pages, whereas the Ministry of Health website had the lowest.

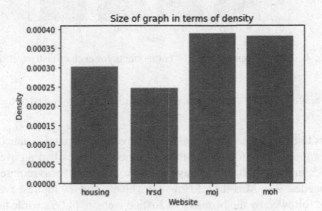

Fig. 2. Density of each ministry website's graph.

The OUT components included only the OUT internal pages of each website, as these were the only type visualized in the dataset. These parts of the websites were not easily navigable, as they did not provide links back to the cores of the websites. As shown in Fig. 4, the Ministry of Human Resources and Social Development website had

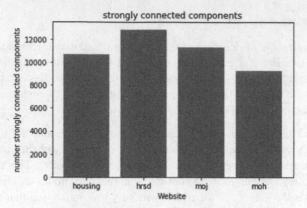

Fig. 3. Number of strongly connected components for each ministry website.

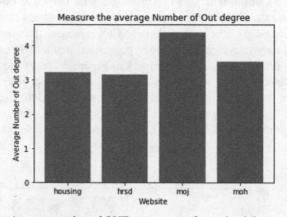

Fig. 4. Average number of OUT components for each ministry website.

the lowest average of OUT components, indicating that it was easier to navigate than the other websites.

Average Directed Distance. We calculated the average directed distance in each ministry website's graph. It is found that the examined websites had an average directed distance of 2–5, indicating that an average of two to five clicks was required to reach the information needed. The Ministry of Housing website had the highest average directed distance (4.6), followed by the Ministry of Justice website (4.06), while the Ministry of Human Resources and Social Development had the lowest average (nearly 2).

Graph Diameters. The graph diameters were calculated in terms of the longest path between a selected random node and all its neighbors in the graph. In fact, when the graph diameter is measured, then the worst-case scenario for website navigation is determined.

An average of 4 hyperlinks was needed to reach the required information. Three websites were below this average, whereas the Ministry of Housing website had a diameter of 8.

The investigation of the graph diameters showed that the site map pages of some websites connected other pages in the diameter. This was especially noticeable for websites with a diameter of 4, such as the Ministry of Justice website, where the sitemap page was placed in the second node connecting the first node with the other node in the diameter. Some websites constructed the diameter paths from their home pages, which means to reach any target page in a diameter the user needs to go back to the home page to reach it. However, the largest diameter was recorded for the Ministry of Housing website and was not via its home page or site map.

Average Degree of Nodes. The average degree of nodes for each website is shown in Fig. 5. The Ministry of Justice website had the highest average degree (4.39), while the Ministry of Human Resources and Social Development website had the lowest (3.16). As previously mentioned, the number of nodes in each graph ranged from 9,292 to 12,894.

Average Cluster Coefficient. The ACCs of each graph are shown in Fig. 6. The ACCs ranged from just below 0.002 (Ministry of Human Resources and Social Development website) to nearly 0.005 (Ministry of Health website). These low ACCs indicated that the graphs included numerous weak ties.

Closeness Centralization. To determine the closeness centralization of each website, we first calculated the closeness centralization of each node that represented the path to its closest neighbor and then computed the closeness centralization of the whole graph (Fig. 7). The Ministry of Justice website had the highest closeness centralization (8.55), followed by the Ministry of Human Resources and Social Development (8.26) and Ministry of Health websites (8.22). The Ministry of Housing had the lowest closeness centralization (3.84).

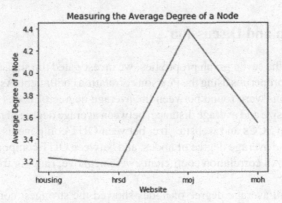

Fig. 5. Average degree of nodes.

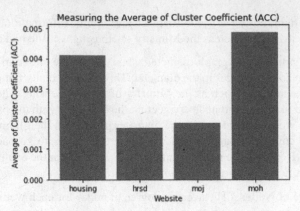

Fig. 6. Average cluster coefficients.

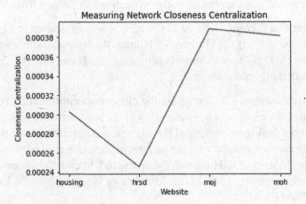

Fig. 7. Closeness centralization of each graph.

6   Evaluation and Discussion

After measuring the seven graph proprieties, we investigated the statistical relationships between pairs of properties using the Pearson correlation coefficient. As shown in Table 3, several correlations were found between the average degree of nodes and website size, between website size and average distance, between average degree of nodes and average distance, between SCCs and website size, between OUT components and website size, between SCCs and average degree of nodes, and between OUT components and average degree of nodes. All correlation coefficients were negative, ranging from very strong to very weak.

The SCCs and average degree of nodes showed the strongest correlation (−0.95), followed by the OUT components and average degree of nodes (−0.47) and the average degree of nodes and average distance (−0.42). On the other hand, the OUT components and website size showed a weak correlation (−0.28), while average distance and website size (−0.16), average degree of nodes and website size (−0.15), and SCCs and website size (−0.12) also exhibited very weak correlations.

We assessed the statistical significance of these correlations using the t-test (Table 3). The null hypothesis was that the observed correlations were not significant. The null hypothesis was accepted for all correlations, except for the correlation between SCCs and average degree of nodes, which was rejected at a 0.05 significance level.

Table 3. Correlation coefficients, t-values, and p-values.

Correlation	r	t-value	p-value
Average degree of nodes and average distance	−0.42	0.19	0.58
Average degree of nodes and website size	−0.15	−16.80	0.85
Average distance and website size	−0.16	14.77	0.84
Website size and SCCs	−0.12	14.77	0.89
Website size and OUT components	−0.28	2.41	0.72
Average degree of nodes and SCCs	−0.95	−0.94	0.05
Average degree of nodes and OUT components	−0.47	2.94	0.53

7 Conclusions

In this study, we performed a quantitative evaluation of the internal structures of four Saudi e-government websites to assess their ease of navigation using a web structure mining methodology adapted from [6]. We studied the websites of the Ministry of Health, the Ministry of Municipal & Rural Affairs & Housing, the Ministry of Human Resources and Social Development, and the Ministry of Justice. After pre-processing the data, we constructed graphs of the ministries' websites and then measured seven graph properties: graph size, strongly connected components, OUT components, average degree of nodes, average distance, average cluster coefficient, and graph closeness centralization. We found a strong and statistically significant negative correlation between the number of SCCs and the average degree of nodes.

Our results support previous studies [5, 6] showing that evaluating the internal structures of websites is a useful and inexpensive tool compared to other methods, such as surveys and webometrics. We plan to expand this study by assessing the significance of each graph property and investigating other properties. Moreover, we intend to combine this methodology with other methods, such as webometrics, to analyze larger e-government website datasets.

References

1. Howard, M.: E-government across the globe: how will 'e' change government. e-Government **90**, 80 (2001)
2. United National Platform: About Unified National Platform. https://www.my.gov.sa/wps/por tal/snp/aboutPortal/!ut/p/z0/04_Sj9CPykssy0xPLMnMz0vMAfIjo8zivQIsTAwdDQz9_d29 TAwCnQ1DjUy9wgwLEz1g1Pz9AuyHRUBI89e_A!!/. Accessed 4 Sept 2022

3. United National Platform: Digital Transformation. https://www.my.gov.sa/wps/portal/snp/aboutksa/digitaltransformation. Accessed 7 Sept 2022
4. United National Platform: Gov. Agencies Directory. https://www.my.gov.sa/wps/portal/snp/agecies/!ut/p/z1/jY9ND4IwDIZ_iweO0k6YEm_owbjEoCEg7mLATCCBjcAU_fcSvRj87K3N87R9gUMEXMnPI11rmRcdP2Oj_ds7djEReJ5C2bjZk6CEWUhok9h2wMsOuuA1cRz_ZAgUuD_-PihXPzl0J2O3gPe_3iDnw5w4CnhoekV2ZWE4KvBZHUYvaPNXdONO6aqYGGti2rZnkMjUPqjTwnZCpRkP0zEFVBtFlOeTJtR3cAJ1xbQ0!/dz/d5/L2dBISEvZ0FBIS9nQSEh/. Accessed 4 Sept 2022
5. Petricek, V., Escher, T., Cox, I., Margetts, H.: The web structure of e-government-developing a methodology for quantitative evaluation, In: Proceedings of the 15th international conference on World Wide Web, pp. 669–678 (2006)
6. Alqurashi, T., Wang, W.: A graph based methodology for web structure mining-with a case study on the webs of UK Universities, In: Proceedings of the 4th International Conference on Web Intelligence, Mining and Semantics (WIMS 2014), pp. 1–11 (2014)
7. Eirinaki, M.: Web mining: a roadmap. Int. J. Knowl. Based Comput. Syst. 3(2) (2015)
8. Eidaroos, A.M., Probets, S.G., Dearnley, J.A.: Heuristic evaluation for e-Government websites in Saudi Arabia. In: Aloqbi, A., Alsini, I., Alzimani, K. (eds.) Proceedings of the SIC: The Third Saudi International Conference, p. 5. Saudi Students Clubs and Schools in the UK and the Republic of Ireland, Guildford (2009)
9. Yesser. Saudi e-Government Program. https://www.yesser.gov.sa/en. Accessed 10 Sept 2022
10. Al-Nuaim, H.: An evaluation framework for Saudi e-government. J. E-Gov. Stud. Best 2011, 1–12 (2011)
11. Hamner, M., Al-Qahtani, F.: Enhancing the case for electronic government in developing nations: a people-centric study focused in Saudi Arabia. Gov. Inf. Q. 26(1), 137–143 (2009)
12. Al-Fakhri, M.O., Cropf, R.A., Higos, G., Kelly, P.: E-government in Saudi Arabia: between promise and reality. Int. J. Electron Gov. Res. 4(2), 59–82 (2008)
13. Shambour, M.K.Y.: Assessing the usability of Hajj and Umrah websites. In: 2021 International Conference on Information Technology (ICIT), pp. 876–881. IEEE (2020)
14. Al-Zahrani, M.: Integrating IS success model with cybersecurity factors for e-government implementation in the Kingdom of Saudi Arabia. Int. J. Electr. Comput. Eng. (IJECE) 10(5), 4937 (2020)
15. El-Sofany, H.F., Al-Tourki, T., Al-Howimel, H., Al-Sadoon, A.: E-government in Saudi Arabia: barriers, challenges, and its role of development. Int. J. Comput. Appl. 48(5), 1–7 (2012)
16. Akram, M., Sulaiman, R.B.: An empirical study to evaluate the accessibility of Arabic websites by low vision users. In: 2020 the 8th International Conference on Information Technology and Multimedia (ICIMU), pp. 206–211. IEEE (2020)
17. Alghamdi, S., Beloff, N.: Towards a comprehensive model for e-government adoption and utilisation analysis: the case of Saudi Arabia, In: Proceedings of the 9th Federated Conference on Computer Science and Information Systems (FedCSIS), vol. 2, pp. 1217–1225. IEEE, Warsaw (2014)
18. United Nations: E-Government Survey 2020 Digital Government in the Decade of Action for Sustainable Development, Gov 11, The United Nations, New York, (2020)
19. Aldrees, A., Gračanin, D.: Cultural usability of E-government portals: a comparative analysis of job seeking web portals between saudi arabia and the united states. In: Soares, M.M., Rosenzweig, E., Marcus, A. (eds.) HCII 2021. LNCS, vol. 12780, pp. 3–17. Springer, Cham (2021). https://doi.org/10.1007/978-3-030-78224-5_1
20. Al-Nuaim, H.: An evaluation framework for Saudi e-government. J. e-Gov. Stud. Best Pract. 1, 1–12 (2011)

21. Thelwall, M.: Conceptualizing documentation on the Web: an evaluation of different heuristic-based models for counting links between university Web sites. J. Am. Soc. Inf. **53**(12), 992–1005 (2002)
22. Payne, N., Thelwall, M.: A statistical analysis of UK academic web links. Cybermetrics (2004)
23. Watts, D., Strogatz, S.: Collective dynamics of "small-world" networks. Nature **393**(6684), 440–442 (1998)

Extracting Digital Biomarkers
for Unobtrusive Stress State Screening
from Multimodal Wearable Data

Berrenur Saylam[(✉)] and Özlem Durmaz İncel

Boğaziçi University, 34342 İstanbul, Turkey
{berrenur.saylam,ozlem.durmaz}@boun.edu.tr

Abstract. With the development of wearable technologies, a new kind of healthcare data has become valuable as medical information. These data provide meaningful information regarding an individual's physiological and psychological states, such as activity level, mood, stress, and cognitive health. These biomarkers are named digital since they are collected from digital devices integrated with various sensors. In this study, we explore digital biomarkers related to stress modality by examining data collected from mobile phones and smartwatches. We utilize machine learning techniques on the Tesserae dataset, precisely Random Forest, to extract stress biomarkers. Using feature selection techniques, we utilize weather, activity, heart rate (HR), stress, sleep, and location (work-home) measurements from wearables to determine the most important stress-related biomarkers. We believe we contribute to interpreting stress biomarkers with a high range of features from different devices. In addition, we classify the 5 different stress levels with the most important features, and our results show that we can achieve 85% overall class accuracy by adjusting class imbalance and adding extra features related to personality characteristics. We perform similar and even better results in recognizing stress states with digital biomarkers in a daily-life scenario targeting a higher number of classes compared to the related studies.

Keywords: Digital biomarkers · wearable computing · machine learning · classification · stress · sensors · daily life

1 Introduction

Clinical biomarkers are objectively-measured and evaluated indicators of the biological processes [1,2]. The biomarkers and the clinical outcomes aim to assist in understanding the factors affecting human health.

It becomes possible to measure health parameters, such as the amount of daily activity, sleep quality, and stress level while working on a task with wearable devices, such as smartwatches, sleep sensors, and step counters, in an ambulatory and continuous manner. This digitalization of the healthcare measurements created the term *digital biomarkers*, which are objective, quantifiable,

© ICST Institute for Computer Sciences, Social Informatics and Telecommunications Engineering 2023
Published by Springer Nature Switzerland AG 2023. All Rights Reserved
S. I. Lopes et al. (Eds.): Edge-IoT 2022/SmartGov 2022, LNICST 510, pp. 130–151, 2023.
https://doi.org/10.1007/978-3-031-35982-8_10

physiological, and behavioral measures collected from wearables and smartphones [3]. The indicators or characteristics for a digital marker could be computed from one or more digital health technologies.

Furthermore, there are different categories of biomarkers in literature [3], such as *diagnostic biomarkers* to detect any disease or condition [4], *pharmacodynamic response biomarkers* to measure changes in response to pharmaco agents [5] and *monitoring biomarkers* to monitor a specific medical condition [6]. Thus, there are mainly three types of physiological outcomes. Outcomes for all three can be measured via sensors. Additionally, outcomes can be measured via questionnaires for the second type, i.e., *pharmacodynamic response biomarkers*. Our study falls into the monitoring biomarkers category since data is collected during participants' daily lives.

In this work, we examine Tesserae dataset [16], which is collected from office workers using smartphones for activity tracking, wearable devices for step-count, sleep and heart rate measurement, and Bluetooth beacons to understand locations such as home, work, and questionnaires for ground truth information. Previous studies which are using the Tesserae dataset (Table 1) focus on understanding the effects of seasons and weather on sleep patterns [10], predicting job performance [17], and predicting mental health from social network data [18]. However, this work focuses on stress level classification and examines the affecting biomarkers. To the best of our knowledge, there is no work considering these aspects on this dataset.

We investigate the extraction of novel biomarkers related to stress with various parameters and modalities, such as mobile phones and wearable devices. We aim to predict the participants' stress levels using the data from wearables and smartphones and find the most important biomarkers, in other words, the features related to stress levels. We rank the features to show which modalities, such as sleep, and activity levels, are more important in classifying stress levels. We have daily stress responses from the participants as the labels. Using these labels, we classified the five stress levels from low to high provided in ground truth data with these important parameters and compared the result with the usage of all parameters using the Random Forest (RF) algorithm. We also investigate the inclusion of parameters related to the participants' personalities.

Since the number of examples in each class is not the same, and some classes have fewer instances, we observed lower recognition performance for these classes. We applied SMOTE (synthetic minority over-sampling) to solve the class imbalance problem. We obtained the best classification result, 85% overall class accuracy, by adding the personality-related parameters in our parameter space and solving the class imbalance issue. In the end, in all cases, we found that the most important parameters are sleep and phone activity modalities. As far as we examined, this is the first study extracting digital biomarkers, in other words, features related to stress state from the Tesserae dataset.

The rest of the paper is organized as follows. In Sect. 2, we explore literature, related to biomarkers and stress monitoring. In Sect. 3, we explain the details of the dataset, the data construction step for our analysis, the data preprocessing step before analysis, and details of the target class, i.e., stress. In Sect. 4, we provide obtained results with feature ranking, modality ranking, and performance details with a discussion and comparison to the related studies. In Sect. 5, we explain our findings and discussion points for further analysis.

2 Related Works

Many related works exist in the literature about biomarkers for various physiological and psychological states [7–12]. In [7], the authors examined the behavioral markers to track physical activity following hospital discharge via data from wearable devices. The idea is to understand the characteristics of the individuals in smartphone and wearable device usage to monitor health-related measurements. They identified four biomarker sets i) more agreeable and conscientious; ii) more active, social, and motivated; iii) more risk-taking and less supported; and iv) less active, social, and risk-taking. Identification of these groups of biomarkers has been made using latent class analysis.

In [8], researchers examined biomarkers of depression state outside of the laboratory. Similar to [7], they collected data with wearable devices and state-of-the-art questionnaires, namely Patient Health Questionnaire (PHQ-9), as a ground truth. PHQ-9 is a standard self-report for depression assessment in clinical contexts [9]. As a methodology, they used multiple regression analysis to predict the PHQ-9 result and find the parameter which can significantly predict the target value, in this case, the PHQ-9 value.

In another study [10], the main idea was to extract the underlying effects of seasons and weather parameters on the sleep data. Similar to the previous work [8], they utilized regression-based modeling. They focused on continuous data collection via wearable devices to differentiate their study from state-of-the-art.

Even though statistical approaches for extracting biomarkers are common in the recent literature, some studies use simple machine-learning (ML) techniques [11,12]. For instance, in [11], the aim was to determine digital biomarkers

Table 1. Studies using the Tesserae dataset in the literature

	Study Aim	Methodology	Result
[10]	Investigation of the effects of seasons and weather on sleep	Construction of an independent model for each variable which is sleep duration, bedtime, and wake-up time. Usage of mixed linear effect model	The strongest effect on wake time and sleep duration especially in the spring season
[17]	Prediction of workers job performance	Extraction of the high-level features with AutoEncoder (AE) usage and gradient analysis to understand the causality relation between features and the target	Prediction of job performance with %75 f1-score. Analyze of different job performance metrics parameters' effects on the model performance
[18]	Prediction of mental health, depression and anxiety, throughout the social network data	Application of network analysis methods for different types of tasks such as depressed and non-depressed positions in network differ or not, difference between network positions lead to depression or anxiety trait difference, dynamic or static network lead to better results on the mental health prediction	Found that the inclusion of dynamics leads to further improvements to the static network data analysis results

for frailty, an essential factor in older adults' recovery process. They examined physical activity parameters, such as percentage time standing, percentage time walking, walking cadence, and longest walking bout, to identify slowness, weakness, exhaustion, and inactivity classes of physical frailty. As a methodology, they utilized ANOVA and binary logistic regression model.

As another example of the usage of ML models in extracting biomarkers, a study [12] on stress and mental health status markers extraction can be given. Again, wearable device measurements are analyzed to determine the self-reported values-this study, different from others, utilized SVM models with different configurations.

We observe that recent studies on biomarkers are utilizing either basic statistical methods, such as ANOVA analysis, or different forms of regression models. When utilizing ML models, state-of-the-art also uses traditional models.

In addition to the biomarkers' literature, there are many studies on stress detection and monitoring [13–15, 19].

In [13], authors examined features from multi-modal smartphone sensors, i.e., accelerometer sensor for physical activity, microphone for social interaction, phone calls and application usage for social activity, etc. They proposed combinations of machine learning techniques such as semi-supervised learning, ensemble methods, and transfer learning to classify three stress levels (low, mid, high).

In [14], researchers added surrounding data to personal stress data to examine whether these improve overall stress detection accuracy. Again, they used three-level stress for classification. They used low-level features from smartphone sensor data, such as average, standard deviation, minimum, maximum, etc. They designed different scenarios on their data and StudentLife [15] data alone and in combination with personal and surroundings data. They reached the highest performance when they combined personal and surrounding data, 79.16% and 81.79% on their collection of data and StudentLife, respectively.

Moreover, stress-related studies also can be classified according to the data collection environment, such as in a controlled laboratory and daily (unobtrusively) environment. In [19], authors extensively explain state-of-the-art using different signal types in different environments. Depending on the modality, different sensor types for measuring physiological changes exist. For instance, accelerometer, body temperature, EDA (electrodermal activity), HR (heart rate), HRV (heart rate variability) [20], and speech are some of the typical sensor types for physiological changes. There is also usage of high-level features extracted from mobile phone usage patterns, physical activity (total number of steps), and screen events.

We observe that literature studies validate their proposed selection of sensor types, data collection environment, and proposed algorithm type. In this study, we contribute to the parameter space of the stress features by examining an extensive set of multi-modal data analyses.

3   Methodology

3.1   Dataset

In this study, we utilize Tesserae Dataset[1] [16]. It is collected to measure office workers' workplace performance via psychological traits and physical character-istics over one year. It consists of data from 757 subjects. A smartphone and Garmin watch are used as data collecting devices.

Data were collected from the phones with an activity tracking application. The participants wore a Garmin watch during the study period. It has 5–7 days of battery life. In addition, Bluetooth beacons have been used to extract information about the location, such as home or office. As complementary data to the non-verbal measurements by devices, they also collected verbal data from social media such as Facebook and LinkedIn, which were not accessible to us.

The University of Notre Dame approved this data collection campaign as a research project, and a consent form has been taken from the participants.

3.2   Ground Truth

For collecting ground truth data, various questionnaires were shared with the participants. These questionnaires are related to job performance, intelligence, mood, anxiety, health measure, exercise, sleep, and stress. At the beginning of the study, participants filled out all questions for each type of survey. The required duration is about one hour to fill. In addition, there are daily survey questions that constitute the summary of each type of measurement. Each questionnaire's overall score corresponds to one column in the daily survey scores file. Thus, it requires only a few minutes to fill every day. Moreover, they collected an end study questionnaire and follow-up survey. However, they were not accessible to us. Thus, the questionnaires have four main parts as in the following.

– Initial Ground Truth
– Daily Surveys
– Exit
– Follow-up Survey

To give an idea about the content of the questionnaires, we summarize them in Table 2. We show the ones we have access to using * mark.

3.3   Dataset Construction

In the shared data file, we did not have access to all measurements as stated in the previous section. We made our analysis on the reduced data. Even if detailed sampling measurements are sampled from the wearable device from 3 min to 15 min, depending on the data modalities, we made our analysis on daily bases. The used file details can be seen in Table 3.

---

[1] https://tesserae.nd.edu/.

Table 2. Details of the questionnaires

Questionnaires	Content
Initial Ground Truth (IGTB)	In-Role Behavior (IRB), Individual Task Proficiency (ITP), Organizational Citizenship Behavior (OCB), Interpersonal and Organizational Deviance Scale (IOD), Shipley Abstraction*, Shipley Vocabulary*, Big Five Inventory* (BFI), Positive and Negative Affect* Schedule (PANAS), State-Trait Anxiety Inventory* (STAI), MITRE modified Alcohol Use Disorders (AUDIT MITRE), Modified Global Adult Tobacco Survey (Modified GATS), International Physical Activity Questionnaire* (IPAQ), Pittsburgh Sleep Quality Index* (PSQI)
Daily Surveys	In-Role Behavior (IRB), Individual Task Proficiency (ITP), Organizational Citizenship Behavior (OCB), Counterproductive Workplace Behavior (CWB), Big Five Inventory* (BFI), Positive and Negative Affect Schedule* (PANAS), Omnibus Anxiety Question*, Tobacco Use Assessment, MITRE Omnibus Stress Question*, MITRE Alcohol Use Assessment, MITRE Physical Activity Assessment* MITRE Sleep Assessment*, MITRE Context Assessment
Exit Battery	State-Trait Anxiety Inventory (STAI), Positive and Negative Affect Schedule (PANAS), Morningness-Eveningness Questionnaire (MEQ), Emotional Regulation, Emotional Intelligence, Pro-social Motivational
Followup	Life events, sick days, vacation days

Even though they collected data from 757 participants, we had access to 727 participants' data. Furthermore, although it is stated[2] that 56 days of the daily survey is collected, we observed 61 days of daily survey answers from some of the participants. To construct our dataset, we merged the files stated in Table 3 according to *ParticipantID* and *Timestamp*. We obtained wearable and ground truth data for each participant on a daily basis. While merging, we noticed that for some participants, the amount of data from wearables is more than ground truth survey answers (it means they collected more data with the devices than the planned data collection period). However, as we need the ground truth information for our analysis, we considered participants' data that only have ground

---

[2] https://osf.io/yvw2f/wiki/EMAs/.

Table 3. Details of the constructed data for analysis

Data Folder	Used Data File				
Context	Weather (78)				
Garmin Summary	Activity (8)	Daily (25)	HR (11)	Stress (11)	Sleep (7)
Mixed	Phone Activity (128)	HR WorkDesk Home (7)			
Ground Truth	Daily Scores (19)				

truth responses, i.e., responses to the daily surveys. After constructing the data file, we have 36294 rows of data coming from all participants. If we had 61 days of ground truth for everyone, it must be 44347 rows of data. Thus, it is clear that we do not have survey answers from all participants for precisely 61 days. In addition, we merged files by considering the common columns in each file. Thus, as we have common columns in each file, such as *ParticipantID*, *Timestamp*, and *Date*, we did not add them in the final construction since a one-time indication is sufficient in the whole dataset. For this reason, we obtained fewer columns (269) compared to the sum of each data file's column number (294), which are given in detail in Table 3 between the parentheses. In the final data, we have 269 columns where 15 of them are the ground truth. Here, 15 columns coming from the ground truth which are *survey name, stress, anxiety, sleep, positive affect, negative affect, extraversion, agreeableness, conscientiousness, neuroticism, openness, total phone activity duration, survey sent time, survey start time, survey finish time.* The rest of the columns from the other modalities are not given explicitly since their volume is quite large. In this section, we explained only the construction of the data. We preprocess it for further analysis, which is explained in Sect. 3.5.

3.4   Details of the Stress Classes

We selected stress as our dependent variable in the scope of this study, and we examined its distribution in detail. In Fig. 1, one can see that there is a class imbalance. We have a few instances from some classes, especially from 4*th* and 5*th* classes. The model may fail to recognize them due to insufficient examples. To solve this issue, we applied SMOTE technique. After the implementation, we got 57150 rows for both our experiments which are explained in detail in Sect. 3.5, and column numbers remained the same. Here, classes 1 and 5 correspond to very low stress and very high-stress levels, respectively. To show the effect on the model performance, we will provide model results with class imbalance along with performance after applying SMOTE in Sect. 4.

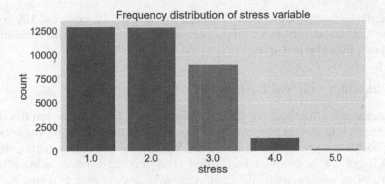

Fig. 1. Distribution of stress classes

3.5 Data Preprocessing

We deleted irrelevant attributes for our analysis, such as *survey name*, *survey sent time*, *survey start time*, and *survey end time*. We selected the stress variable among ground truth variables as a target variable. Nine missing values were in the stress column over all participants' data, and we deleted rows corresponding to them rather than applying an imputation method for simplicity.

We also examined missing values among the independent variables. Some attributes were never collected from some participants. Thus, the imputation methodology could not be applied for these attributes. Among them, if there is a lack of many participants' data, their removal by row leads to a high decrease in our dataset. Instead, we deleted those columns. These are *act (activity) still, light mean, garmin hr (heart rate) min, garmin hr max, garmin hr median, garmin hr mean, garmin hr std, ave (average) hr at work, ave hr at desk, ave hr at desk, ave hr not at work, call in num (number), call in duration, call out num, call out duration, call miss num*, and their derivatives according to time episodes. However, when we have data columns with missing values at the person level, we imputed them by applying the mean operation for each participant. After this preprocessing step, we got 31772 rows and 195 columns.

In order to see the impact of personality attributes in our prediction analysis, we designed two experiments. In the first experiment, the ground truth attributes other than the stress level; extraversion, agreeableness, conscientiousness, neuroticism, openness, anxiety, sleep, positive affect, and negative affect were deleted from the constructed data file. Since we did not include personality-related columns from big five personality survey, we named this dataset as *without personality dataset*. Thus, we have 31772 rows and 185 columns. In the second experiment, we included these parameters in our feature space for the analysis rather than removing them as in the first experiment. Since we have personality information in the constructed data file, it is named as *with personality dataset*. Please note that as additional information, it does not only include personality-related attributes, which are extraversion, agreeableness, conscientiousness, neuroticism, and openness; there are also anxiety, sleep, positive affect, and negative affect attributes. In the end, we have 31772 rows and 195 columns. The last column is the stress level, our target variable, and the remaining 194 columns include the features.

3.6 Classifier and Validation

As a classification method, we used Random Forest (RF) algorithm in our analyses because it is an ensemble method and perform better among the other used methods in literature in this domain [19]. We applied hyper-parameter optimization with quite a large space and found that in scikit-learn n_estimators 1000, criterion *gini*, min_sample_split 2, min_samples_leaf 1, max_features *sqrt* combination reveal the best performance. Thus, we continued with that setup. In addition, we ran RF with different train/test split sizes. As we increased train size, we got higher accuracy scores. However, to overcome over-fitting, 80% and 20% train and test size are chosen, respectively.

4 Results

4.1 Results on Without Personality Dataset

In this section, we work on data with 185 columns where there are no personality information-related columns and other attributes such as anxiety, sleep, and positive and negative affect. First, we present the results of the imbalanced stress class. We provide the most important feature ranking, i.e., biomarkers and corresponding classification results. Then, we list important features and classification results when we solve imbalance via SMOTE application.

With Class Imbalance

– **Most important biomarkers**
   We started with 184 independent biomarkers. We want to select only the important parameters within the parameter space that greatly impact the target, i.e., stress. Therefore, we applied Random Forest feature selection to extract the most important biomarkers. The most important 20 features are shown in Fig. 2. To see the effect of modalities, we rank these biomarkers according to their corresponding modalities by assigning an importance value, e.g., 20 for the most important one and subtracting by one for the up-comings. Then, we sum and obtain modality ranking in Fig. 3a. There, we see that the most important features come from phone activity, sleep, HR, stress, activity, and daily modalities calculated according to Table 3.
   In Fig. 4, we see significant changes between stress classes for each type of marker. The amount of the effects are different and can be seen in Fig. 2. For instance, the most important marker is wake-up time according to the feature ranking. When we examine its relation with stress classes in Fig. 4a, we notice that the wake-up time interval becomes narrow concerning the

increase in the stress level. Thus, it is found that the feature ranking affects the stress level. Please note that *stress* feature, from Garmin based on heart rate variability measures (the amount of time between consecutive heartbeats), has an important effect on the target stress class. It can be interpreted that the stress measurements from the Garmin confirm the subjective stress score collected as ground truth.

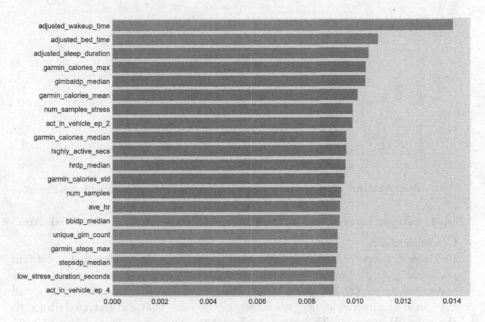

Fig. 2. Feature ranking with class imbalance without personality

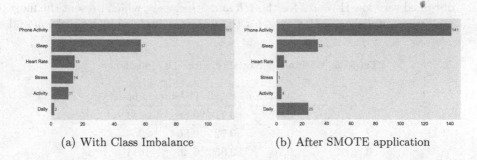

(a) With Class Imbalance   (b) After SMOTE application

Fig. 3. Ranking of biomarkers' corresponding modalities: Without Personality Dataset

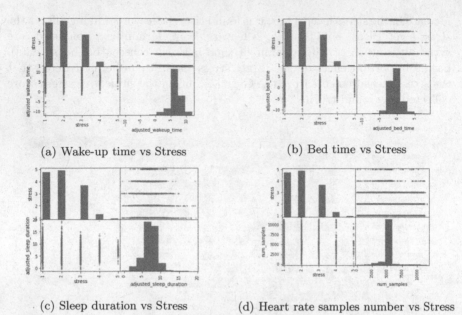

(a) Wake-up time vs Stress

(b) Bed time vs Stress

(c) Sleep duration vs Stress

(d) Heart rate samples number vs Stress

Fig. 4. Relation between some of the features with the stress for imbalanced data

– **Classification**

In Table 4, we present the classification performance score details for *without personality dataset* in original form. We observed identical performance scores presented as in Table 4 when using 107 out of 184 features. Thus, to avoid the curse of dimensionality, we removed the ones that did not contribute to the overall accuracy. To better explain the results, we shared the first 20 important ones in Fig. 2.

We applied RF classification to these selected 107 features (biomarkers). The detailed classification results are in Table 4. As we have a class imbalance, we obtained very low f1-scores for the 4*th* and 5*th* classes, which present the most highly stressful classes. However, for these classes, we have high precision and

Table 4. Without personality with class imbalance

	precision	recall	f1-score	support
1	0.65	0.71	0.68	2244
2	0.52	0.72	0.60	2205
3	0.70	0.35	0.46	1611
4	0.97	0.12	0.21	251
5	0.92	0.25	0.39	44
accuracy			0.60	6355
macro avg	0.75	0.43	0.47	6355
weighted avg	0.63	0.60	0.58	6355

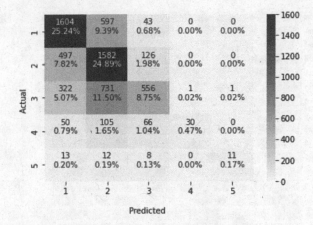

Fig. 5. Confusion matrix without personality with imbalance

low recall. It can be interpreted as correctly predicted labels; however, actual instances belonging to these classes are misclassified. We observed lower f1-score even in classes with high instances (1*st*, 2*nd*); 0.68 and 0.60 respectively. In addition, we provide a confusion matrix in Fig. 5. Class 1 is mostly confused with the 2*nd* class. In the confusion matrix, the percentages are distributed over each pair. Thus, the sum of all percentages corresponds to 100%.

Performance After Applying SMOTE. To resolve the class imbalance, we applied the SMOTE technique. The idea is to produce synthetic data by keeping the same distribution of each class. Before applying SMOTE, the number of instances for each stress class was 10991, 11430, 7935, 1197, and 219 for classes 1 to 5 respectively; after SMOTE, we have 11430 instances for each class. Thus, the number of rows increases to 57150 from 31772.

- **Most important biomarkers**
  Similarly, we applied RF feature selection and extracted most important 20 biomarkers in Fig. 6. Even though the features selected in the imbalanced version are different, as we saw in Fig. 3b that the ranking of the modalities is the same for the first ones, which are phone activity and sleep modalities. However, there is a slight change in the ranking of HR, daily, stress, and activity modalities.
- **Classification**
  Classification result and confusion matrix can be seen in Table 5 and Fig. 7. We see the effect of balancing the classes. Overall class accuracy performance increased from 0.60 to 0.78. However, when we examine it in detail, we notice that this improvement comes from the 4*th* and 5*th* classes which have lower instances than other classes. The performance of the remaining classes was approximately the same except for the 3*rd* class, which has slightly increased.

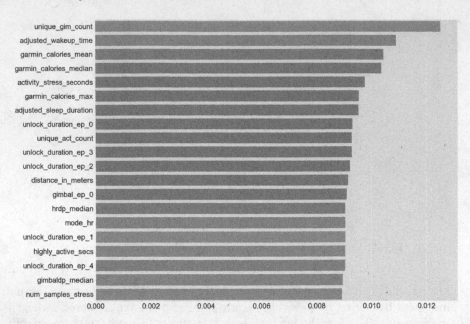

Fig. 6. Feature ranking after SMOTE without personality

Table 5. Without personality after SMOTE

	precision	recall	f1-score	support
1	0.66	0.70	0.68	2306
2	0.58	0.61	0.59	2212
3	0.75	0.62	0.68	2305
4	0.92	0.98	0.95	2320
5	1.00	1.00	1.00	2287
accuracy			0.78	11430
macro avg	0.78	0.78	0.78	11430
weighted avg	0.78	0.78	0.78	11430

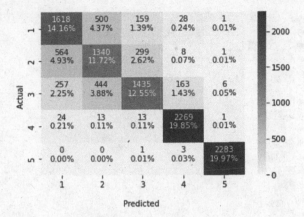

Fig. 7. Confusion matrix without personality balanced data

4.2   With Personality Dataset Results

In this experiment, we add personality and other parameters collected during the ground truth part into our parameter space. We repeat the same process. Here, we deal with 194 independent variables, and our target is again the stress variable.

With Class Imbalance

– **Biomarkers**

Since we added new parameters after feature selection, we observed them in the new feature ranking in Fig. 8. We observed 7 over 10 recently added parameters among the most important biomarkers. The two overwhelming important biomarkers are anxiety and negative affection over stress. This result is coherent with the literature [21,22]. It is stated that there are two types of stress; acute and chronic [21]. The triggering factor for the acute stress may be the anxiety [22]. Thus, it is expected that it is found among the most affecting factors.

The general ranking of the modalities is shown in Fig. 9a. Therefore, we can say that sleep and phone activity modalities keep their places of importance, and recently added features occur in our ranking. In Fig. 10, we share the *anxiety, agreeableness, consciousness, neuroticism* versus stress distribution. There are slightly visible effects between stress classes, especially for the distinction of the 5*th* class from the rest. For instance, we can see an effect where the range of these features become narrow when stress level increase. We see the effect of the newly added parameters on the stress.

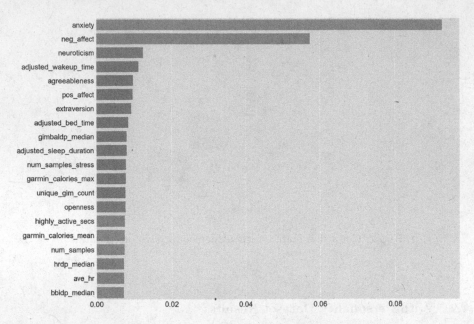

Fig. 8. Feature ranking with class imbalance with personality

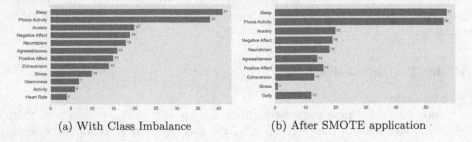

(a) With Class Imbalance   (b) After SMOTE application

Fig. 9. Ranking of biomarkers' corresponding modalities: Personality Dataset

– **Classification**

In Table 6, we observe that even with a class imbalance on the target variable, we got higher f1 scores compared to the *without personality* dataset. Thus, we can say that these parameters improve the overall result accuracy from 0.60 to 0.71. The detailed confusion matrix can be seen in Fig. 11.

Performance After Applying SMOTE

– **Biomarkers**

Again, we apply SMOTE to solve the imbalance issue in stress classes. The parameter space is the only difference from the *without personality* dataset.

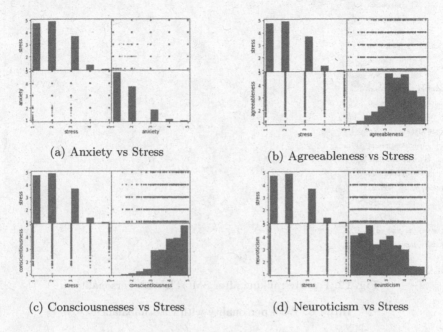

(a) Anxiety vs Stress

(b) Agreeableness vs Stress

(c) Consciousnesses vs Stress

(d) Neuroticism vs Stress

Fig. 10. Pair relation some of the features with the stress for imbalanced data

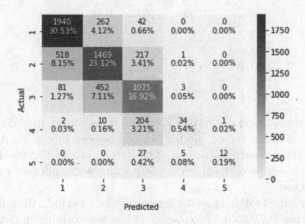

Fig. 11. Confusion matrix with personality with imbalance

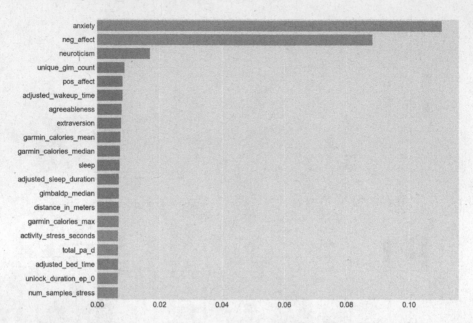

Fig. 12. Feature ranking after SMOTE with personality

Table 6. With personality with class imbalance

	precision	recall	f1-score	support
1	0.76	0.86	0.81	2244
2	0.67	0.67	0.67	2205
3	0.69	0.67	0.68	1611
4	0.79	0.14	0.23	251
5	0.92	0.27	0.42	44
accuracy			0.71	6355
macro avg	0.77	0.52	0.56	6355
weighted avg	0.71	0.71	0.70	6355

The row numbers after the SMOTE remain the same compared to *without personality* dataset. Extracted biomarkers can be seen in Fig. 12. After SMOTE, the importance of order changed. The details are in Fig. 9b. Phone-related features rank up. Sleep features are important with different ratios.

- **Classification**

We see the effect of balanced classes. Overall performance in accuracy is increased from 0.71 to 0.85. However, when we examine in detail, we notice that this improvement comes from the 4*th* and 5*th* classes, which have lower instances than other classes similar to *without personality dataset results* in Sect. 4.1 after SMOTE application. The other classes' performance remained quite the same except for the 3*rd* one, which increased from 0.68 to 0.81 f1-score. Performance details can be seen in Table 7 and confusion matrix in Fig. 13.

Table 7. With personality after SMOTE

	precision	recall	f1-score	support
1	0.77	0.87	0.82	2306
2	0.71	0.62	0.66	2212
3	0.82	0.79	0.81	2305
4	0.95	0.99	0.97	2320
5	1.00	1,00	1.00	2287
accuracy			0.85	11430
macro avg	0.85	0.85	0.85	11430
weighted avg	0.85	0.85	0.85	11430

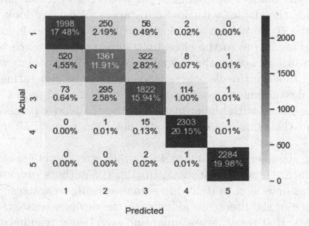

Fig. 13. Confusion matrix with personality balanced data

4.3   Discussion and Comparison

Considering our two different experiments and their sub-scenarios, we obtained higher classification results by including ground truth parameters about personality in our parameter space. These parameters are extraversion, openness, neuroticism, agreeableness, consciousness, and mood-related parameters, such as positive and negative affect. In addition, we observe that they are selected among the most important parameters after feature ranking impacting the stress state and increasing the classification scores. For instance, we obtain 0.60 accuracy (Table 4) when they are not included the analysis, while we have 0.71 accuracy (Table 6) when we add them. The classification performances are even higher when we apply SMOTE and solve the class imbalance problem, which is 0.78 (Table 5) when these parameters are not considered, and 0.85 accuracy is achieved (Table 7) when they are taken into account. The most important ones are anxiety and negative affection. Intuitively, these are highly related to stress levels. Therefore, their usage for further analysis may be a helpful approach. Besides the personality-related parameters, sleep and phone activity-related markers are the most important ones in all cases (Fig. 3 and Fig. 9). In [23], authors found a strong relationship between sleep and stress. Also, in [24], health-related factors such as sleep patterns are found among the important ones affecting stress. Moreover, in study [25], researchers reveal the relationship between positive affect and well-being with sleep. Thus, they are also related to stress due to the relationship between sleep and stress. In [26], again, sleep is found to be related to the mood state. Furthermore, the relationship between exercise and anxiety decrease is examined and found related. Thus, our results aligned with the literature.

We also observed significant performance improvement after applying SMOTE since the number of instances per stress class became similar. We can better recognize the classes with lower instances. When we look in detail, we observe that the f1-score from the classes of lower instances is lower than the other classes. This is due to the class imbalance problem. Since we have fewer instances than other classes, the model fails to recognize them well. After we apply SMOTE to solve the class imbalance problem by generating data similar to the current measurements, we obtain higher final class f1 scores. As it was not the case for the classes with higher instances, they had lower precision rates than the others, and their final class scores did not change much after the SMOTE application.

Comparing classifier performance with other stress level classification studies in the literature is also important. In [19], the authors prepared a detailed survey on stress detection in daily life scenarios using wearables. They present the performance in the literature along with the devices, sensors, and methods used. We observe that we achieve similar and even better results considering the ambulatory scenarios in the literature [19] even with a higher number of classes. In [27], they used speech data, applied GMM (Gaussian Mixture Model), and obtained 80.5% accuracy in the stress and relaxed states classification. Another high result is presented in [28]. They received 76% accuracy using *blood volume pulse, skin temperature, electro-dermal activity (EDA), heart rate variability, heart rate* parameters applying Random Forest on two classes (stressed, relaxed) problem.

In addition to RF, we also applied deep learning (DL) methods as they performed better in literature [29]. We used MLP (Multi-layer Perceptron). We performed hyper-parameter optimization with grid search in scikit-learn and found that activation *relu*, alpha 0.0001, hidden layer 30, solver *adam* reveal the best performance. However, overall class performances for our scenarios with MLP compared to RF are lower by about 20%. For instance, for our best case (with personality and with SMOTE), we have 85% with RF but 63% with MLP. As these results were not promising, we did not include their details in this study.

5   Conclusion and Future Work

In this study, we examined the digital biomarkers related to stress state since they become valuable information for well-being. We used the Tesserae dataset, collected from office workers. There have been several different modalities. We used the Machine Learning technique to examine these markers, specifically the Random Forest algorithm. We extracted them by dealing with multi-modal data. Also, we made classification with selected biomarkers which refer to high importance in *stress* class. We applied SMOTE technique to solve the imbalance issue in the target class. We also analyzed the impact of using personality-related parameters. In all cases, phone activity and sleep modalities-related markers are the most relevant to *stress*. Highest classification accuracy is 85% using *with personality dataset* after applying SMOTE. Our findings confirm the literature that examines the statistical relationship between sleep, well-being, stress, positive affect, mood, and physical activity modalities [23–26]. We contribute by working all these modalities in one study in a multi-modal manner by applying machine learning methods over wearable and survey data collected in an unrestricted environment.

We want to point out some improvements for further studies. We excluded collected wearable and mobile phone data without ground truth. This amount is vast since there is almost one-year collection of data from wearables for some participants. Thus, one further approach may be an imputation of ground truth data corresponding to these data to use in the processing. In addition, we did not consider the time-related aspects in this study. For instance, there may be changes in stress levels according to the days of the week. It is intuitively expected that one may have a lower stress level during weekends and holidays. Furthermore, we will explore different DL methods, such as CNN and LSTM. We will consider these aspects in our future studies.

Acknowledgment. Tübitak Bideb 2211-A academic reward is gratefully acknowledged. This work is supported by the Turkish Directorate of Strategy and Budget under the TAM Project number 2007K12-873.

References

1. FDA-NIH Biomarker Working Group: BEST (Biomarkers, EndpointS, and other Tools) resource 2016. Silver Spring, MD, US FDA (2016)
2. Frank, R., Hargreaves, R.: Clinical biomarkers in drug discovery and development. Nat. Rev. Drug Discov. **2**(7), 566–580 (2003)

3. Srikanth, V., et al.: Digital biomarkers: convergence of digital health technologies and biomarkers. NPJ Digital Med. **5**(1) (2022)
4. Perez, M.V., et al.: Large-scale assessment of a smartwatch to identify atrial fibrillation. New England J. Med. **381**(20), 1909–1917 (2019)
5. Mahadevan, N., et al.: Development of digital biomarkers for resting tremor and bradykinesia using a wrist-worn wearable device. NPJ Digital Med. **3**(1), 1–12 (2020)
6. Andrzejewski, K.L., et al.: Wearable sensors in Huntington disease: a pilot study. J. Huntington's Dis. **5**(2), 199–206 (2016)
7. Fendrich, S.J., Balachandran, M., Patel, M.S.: Association between behavioral phenotypes and sustained use of smartphones and wearable devices to remotely monitor physical activity. Sci. Rep. **11**(1), 1–12 (2021)
8. Mandryk, R.L., et al.: Remote assessment of depression using digital biomarkers from cognitive tasks. Front. Psychol. **12** (2021)
9. Kroenke, K., Spitzer, R.L., Williams, J.B.W.: The PHQ-9: validity of a brief depression severity measure. J. Gen. Internal Med. **16**(9), 606–613 (2001)
10. Mattingly, S.M., et al.: The effects of seasons and weather on sleep patterns measured through longitudinal multimodal sensing. NPJ Digital Med. **4**(1), 1–15 (2021)
11. Park, C., et al.: Digital biomarkers of physical frailty and frailty phenotypes using sensor-based physical activity and machine learning. Sensors **21**(16), 5289 (2021)
12. Sano, A., et al.: Identifying objective physiological markers and modifiable behaviors for self-reported stress and mental health status using wearable sensors and mobile phones: observational study. J. Med. Internet Res. **20**(6), e9410 (2018)
13. Maxhuni, A., et al.: Stress modelling and prediction in presence of scarce data. J. Biomed. Inform. **63**, 344–356 (2016)
14. Muñoz, S., et al.: Prediction of stress levels in the workplace using surrounding stress. Inf. Process. Manage. **59**(6), 103064 (2022)
15. Wang, R., et al.: StudentLife: assessing mental health, academic performance and behavioral trends of college students using smartphones. In: Proceedings of the 2014 ACM International Joint Conference on Pervasive and Ubiquitous Computing (2014)
16. Mattingly, S.M., et al.: The tesserae project: large-scale, longitudinal, in situ, multimodal sensing of information workers. In: Extended Abstracts of the 2019 CHI Conference on Human Factors in Computing Systems (2019)
17. Mirjafari, S., et al.: Predicting job performance using mobile sensing. IEEE Pervasive Comput. **20**(4), 43–51 (2021)
18. Liu, S., et al.: The power of dynamic social networks to predict individuals' mental health. In: Pacific Symposium on Biocomputing 2020 (2019)
19. Can, Y.S., et al.: Stress detection in daily life scenarios using smart phones and wearable sensors: a survey. J. Biomed. Inform. **92**, 103139 (2019)
20. Taelman, J., et al.: Influence of mental stress on heart rate and heart rate variability. In: Vander Sloten, J., Verdonck, P., Nyssen, M., Haueisen, J. (eds.) 4th European Conference of the International Federation for Medical and Biological Engineering. IFMBE Proceedings, vol. 22. Springer, Cham (2009). https://doi.org/10.1007/978-3-540-89208-3_324
21. Picard, R.W.: Automating the recognition of stress and emotion: from lab to real-world impact. IEEE MultiMedia **23**(3), 3–7 (2016)
22. England, M.J., et al.: Epilepsy across the spectrum: promoting health and understanding: a summary of the Institute of Medicine report. Epilepsy Behav. **25**(2), 266–276 (2012)

23. Marcusson-Clavertz, D., et al.: Relationships between daily stress responses in everyday life and nightly sleep. J. Behav. Med. 1–15 (2022)
24. Gedam, S., Paul, S.: A review on mental stress detection using wearable sensors and machine learning techniques. IEEE Access **9**, 84045–84066 (2021)
25. Steptoe, A., et al.: Positive affect, psychological well-being, and good sleep. J. Psychosom. Res. **64**(4), 409–415 (2008)
26. Pilcher, J.J., Huffcutt, A.I.: Effects of sleep deprivation on performance: a meta-analysis. Sleep **19**(4), 318–326 (1996)
27. Lu, H., et al.: StressSense: detecting stress in unconstrained acoustic environments using smartphones. In: Proceedings of the 2012 ACM Conference on Ubiquitous Computing (2012)
28. Gjoreski, M., et al.: Continuous stress detection using a wrist device: in laboratory and real life. In: Proceedings of the 2016 ACM International Joint Conference on Pervasive and Ubiquitous Computing: Adjunct (2016)
29. Bobade, P., Vani, M.: Stress detection with machine learning and deep learning using multimodal physiological data. In: 2020 Second International Conference on Inventive Research in Computing Applications (ICIRCA). IEEE (2020)

Smart Transportation

Continuous Measurement of Air Pollutant Concentrations in a Roadway Tunnel in Southern Italy

Saverio De Vito[1], Antonio Del Giudice[1(✉)], Gerardo D'Elia[1], Elena Esposito[1], Grazia Fattoruso[1], Sergio Ferlito[1], Fabrizio Formisano[1], Giuseppe Loffredo[1], Ettore Massera[1], Girolamo Di Francia[1], Patrizia Bellucci[2], and Francesca Ciarallo[2]

[1] Centro Ricerche Portici, ENEA (Italian National Agency for New Technologies, Energy and Sustainable Economic Development), Portici, Italy
antonio.delgiudice@enea.it

[2] ANAS (Azienda Nazionale Autonoma Delle Strade Statali) S.p.A. Roma, Rome, Italy

Abstract. Air Quality is of significant concern in modern life. Since pollutants are harmful for health and environment, it is important to measure their concentration in the air. In this work the authors report on a tool for the measurement of the concentration of CO, NO2, O3, VOC and PM in the air in harsh environments such as motorway tunnels or underground transportation system. Inside a tunnel, pollution is for the major part composed of gasses released by vehicles and particulate matters, mainly due to vehicle's brake particles, asphalt erosion and tires wearing. The tool is composed of a network of rugged low-cost solid-state sensor nodes placed in the environment to continuously monitor the gas concentrations and a remote backend that stores, handles and presents the information received via cellular network. The sensor network has been installed in a roadway tunnel in southern Sicily (Italy) and here the authors report preliminary results related to the continuous measurement of CO and NO2. The aim of this work is to contribute to make continuous the monitoring of gases concentrations inside a roadway tunnel. The sensors have been designed to be online for a long period, allowing remote maintenance. The results will be deeply investigated after a long period of data collection. The analysis of data will be useful to pose in place appropriate actions to mitigate dangerous concentrations of gases.

Keywords: Air Quality Sensor Node · Motorway Tunnel air continuous monitoring · Gaseous pollutant

1 Introduction

There is an increasing concern on how human health can be negatively affected by living in busy city environments [1], the major pollutants under concern being: particulate matter (PMx.x), ozone (O3), Nitrogen Dioxide (NO2), Carbon Oxide (CO) and Volatile Organic Compounds (VOC). PM is a mix of particles both solid and liquid derived

© ICST Institute for Computer Sciences, Social Informatics and Telecommunications Engineering 2023
Published by Springer Nature Switzerland AG 2023. All Rights Reserved
S. I. Lopes et al. (Eds.): Edge-IoT 2022/SmartGov 2022, LNICST 510, pp. 155–165, 2023.
https://doi.org/10.1007/978-3-031-35982-8_11

mostly from human activity and combustion of fossil fuels and biomass. Vehicles gas exhausts and the particles produced by rubbing and friction due to braking, tires wearing and asphalt also contribute to increase the concentration of PM [2]. O3 is the result of the photochemical interaction between sun light and vehicle emissions: in a roadway tunnel it is expected to be found mainly due to winds action. NO2 is normally generated by combustion processes so, by vehicular traffic and gas cookers used so frequently yet in housing units and as a result of some industrial transformation processes. VOC are composed of chemical compounds due to vehicles emissions and emissions of solvents from industries. PM10 refers to particles with a diameter of 10 microns or less, these can be inhaled during breathing and can reach and stuck in the lungs. That's not the worst, because PM2.5 which refers to particles with a diameter of 2.5 microns or less, can go beyond the lung barriers and enter the blood system. The consequences on health can be heart and respiratory diseases or even lung cancer. Ozone and nitrogen dioxide can cause asthma, lung diseases as inflammation or reduced lung function and bronchial symptoms. The exposure to polluted air of children and pregnant women has even worse effects. Polluted air is the cause of asthma in children aged 5–18 years and 543000 children per year die of respiratory diseases due to polluted air exposure, the fetal brain growth can be affected by pregnant women exposed to air pollution [1]. As a result, during the last decades air pollution has gained the attention of many organizations and scientists who have studied the phenomenon of exposure to harmful gasses from different points of view.

Road tunnels is an effective alternative to keep traffic away from congestion and to connect two places with the minimum path length. However, due to the tunnel limited ventilation, one can be exposed to pretty high levels of pollutants concentrations. There is another problem inside the tunnel being that AQ measuring instruments can be exposed to different agents like particulate, small animals and water leaks from the above land. In the scientific literature the characterization of tunnel air quality, has been investigated in several works. In [3] the authors conduct a monitoring campaign deploying two devices for the sampling of the air gas concentration at the beginning and at the end of a tunnel. They considered no forced ventilation and only airflow induced by cars movement. The measurement campaign lasted for seven consecutive days. The results are focused on the study of emission factors and for the analyzed case, the authors, emphasize the relevance of the contribution non-exhaust vehicular emissions together with vehicles speed and age, on air quality. In [4] the authors collect samples for seven days not consecutive, between 1 pm and 2 pm that corresponds to the hours when children exit from schools in the city of Guanajuato (Mexico). The measurement campaign revealed that in the tunnel PM concentration exceeds safe limits. In [5] the authors investigate the concentrations of pollutants immediately out of the tunnels that connects Europe and Asia in Istanbul. They deploy two measuring devices at the exit of the tunnel in order to evaluate the impact of the gasses that come from the tunnel on the air quality in proximity of the tunnel taking also into account the speed of the wind, temperature, humidity and traffic volumes. They conclude that the tunnel operation has no adverse effect on the air quality in the city of Istanbul. In [6] also the dependence of PM10 and PM2.5 from vehicle speed has been investigated and the authors conclude that there is a certain dependence from vehicle speed only for PM10. Also, in this case the measurement stations were placed at the entrance and at the exit of the tunnel.

This work is aimed at the presentation of an IoT measurement system, capable of taking air quality related measurements in harsh environments like road tunnels or underground transportation systems, for long periods. The novel approach of this work is in the fact that the system can be used to monitor gas concentrations for long periods and contribute to build an automated system for the continuous monitoring and control of harmful gases concentrations. The system has been installed in the "Galleria San Demetrio" a motorway tunnel in Sicily (Italy) to evaluate car related gas emissions in a three-month period and the results of this first experimental campaign will be here presented and discussed. The system described is conceived to be part of a decision supporting system (DSS) for government and local administrations with the aim to characterize the environment in which it is deployed and support the adoption of the necessary counter measures in order to ensure compliance to air quality safe concentration levels [7]. The system has been designed to last for months, so some precautions have been taken to achieve good levels of physical and software robustness. That long period of time will also provide a large amount of data suitable to characterize the air pollution inside the tunnel in different periods of the year.

In paragraph 2, the measuring system will be described, paragraph 3 describes in detail its deployment in the road tunnel and, finally in paragraph 4 some preliminary results will be presented and discussed.

2   Measurement System

The measurement system is composed of four measuring stations, three installed in the motorway tunnel and the fourth placed in open air, a few kms away from the tunnel. In Fig. 1 a draft of one of the installed Measuring Station (MS) is shown. The MS is composed of a rugged enclosure containing a MONICA sensor node [8, 9], a power supply system, a Raspberry Pi and a Lipari router [10] for remote communication. Data are wirelessly transmitted to a remote backend for the storage and presentation of the inferred information.

Fig. 1. Main components of the measurement station

The MONICA sensor node has all the sensors and the hardware to sample air quantitatively and qualitatively. The Raspberry Pi oversees collected samples, if necessary, making some preliminary calculations and organizing data to be sent to the remote cloud by means of the Lipari Router. The gateway operates by means of the cellular network and sends the data to two remote data base. MONICA communicates with the Raspberry by means of a Bluetooth connection whereas the Raspberry is connected to the router via ethernet cable. The router transfers data packets to two data base by means of an LTE connection.

The next paragraphs describe in detail the main components of the measuring station.

2.1 MONICA

MONICA is the Italian acronym of *MONItoraggio Cooperativo della qualità dell'Aria* (Air Quality Cooperative Monitoring). Essentially it is an IoT device for the continuous monitoring of the concentration of gasses, potentially harmful to health, that can be found in the air because of modern life activities. It has been already used in other air quality measuring campaigns and it represents the core of the measuring system presented in this work [11]. Being also a portable device, MONICA's energy consumption is quite limited, all the components of the boars being low power, overcoming battery duration limits. Moreover, whenever possible, the inactive components are set in sleep mode.

In this work, the node is continuously connected to the electricity grid supply. However, a power supply module with a battery is in charge of provide the voltages to the electronics of the node.

The gaseous pollutants that the board can sense are NO_2 (nitrogen dioxide), CO (carbon monoxide) and O_3 (ozone) and it's suitable for VOC (Volatile Organic compound) measures. For this purpose, an Alphasense array that include the sensors for these three gases has been chosen. The sensors transform the respective gas concentration to a voltage value then an Analog Frontend (AFE) operates the necessary signal conditioning to make the signal presentable to the sampler of the microcontroller (Nucleo LK432C). The ADC is a 12-bit and the sampling frequency has been kept relatively low since the analog signals are slowly varying. There are also digital sensors, this is the case of the temperature/humidity sensor. This sensor is located in the proximity of the AFE and it communicates with the microcontroller by means of a serial protocol.

The node is equipped with two fans operated at fixed speed. The forced ventilation guarantees the minimum air flux for the sensors to follow the concentration dynamics. Finally, MONICA also includes a Particulate Matter sensor. The sensor chosen is the Plantower PMS 7003 that can measure PM1, PM2.5 and PM10. It has been placed in the frontal part of the node ad it has its own fan to force the air into the measuring chamber.

In order to obtain the correct value of the gas concentration from the sensors, the node may require a calibration process that in the specific case consists of two phases: at first, the nodes are characterized in a controlled environment very similar to the one in which they will be deployed, then the nodes can be deployed along with some reference devices for a certain period during the year, that allows to obtain a multivariate calibration function for different periods of the year (summer, winter) [8].

2.2 Roadway Tunnel Measuring Station

The Fig. 2 shows the measuring station. The first specification to comply with, is the reliability of the case that contains the electronics part. It must be resistant to water leakages from the top of the gallery or to the rain in case of open air installation where it is operated only in vertical position. The case has been chosen and modified to resist to possible "animal attacks". Birds, insects, rodents, lizards could damage the electronics inside the case entering from the apertures that are necessary to let the air flow up to the sensors. The case has no switch and nothing else but the supply cable that communicates with external world. All the communication with the remote server, are operated wirelessly. The power supply is taken from the electric grid connection (220Vac). Inside, a power transformation is operated in order to supply the different devices at the proper voltage level. The case is in plastic so that electromagnetic waves can freely pass through.

Fig. 2. The Measuring Station rugged enclosure. On the left, are clearly visible the two apertures of about 5 sqcm required for the air to flow inside the enclosure and up to the sensors.

The system operates by means of a software that resides both on the MONICA node and on the Raspberry. The code that controls the node is written in C and basically consists of a loop that in turn asks the sensors to measure and transmit the obtained data. Sensors are both digital or analog. The firsts are simply periodically polled and the values are listed in a JSON packet that is successively sent. The analog sensors are sampled by means a ADC. The code that controls the Raspberry is written in Python. The system and the code have been designed taking care to ask for minimum or even null maintenance for months. In case of glitch in the electric network it can happen that the system needs a reboot. During restart the raspberry has been set so that it restarts sequentially all the modules for the normal operation and the Bluetooth module for connection with the node. That function has been achieved also thanks to PM2 [12]. PM2 is a process manager that automatically handles the execution of the processes and in case of anomalous halting it restarts the process. PM2 registers in a log file all the events and the number of restarts of the processes that have occurred. It is also possible to remotely access to the raspberry by means of a Remote Access Software. In that way it is possible to update the software and check for the correct operation of the system.

2.3 Remote Backend

The remote backend is a software that resides on remote machines that is responsible of the collection of the information on the monitored parameters. Both the measuring station and the remote servers are constantly connected to the data network. The measurement station sends a JSON packet containing all the measurements from the sensors every four minutes so that 360 samples per day are collected. The data are sent by the Python code on the Raspberry of the measurement station which interacts with the backend server by means of RESTful API. The data base is a MongoDB. System reliability is increased using simultaneously two servers to receive data. These two act as data lake repository and it is also possible to implement some complimentary services such as data presentation and alerts. The measurement station is capable to send some specific alarms in case of system faults. Furthermore, in case of unexpected halting of the system an email message with the error code is sent to the system administrator.

3 Deployments

The measuring campaign is intended to assess the air quality in two different places with two different deployments. The first one is in open air and installed on the viaduct San Paolo in the city of Catania (Sicily, Italy) above the entrance of the tunnel Gagliano (latitude: 37.5499 longitude: 15.0740). This installation consists of a single measuring station designed to be resistant to rain and to hot temperatures caused by the continuous exposure to sun. This measurement station will continuously monitor the quality of the air in proximity of one side of the tunnel openings where there is the entrance for a carriageway and the exit of the other one (Fig. 3). This device is active from February the 12th 2022. The city electrical network provides power supply to the device, and it is connected to the internet network by means of a router always active.

Fig. 3. Open air installation, Viaduct San Paolo, Catania, Sicily, Italy. The installation site on the left, while on the right it is observable a detail of the measuring station installation.

The second deployment is inside the tunnel called in Italian San Demetrio 20 km south the first deployment in the Siracusa direction (latitude: 37.36084, longitude: 15.0474463) (Fig. 4). This installation consists of three measuring devices installed in three emergency areas inside the tunnel. The measuring systems have been made rugged to resist to water leakages inside the gallery but also to the intrusion af small animals or insect that could compromise the system integrity. Nevertheless, all the necessary precautions have been taken to ensure that the air could easily flow inside the device and reach the sensible parts for the measurements. For this purpose, the fan already active on the MONICA have been exploited. One of three systems has been installed on March the 28th 2022 while the remaining two have been installed on June the 3rd 2022.

Fig. 4. In tunnel deployment, San Demetrio Tunnel, Sicily Italy

Accordingly to the distances imposed by the emergency areas, the measuring systems have been posed: close to the entrance, in the middle and close to the exit of the tunnel.

4   Results

The results of that work, essentially prove that the devices installed are working correctly. Inferred information can be extracted once more data will be available with time. In Fig. 5, CO measurements recorded by the three devices inside the tunnel are reported in the period from June the 4th to June the 15th together with the corresponding temperature, T and relative humidity, recorded at the same site. CO has been evaluated using two calibration methods: the sensor own datasheet (factory calibration) and a so-called field-calibration, obtained using data recorded in field measurements although in different sites. Both calibrations show that CO ranges around 1 to 4 mg/m3 in the tunnel (Fig. 5), far beyond the concentrations observed outdoor and reported in Fig. 7. NO2 has been evaluated considering the same two calibrations, factory and in field calibration. One can observe that for the indoor installation the curve ranges from 100 μg/m^3 to 200 μg/m^3 (Fig. 6) and for outdoor installation the curve ranges from 50 μg/m^3 to 100 μg/m$^{3.}$ (Fig. 7). The NO2 trend seems temperature dependent, this will be assessed once traffic data will be available.

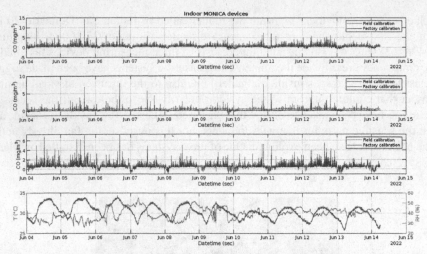

Fig. 5. Tunnel installation a) **CO** trend (the red curve is relative to the calibration in field, blue curve refers to the standard calibration) b) Temperature (blue) and humidity (red). (Color figure online)

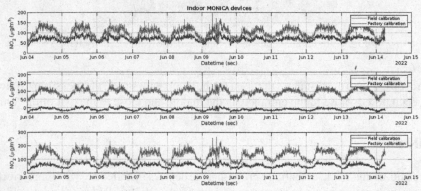

Fig. 6. Tunnel installation a) **NO2** trend in μg/m^3 for the indoor installation (the red curve is relative to the calibration in field, blue curve refers to the standard calibration). (Color figure online)

Figure 8 shows the trend of particulate matter 2.5 measured by the three devices installed inside the tunnel. The graphs show the factory calibration. There are some peaks in the graphs that need to be investigated and compared with traffic data that will be available at the end of the measuring campaign. In Fig. 9, PM2.5 behavior for outdoor installation is shown.

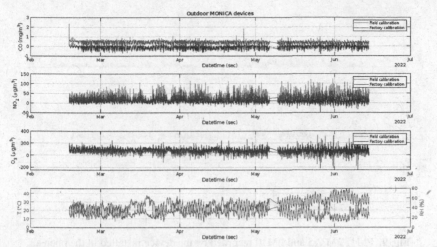

Fig. 7. Outdoor installation. a) Gas concentrations trend (the red curve is relative to the calibration in field, blue curve refers to the standard calibration) b) Temperature (blue) and humidity (red). (Color figure online)

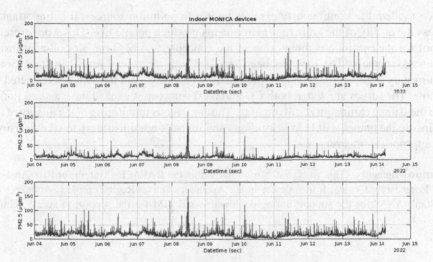

Fig. 8. PM2.5 recorded by the three devices installed in the tunnel.

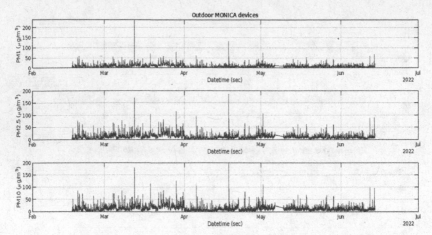

Fig. 9. PM1, PM 2.5 and PM10 recorded by the device installed in the open air.

5 Conclusions

Since modern life continuously exposes people to pollution sources, it is important to assess the quality of the air in the environments in which people live. This work presents a tool for the continuous monitoring of the concentration of some air pollutant inside motorway tunnels. The tool has been installed in a motorway tunnel in Italy. Some preliminary results have been here presented as resulting from the samples collected up to now. The curves show that both CO and NO2 sometimes exceed the standard limits. The measuring campaign is still ongoing. The continuous monitoring of the quality of the air inside the tunnel will help institutions and tunnel's administrators to take decisions for appropriate interventions.

Acknowledgments. This work was carried out within the RAFAEL (System for Risk Analysis and Forecast for Critical Infrastructure in the Apennines Dorsal Region) project. Authors wish to thank ANAS for the support during deployment and TIM for the support to access cellular network.

References

1. https://www.who.int/news-room/spotlight/how-air-pollution-is-destroying-our-health. Accessed 29 Aug 2022
2. https://www.researchgate.net/publication/322307951_Particulate_Matter_from_the_ Road_Surface_Abrasion_as_a_Problem_of_Non-Exhaust_Emission_Control.   Accessed 29 August 2022
3. Raparthi, N., Debbarma, S., Phuleria, H.C.: Development of real-world emission factors for on-road vehicles from motorway tunnel measurements. Environmental Science. https://doi. org/10.1016/j.aeaoa.2021.100113

4. Zamorategui-Molina, A., Gutiérrez-Ortega, N.L., Baltazar-Vera, J.C., Del Ángel-Soto, J., Tirado-Torres, D.: Carbon monoxide and particulate matter concentrations inside the road tunnels of Guanajuato City. Mexico. Aerosol Air Qual. Res. **21**, 210039 (2021). https://doi.org/10.4209/aaqr.210039

5. Gokce, H.B., Arıoğlu, E., Copty, N.K., Onay, T.T., Gun, B.: Exterior air quality monitoring for the Eurasia Tunnel in Istanbul, Turkey. Science of the Total Environment (IF10.753), Pub Date: 2019–09–07. https://doi.org/10.1016/j.scitotenv.2019.134312

6. Gillies, J.A., Gertler, A.W., Sagebiel, J.C., Dippel, W.A.: On-road particulate matter (PM2.5 and PM10) emissions in the Sepulveda Tunnel, Los Angeles, California. Environ. Sci. Technol. **35**(6), 1054–1063 (2001). https://doi.org/10.1021/es991320p

7. https://www.who.int/news-room/feature-stories/detail/what-are-the-who-air-quality-guidel ines. Accessed 29 Aug 2022

8. De Vito, S., et al.: Crowdsensing IoT architecture for pervasive air quality and exposome monitoring: design, development, calibration, and long-term validation. Sensors **21**, 5219 (2021). https://doi.org/10.3390/s21155219

9. De Vito, S., et al.: Hyper resoluted Air Quality maps in urban environment with crowdsensed data from intelligent low cost sensors. In: 2022 IEEE International Symposium on Olfaction and Electronic Nose (ISOEN), pp. 1–4 (2022). https://doi.org/10.1109/ISOEN54820.2022. 9789614

10. https://www.tiesse.com/download/datasheet-lipari-5100/

11. https://uiaairheritage-portici.it/. Accessed 29 Aug 2022

12. https://pm2.keymetrics.io/. Accessed 29 Aug 2022

Rating Urban Transport Services Quality Using a Sentiment Analysis Approach

Orlando Belo[✉] and Ricardo Milhazes

ALGORITMI Research Centre/LASI, University of Minho, Braga, Portugal
obelo@di.uminho.pt

Abstract. Urban transport systems are recognized as one of the most relevant pillars in the operation of a city, as well as in the quality of service they provide to its inhabitants and visitors. Today, transport network management and control systems play a key role in ensuring their operation, and planning new services in accordance with some specific requirements. Some of these services provide means to users for expressing their opinions about the services they used. When properly treated and analyzed, the opinions reveal very relevant information, both positive and negative, about the operation of public transport companies, which can be used to identify risk situations, malfunctions, or emerging threats, among other things. From the identification of these situations, transport companies can improve their image, attenuating or eliminating such critical and undesirable situations and, consequently, increasing the quality of the service they use and their earnings. In this paper, we present and discuss a system for analyzing complaints about services provided by a public transport company, in order to identify sentiments expressed in complaint texts and establish a complaint-index reflecting the negativity level of the complaint.

Keywords: Customer Analytics · Customer Opinion Analysis · Service Assessment · Sentiment Analysis · Smart-City Governance

1 Introduction

Regardless of the level of sophistication, the governance of smart city systems [1, 2] is strongly based on their information systems and infrastructures, whether physical or logical, and on the people who promote, design and manage them. However, we know that there are many other aspects that must be taken into account when applying and implementing governmental actions. The opinion of the inhabitants (and visitors) of a city is certainly one of these aspects. Probably one of the most important. Today, people share their opinions and discuss the most varied real-life topics on social media [3]. They use social networks for publicizing an event, sharing an idea, or revealing their experiences with companies. A significant part of these opinions is supported by the knowledge people have about specific practical situations, occurred in the city, which should be analyzed for getting useful information and helping manage companies or the services they promote and provide.

© ICST Institute for Computer Sciences, Social Informatics and Telecommunications Engineering 2023
Published by Springer Nature Switzerland AG 2023. All Rights Reserved
S. I. Lopes et al. (Eds.): Edge-IoT 2022/SmartGov 2022, LNICST 510, pp. 166–175, 2023.
https://doi.org/10.1007/978-3-031-35982-8_12

Urban transport has raised numerous challenges in the context of smart cities [4]. Its development has involved the design and implementation of a wide range of systems, both physical and logical, specifically oriented for improving the quality of the services, and integration into the city's ecosystem, in order to reduce or limit the use of individual transportation means, and improve the quality of living in a city. However, independently from the offer, quality and sophistication of physical means, we must emphasize the importance of the data we have access to about city systems functioning, and how their urban transports operate. The analysis of urban data [5], which comes from many diverse sources, should lead to the improvement and sophistication processes implemented in a smart city.

Currently, in most data analysis processes, analysts and decision makers give great importance to everything that people, in general, post on social networks, such as general comments, experience reports, preferences, or opinions about services or goods they purchased. However, opinions are the ones that attract more attention of analysts. An opinion expressed by a person in any social network or in a specialized reviewing system, in a matter of seconds, can positively or negatively influence a large number of other people, and may eventually affect the credibility of a service or even an entire company. The analysis of such opinions allow for inferring the sentiments customers expressed in the texts, which provide valuable information for reinforcing customers' profiles and improving understanding about customers habits, preferences, well-being, or trends.

The implementation of customer analytics systems [6] in urban transports [7] companies with the ability for developing sentiment analysis processes allow for knowing what a customer thinks (feels) about a service or product of the company. This is very valuable for the company. It helps for assessing its image for customers, identifying and reducing management risks or for increasing revenues, among other things. It gives information about the experience customers had using urban transports. Sentiment analysis [8] can be an important instrument for urban transports companies for assessing performance and quality of service in a city. All the technological means set on a smart city may contribute to promote mechanisms for opinion gathering, conciliating what habitants "feel" about the city, in a global view, or about a company or a service, in particular. Sentiment analysis may add value to smart cities governance.

In this paper, we present a sentiment analysis system (a test bed) developed for creating a complaint-index for a public transport company, using sentiments expressed in a set of complaint texts that customers posted on some Web sites. With this work, we want to highlight the contributions of sentiment analysis may give for the identification of problems and needs of urban transports in a city based on customer opinions expressed in subjective texts. Combined with other advanced technologies such as business intelligence, cloud computing, Internet of Things (IoT), or big data, sentiment analysis may improve customer analytics, taking smart cities governance applications to a new level of sophistication. In order to demonstrate the index assessment model as well as the usefulness of the system conceived, we collected from the Web a very diverse set of customers' complaints about urban transports, which we assumed to belong to a fictitious urban transport company idealized by us. Even so, the data we collected is real. Thus, using sentiment analysis, we processed complaint texts, as well as a set of categorical elements referred by customers (bus, driver, accessibility, lifetime, cost, etc.), and we created the referred index for the company. Knowing the value of this index, company managers have the possibility to know the status and the "image" of the company, identifying threads and tendencies of using urban transports or defining new strategies for improving company's services. The rest of the paper includes three more sections, namely: Sect. 2, which exposes and discusses some sentiment analysis fundamentals and applications; Sect. 3, which presents the sentiment analysis system we designed and implemented; and Sect. 4, which includes conclusions and some future research lines for improving and extending the current implementation of the system.

2   Related Work

Smart cities [4] has been a field of excellence for numerous cutting-edge technologies, involving numerous areas of information and communication technologies. From the use of conventional data processing to the application of artificial intelligence techniques [9], there are numerous areas of knowledge involved in the progression and development of the most innovative smart cities initiatives and, in particular, with their governance. Artificial intelligence, for example, has been introduce intensively in many smart cities applications, oriented for developing monitoring and control applications, for the most common smart city systems, and improving data processing and analysis of data for getting valuable information for sustaining the regular functioning of a city [10]. In this domain, we may find several cases of applications involving the use of sophisticated machine learning techniques [11] in healthcare, smart traffic management and transportation, environment monitoring, identification of road surface conditions, public safety, or electrical smart grids, among many others [12]. The use of machine learning applications in smart cities allows for better predictions about events or issues not planned or expected. This is the basis to promote proactive management and control of services and facilities of a smart city. One of the most attractive application aspects of machine learning is opinion analysis, also called as sentiment analysis. Its application in smart cities, with particular emphasis on its management and governance aspects, has great potential and, when properly applied, can contribute very effectively for rationalizing and improving services provided by a city. Let us see how.

In our daily life, each of us observes, analyses and manifests opinions in countless ways, for different kind of situations. Two different people can interpret and react differently to the same thing, revealing different opinions and sentiments. If we observe carefully our daily lives, the most common and intuitive way of identifying whether a person doing well (or not) is through the sentiments they shown about a certain subject or situation. We can express these sentiments in different ways. The textual format is the most regular. It is not difficult for us to read a text and identify the sentiments expressed in the text. However, even for a person, gathering sentiments, as a reader, may be complicated, as sentiments expressed in text can have a different meaning and weight for the author of the text.

Sentiment analysis [8, 13] is currently one of the most active and interesting areas of work in the domain of customer satisfaction and profiling. Knowing what a customer thinks (feels) about a service or a product is very precious and valuable for a company that cares about its image and wants to improve its relationship with customers or guarantee their loyalty over time. All these aspects make possible to improve company's well-being, as well as increase its influence in the market in which it operates. Consequently, sentiment analysis may contribute to increase company's earnings and reputation, through the improvement of its services and its quality of products.

Currently, sentiment analysis can positively influence a vast number of application areas. Companies like Microsoft or Google have already developed their own sentiment analysis solutions. In [14] we can find an interesting list of application cases of sentiment analysis processes. From the wide range of applications presented, we highlight, for example: stock market forecasting, which despite being an extremely speculative market allows us to make predictions, since several factors, such as consumer opinions, influence it. Several authors have worked on this application domain. For example, Bollen et al. [15] tested the impact of the mood revealed on Twitter on the financial data provided by the Dow Jones Industrial Average (DIJA) market index; intelligent marketing, which helps to determine, among other things, the success of an advertising campaign, taking into account the opinions of consumers. For understanding market trends, Li and Li [16] created an intelligent marketing system using opinions of microblogs, by observing the fluctuations of sentiments on a particular topic; or recommendation systems, which are very useful tools for helping the definition or adjustment of plans for making systems and services more pleasant for users. These systems can include mechanisms for analyzing users' opinions and assessing their feelings about different areas of working for inferring customer's preferences or trends. Li and Shiu [17] developed a recommendation system that provides a list of users to whom an advertisement should be provided, taking into account the preferences shown by them on social networks.

However, the process of machine-learning-based sentiment analysis [18] used for establishing a sentiment rating for opinions expressed in texts is not a simple process. Before the application of sentiment analysis mechanisms, the texts collected containing the opinions need to be prepared, in order to be adapted to a format suitable for machine learning algorithms. This is necessary because people usually express their feelings in very different ways of writing, using simple and complex sentences and very diverse vocabulary. Often, they also use references of irony or sarcasm, revealing emotions, opinions or ideas, or insert graphical symbols in texts, such as emoji, for revealing their current state of mind, enhancing a specific part of the text, or simply for breaking the "monotony" of the text. To do all this tasks, sentiment analysts combine natural language processing [19] with text mining [20] techniques, for removing special characters, correct syntactic errors, interpret images and symbols (when possible) and, mainly, to identify concepts and relationships embedded in opinion texts. All these elements are essential for sentiment classification and rating.

In the next section, we will present and discuss a concrete application of sentiment analysis to a real-world problem we can find in the environment of a city. Our main goal was to evaluate the application of sentiment analysis on smart cities, designing and implementing a system for analyzing use complaints of an urban transport company, and establishing a kind of severity rate for the complaints presented. Based on this indicator, we believe that it is possible to get valuable information for improving the company's quality of service and increasing the well-being and the quality of life of its customers.

3 The Sentiment Analysis System

3.1 The Application Case

During the last few years, we have done some research and development work in the field of sentiment analysis. Despite the great attractiveness of this domain, as well as the practical interest of its application, a significant number of works do not revealed a satisfactory level of confidence. This is critical when we are dealing with real-world applications. Using the knowledge and experience obtained in the development of a previous sentiment analysis system, we decided to make a new experience using a different perspective of sentiment analysis processes application. In the majority of the applications studied, we take into account opinion texts about companies' services or goods, which revealed usually a positive, neutral or negative rating of the sentiments expressed in those texts. In this work, we tried a slightly different approach, at least regarding sentiment classification (rating) and its scale of values. We used texts related to complaints that customers of an urban transport company posted on some specific Web sites, concerning the services provided and transport means used. By nature, we know that a complaint reports negative sentiments about something. In our case, it simply reveals situations of bad quality of service and unpleasant occurrences in transport means, among other things. To sustain our sentiment classification process application, we gathered a set of complaint texts, from different customers of urban transport companies. We assumed that all the complaints were about a same company, which we used an application case of sentiment analysis in one of the most critical system of smart cities – urban transport services.

We decided to classify complaints of this fictitious company for identifying and classifying sentiments expressed in complaints. With the prediction rates obtained, we would establish a complaint-index as an indicator of the severity of the complaint, as well as see the impact of some complaint elements in that rating. Complaint elements categorize the services of the urban transport company, according seven analysis classes, namely: "vehicle", "service", "employee", "health", "route", "park" and "other". Each class integrates several complaint elements. For example, the class "vehicle" has elements such as "bus", "noise", "accessibility", "velocity" or "motor", while the class "employee" contains other different elements, such as "driver", "education", "attitude", or "attendance". The use of complaint elements and the measurement of their impact in the sentiment rate predicted add value to a conventional sentiment analysis process.

3.2 The Sentiment Analysis Approach

We have different approaches for implementing sentiment analysis processes. Regardless of the alternative adopted, it is important to ensure that the process of sentiment analysis is not carried out in an ad hoc manner, but using a methodology already tested and applied. One of the most relevant approaches in the field was proposed by Birjali et al. [21]. These authors outlined and explained the essential tasks of a sentiment analysis process – selecting and extracting data, processing data, classifying sentiments, and visualization of results. In our application, we only designed and developed mechanisms for implementing two of these main tasks, namely: processing data and classifying sentiments. For the remaining tasks, we used autonomously a specific set of tools that are not in the conventional classifying sentiments program pipelining (Fig. 1).

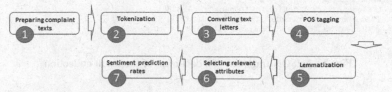

Fig. 1. The task diagram of the sentiment analysis process

To start the processing data task, we needed to prepare the complaint texts. Then the classifying system initiates their pre-processing, doing the tokenization of the texts, isolating texts' words, separating sentences, small phrases, symbols or other types of tokens into single words, and then converting all letters to lowercase before starting POS tagging – the identification of the grammatical class of each word presented in the texts. Finishing POS tagging, the system proceeds doing the lemmatization task for grouping different forms of the same word. As happened in other sentiment analysis implementations, we selected Term Frequency-Inverse Document Frequency (TF-IDF) [22] for selecting relevant attributes, labelling them and storing in vector structures for later use on the classifying task.

Initially, for rating sentiments, we developed several classification models. However, after their validation, and based on the results we got, we decided to apply only a model based on support vector machines [23]. However, even for this model, the confidence of the results was not strong. We verified that was due to the difficulty of the system in classifying the texts in more than two or three classes. Thus, we processed again the machine learning model, classifying this time the sentiments on a 1 to 5 scale, taking into account as well the classification of the "polarity" feature, containing negative, positive and neutral classes. In the next section, we present and discuss the new set of results.

3.3 Result Analysis

In order to analyze the urban transport company sentiment index, we stored the results in a document store, creating a specific document collection (Fig. 2) structured to receive complaint texts, sentiment prediction rates (global and per complaint text) and the impact of each defined complaint element in results. The document store allows us to analyze sentiment rates in a very flexible way, providing means to navigate the classification data, accordingly to each complaint text or following the hierarchical structure of the complaint elements (ELEMENT > > CLASS), or performing analytical operations, such as filtering, crossing, pivoting, drilling-down or rolling-up over the complaint data.

Table 1 presents a summary of the results we got using the support vector machine approach in our application case. As referred before, the complaint-index (the predicted sentiment rate) reflects the negativity level of the complaint in a scale of 1 to 5, being '1' the worst case, which means a very critical situation. Thus, the index reveals how serious is the complaint as well shows the complaint elements (or their class) that influenced the

```
{
  "Id": "0021",
  "Complaint Text": "(…) it is completely unacceptable to have to wait (…) for
  a bus (…)45 minutes late (…) stayed another 10 minutes at the bus stop (…)",
  "Rate_Prediction": "1",
  "Elements_Impact": [
    {"Element": "education", "Impact": "0.333"},
    {"Element": "attitude","Impact": "0.333"},
    {"Element": "driver","Impact": "0.33"}]
}
```

Fig. 2. A JSON fragment of a document of the result collection

Table 1. Complaint assessment results

The Urban Transport Company Application Case	
Nr. of complaint texts	38
Avg. Prediction rate (sentiment rate)	**1.520**
Nr. of classes of complaint elements	7

calculus of the index value. In our case, the average prediction rate reveals that the urban transport company has very serious complaints (having values between 1 and 2, the worst values in the global sentiment analysis scale) sustained by the negative sentiments expressed in customers' complaint texts.

Customers tend to be positive when they rate something (a service or a good) or express their opinions. As expected, this was not the case in the complaint texts posted in the Web sites we consulted. About 66% of the complaints contains terms expressing very negative sentiments, which reveals the great displeasure of customers with the services provided by the company. In Fig. 3, we can see the distribution of customer ratings (a) and the prediction rates of the system for each assessment value (b).

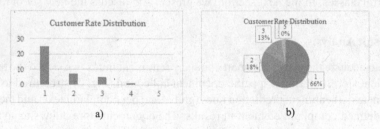

Fig. 3. Customer and system classification rates distribution

The analysis of the results, concerning the various complaint elements (bus, driver, attitude, education, conditions, time, etc.) we considered, as well as their respective classes (vehicle, service, employee, etc.) (Fig. 4), revealed some interesting aspects. We can see that the classes "vehicle", "service" and "employee" of complaint elements occupy the top 3 of the results, having more references in the complaint texts that originated the sentiment rates. As a simple curiosity, we noted that in the class "employee" the complaint elements more referred were "driver", "attitude" and "education".

The utility of these results is relative, depending a lot on each analyst and decision-maker. However, within the scope of our application case study, we may say that the urban transport company has serious problems with its staff and vehicles it uses. In our opinion, results like these alerts for very critical situations we should analyze carefully, seeing with detail the complaints that referred them. Then, it will be necessary to define and apply concrete measures to solve the problems identified and to improve the quality of the service provided by the urban transport company. This is one possible analysis that we can made based on the results of our application case study.

Fig. 4. The distribution of the complaint element classes

4   Conclusions and Future Work

Sentiment analysis applications are still far from providing results having high levels of confidence. During the last few years, a wide range of techniques have been created and developed for identifying and classifying feelings expressed in unstructured texts. The evolution of these techniques has been extraordinary. Today, they are already very useful analysis instruments for any company worried about its well-being and performance. They have the ability to provide information and reinforce company's knowledge, with specific-oriented customers' data, sustaining better business relationships between them and company. Today, in addition to the information regularly extracted from analysis processes of conventional data, this reinforcement is carried out based on the subjectivity, explicit or implicit, contained in the opinion messages of its customers or users. Sentiment analysis is a "step forward" in customer analytics.

In this paper, we presented a sentiment analysis system for evaluating the business status of an urban transport company, based on the complaints presented by its customers. Complaint texts were extract from real-world Web sites, and report negative events or situations related to urban transport services. We can use text sentiment analysis identifying situations of risk, service losses, or emerging threats, for example. Having the identification of these situations, an urban transport company may improve the services it provides, as well as attenuate (or even eliminate) undesirable business situations. Despite the urban transport data we used is real, our application case study is fictitious.

We conceived and designed it specifically for this work, with the goal to evaluate and analyze possible contributions of sentiment analysis for smart cities.

The results we got are equivalent to the ones described in the literature for similar problems, even in cases like the one we had deal when applied to a ternary classification problem. The value of the index reveals how serious are the complaints, as well shows the influence of relevant class complaint elements, such as employee service or vehicle in its impact. As seen before, in our application case, for example, a value of '1' for the sentiment index indicates a very bad situation, and as so should be analyzed seriously. Considering this, we realize how the status of the company is accordingly the complaints expressed by customers. This will be useful to company's managers for identifying risks, or trends and establish correction measures to eliminate or attenuate critical situations like the ones described in complaint texts.

As future work, we intend to refine and improve some tasks in the process we implemented. For example, it will be necessary automating the way we select and extract opinion data, for gathering a greater number of opinion texts, improving preprocessing tasks, and incorporating more efficient filtering and correction text means. Additionally, we need to apply the system to a real world case for getting a more effective validation and proof. This will contribute for showing that sentiment analysis applications could be applied effectively for improving services, and contributing to sustain and ensure a good image for urban transport companies, using advanced software components, such as sentiment analysis, for reinforcing smart cities initiatives.

Acknowledgements. This work has been supported by FCT – Fundação para a Ciência e Tecnologia within the R&D Units Project Scope: UIDB/00319/2020.

References

1. Moura, F., Silva, J.: Smart cities: definitions, evolution of the concept and examples of initiatives. In Encyclopedia of the UN Sustainable Development Goals book series (ENUNSDG) (2019). https://doi.org/10.1007/978-3-319-71059-4_6-1
2. Bernardo, M.: Smart City Governance: From E-Government to Smart Governance. In Carvalho, L.C., (eds.), Handbook of Research on Entrepreneurial Development and Innovation Within Smart Cities, pp. 290–326). IGI Global (2017). https://doi.org/10.4018/978-1-5225-1978-2.ch014
3. Burbach, L., Halbach, P., Ziefle, M., Valdez, A.: opinion formation on the internet: the influence of personality, network structure, and content on sharing messages online. Front. Artifi. Intell. 3 (2020) https://doi.org/10.3389/frai.2020.00045
4. Bubelíny, O., Kubina, M.: Impact of the concept Smart City on public transport. Trans. Res. Proc. **55**, 1361–1367 (2021). https://doi.org/10.1016/j.trpro.2021.07.120
5. Behnisch, M., Hecht, R., Herold, H., Jiang, B.: Urban big data analytics and morphology. Environm. Planning B: Urban Analyt. City Sci. **46**(7), 1203–1205 (2019). https://doi.org/10.1177/2399808319870016
6. Kitchens, B., Dobolyi, D., Li, J., Abbasi, A.: Advanced customer analytics: strategic value through integration of relationship-oriented big data. J. Managem. Inf. Syst. **35**(2), 540–574 (2018). https://doi.org/10.1080/07421222.2018.1451957
7. Wu, M., Yan, B., Huang, Y., Sarker, M.N.I.: Big Data-Driven urban management: potential for urban sustainability. Land **11**(5), 680 (2022). https://doi.org/10.3390/land11050680

8. El-Din, M.D.: A survey on sentiment analysis challenges. J. King Saud Univ.- Eng. Sci. (2016). https://doi.org/10.1016/j.jksues.2016.04.002

9. Buttice, C.: Top 14 AI Use Cases: Artificial Intelligence in Smart Cities (March 27 2020). https://www.techopedia.com/top-14-ai-use-cases-artificial-intelligence-in-smart-cities/2/34049. (Accessed 30 Sep 2022)

10. Jnr, B.A.: A case-based reasoning recommender system for sustainable smart city development. AI Soc. **36**, 159–183 (2021)

11. Hurbean, L., Danaiata, D., Militaru, F., Dodea, A.-M., Negovan, A.-M.: Open data based machine learning applications in smart cities: a systematic literature review. Electronics **10**(23), 2997 (2021). https://doi.org/10.3390/electronics10232997

12. Badar, M., Rahman, S.: Machine learning approaches in smart cities. In: Machine Learning Approaches in Smart Cities, Springer, Publication in "Studies in Computational Intelligence", MIDATASMART (2020). https://doi.org/10.1007/978-981-19-2535-1_9

13. Routray, P., Swain, C., Mishra, S.: A survey on sentiment analysis. Int. J. Comput. Applicat. **76**(10) 0975 – 8887 (2013)

14. Ravi, K., Ravi, V.: A survey on opinion mining and sentiment analysis: Tasks, approaches and applications. Knowl.-Based Syst. **89**, 14–46 (2015)

15. Bollen, J., Mao, H., Zeng, X.: Twitter mood predicts the stock market. J. Comput. Sci. (2011). https://doi.org/10.1016/j.jocs.2010.12.007

16. Li, Y., Li, T.: Deriving market intelligence from microblogs. Decis. Support Syst. (2013). https://doi.org/10.1016/j.dss.2013.01.023

17. Li, Y., Shiu, Y.: a diffusion mechanism for social advertising over microblogs. Decis. Support Syst. (2012). https://doi.org/10.1016/j.dss.2012.02.012

18. Zhang, L., Wang, S., Liu, B.: Deep learning for sentiment analysis: A survey. WIREs Data Mining Knowl. Dis. **8**(4) (2018). https://doi.org/10.1002/widm.1253

19. Sharma, A.: Natural language processing and sentiment analysis, in international research. J. Comput. Sci. **8**(10), 237 (2021). https://doi.org/10.26562/irjcs.2021.v0810.001

20. Maheswari, M.: Text mining: survey on techniques and applications. Int. J. Sci. Res. (IJSR) **6**(6) (2017)

21. Birjali, M., Kasri, M., Beni-Hssane, A.: A Comprehensive Survey on Sentiment Analysis: Approaches, Challenges and Trends, Knowledge-Based Systems, vol. 226 (2021).https://doi.org/10.1016/j.knosys.2021.107134

22. Simha, A.: Understanding TF-IDF for Machine Learning, A gentle introduction to term frequency-inverse document frequency (October 2021). https://www.simplilearn.com/real-impact-social-media-article. (Accessed 9 May 2022)

23. Srivastava, D., Bhambhu, L.: Data classification using support vector machine. In J. Theoret. Appli. Inform. Technol. **12**(1), 1–7 (2010)

Author Index

A

Alharbi, Zahyah H. 117
Alqurashi, Tahani M. 117
Azevedo, Rolando 29

B

Barros, Daniel 3
Barros, Paulo 59
Bellucci, Patrizia 155
Belo, Orlando 166
Bhuiyan, Tanvir 87
Blanco-Novoa, Oscar 59

C

Cao, Houze 75
Cardoso, Bruno 16
Chellappan, Sriram 87
Ciarallo, Francesca 155
Costa, Joana 16

D

D'Elia, Gerardo 155
De Vito, Saverio 155
Del Giudice, Antonio 155
Di Francia, Girolamo 155
Durmaz İncel, Özlem 130

E

Esposito, Elena 155

F

Fattoruso, Grazia 155
Ferlito, Sergio 155
Fernández-Caramés, Tiago M. 3, 59
Formisano, Fabrizio 155
Fraga-Lamas, Paula 3, 59

G

Gonzales, Kenneth John G. 43

J

Joutsijoki, Henry 102

K

Karppi, Ilari 102

L

Loffredo, Giuseppe 155
Lopes, Sérgio Ivan 3, 29, 59

M

Mäenpää, Sari 102
Massera, Ettore 155
Milhazes, Ricardo 166

N

Nolasco, Jan Kyle Lewis T. 43

P

Pinto, André 29

R

Ribeiro, Bernardete 16

S

Sankala, Iina 102
Saylam, Berrenur 130
Silva, Catarina 16
Sombrito, Sean Arthur E. 43

T

Tiglao, Nestor Michael C. 43

X

Xue, Meng 75

Y

Yi, Hye Seon 87

© ICST Institute for Computer Sciences, Social Informatics and Telecommunications Engineering 2023
Published by Springer Nature Switzerland AG 2023. All Rights Reserved
S. I. Lopes et al. (Eds.): Edge-IoT 2022/SmartGov 2022, LNICST 510, p. 177, 2023.
https://doi.org/10.1007/978-3-031-35982-8

Printed in the United States
by Baker & Taylor Publisher Services

Printed in the United States
by Baker & Taylor Publisher Services